Designing Screen Interfaces
in C

AUGUST   Joint Application Design
BAUDIN   Manufacturing Systems Analysis with Application to Production Scheduling
BELLIN and SUCHMAN   Structured Systems Development Manual
BLOCK   The Politics of Projects
BODDIE   Crunch Mode: Building Effective Systems on a Tight Schedule
BOULDIN   Agents of Change: Managing the Introduction of Automated Tools
BRILL   Building Controls into Structure Systems
BRILL   Techniques of EDP Project Management: A Book of Readings
CHANG   Principles of Visual Programming Systems
COAD and YOURDON   Object-Oriented Analysis
CONNELL and SHAFER   Structured Rapid Prototyping
CONSTANTINE and YOURDON   Structured Design: Fundamentals of a Discipline
     of Computer Program and Systems Design
DeGRACE and STAHL   Wicked Problems, Righteous Solutions: A Catalogue of Modern
     Software Engineering Paradigms
DeMARCO   Concise Notes of Software Engineering
DeMARCO   Controlling Software Projects
DeMARCO   Structured Analysis and System Specification
DeSALVO and LIEBOWITZ   Managing Artificial Intelligence and Expert Systems
FLAVIN   Fundamental Concepts in Information Modeling
FOLLMAN   Business Applications with Microcomputers
FOURNIER   Practical Guide to Structured System Development and Maintenance
FRANTZEN and McEVOY   A Game Plan for Systems Development
FRENCH   Business Knowledge Investment
GLASS   Software Conflict: Essays on the Art and Science of Software Engineering
GROCHOW   SAA: A Manager's Guide to Implementing
KELLER   The Practice of Structured Analysis: Exploding Myths
KING   Current Practices in Software Development: A Guide to Successful Systems
LIEBOWITZ and DeSALVO   Structuring Expert Systems: Domain, Design, and Development
MARTIN   Transaction Processing Facility: A Guide for Application Programmers
McMENAMIN and PALMER   Essential System Analyis
ORR   Structured Systems Development
PAGE-JONES   Practical Guide to Structured Systems Design, 2/E
PETERS   Software Design: Methods and Techniques
PINSON   Designing Screen Interfaces in C
RIPPS   An Implementation Guide to Real-Time Programming
RODGERS   UNIX® Database Management Systems
RUHL   The Programmer's Survival Guide
SCHLAER and MELLOR   Object-Oriented Systems Analysis: Modeling the World in Data
TOIGO   Diaster Recovery Planning: Managing Risk and Catastrophe in Information Systems
VESELY   Strategic Data Management: The Key to Corporate Competitiveness
WARD   Systems Development Without Pain
WARD and MELLOR   Structured Development for Real-Time Systems
WEINBERG   Structured Analysis
YOURDON   Managing the Structured Techniques, 4/E
YOURDON   Managing the System Life Cycle, 2/E
YOURDON   Modern Structured Analysis
YOURDON   Structured Walkthroughs, 4/E
YOURDON   Techniques of Program Structure and Design

Designing Screen Interfaces in C

James L. Pinson

Network Specialist
University Computing and Network Services
University of Georgia

YOURDON PRESS
Prentice Hall Building
Englewood Cliffs, New Jersey 07632

Library of Congress Cataloging-in-Publication Data

Pinson, James L.
  Designing screen interfaces in C / James Pinson.
      p.   cm. -- (Yourdon Press computing series)
  Includes bibliographical references and index.
  ISBN 0-13-201583-8
  1. C (Computer program language) 2. Computer interfaces.
3. Information display systems.   I. Title. II. Series.
QA76.73.C15P533   1991
005.265--dc20   90-40860
                                                          CIP

Editorial/production supervision
  and interior design: *Harriet Tellem*
Cover design: *Lundgren Graphics*
Manufacturing buyers: *Kelly Behr/Susan Brunke*

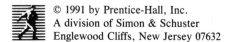
The publisher offers discounts on this book when ordered
in bulk quantities. For more information, write:

> Special Sales/College Marketing
> Prentice-Hall, Inc.
> College Technical and Reference Division
> Englewood Cliffs, New Jersey 07632

Printed in the United States of America
10 9 8 7 6 5 4 3

ISBN 0-13-201583-8

Prentice-Hall International (UK) Limitd, *London*
Prentice-Hall of Australia Pty. Limited, *Sydney*
Prentice-Hall Canada Inc., *Toronto*
Prentice-Hall Hispanoamericana, S.A., *Mexico*
Prentice-Hall of India Private Limited, *New Delhi*
Prentice-Hall of Japan, Inc., *Tokyo*
Simon & Schuster Asia Pte. Ltd., *Singapore*
Editora Prentice-Hall do Brasil, Ltda., *Rio de Janeiro*

To Chantal

Contents

Chapter 3   Menu Design   **116**

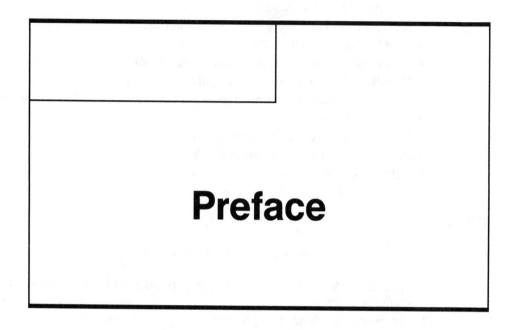

Preface

This book is designed to aid C programmers in the creation of functional, intuitive screen interfaces.

We will cover in depth the construction of a screen and window function library, and use it to build menu systems similar to those found in popular commercial software packages.

Programs will be presented that will allow you to produce:

- A window-based screen interface.
- Moving light bar menus (as in Lotus 1-2-3).
- Multilevel light bar menus.
- Pop-up menus.
- Dialogue boxes.
- Pull-down menus.
- Field editors.
- Data input screens.
- List selection windows.
- Directory functions (for file selection).
- Context-specific help screens.
- Help screen editors.

In the process of building these systems, we cover concepts and techniques for:

- Performing BIOS interrupts.
- High-speed direct writing to the screen buffer.
- Avoiding snow on CGA displays.
- Producing "instant" screen updates with virtual screens.
- Virtual window creation and manipulation.
- Assuring compatibility with multitasking environments such as DESQview.
- User friendly menu design.
- Data input and verification techniques.
- Obtaining directory information for DOS.
- Help screen creation and display.

GOALS

The purpose of this book is to provide the reader with:

1. Programs that can be used as they are, or adapted for the individual programmer's needs.
2. The concepts behind each program.
3. Explanations of programming techniques used to build these programs.

PORTABILITY

Throughout this book we will strive for portability within the MS-DOS/IBM-DOS world.

For the user of our programs this means that the programs should work right the first time they are run. The programs require no special drivers such as ANSI.SYS, no alteration of config.sys files, and no need to buy special windowing operating systems or DOS shells. The software will work successfully with all popular video cards (CGA, MDA, Hercules, EGA, and VGA). Software based on this approach will have the widest possible audience, applicable to virtually every IBM PC and clone made.

For the programmer, portability means having a choice of compilers. We will avoid using compiler-specific graphic/window libraries. *Everything we need we will build*. The code created is memory-model independent; that is, all programs will compile under all Turbo C and QuickC memory models.

The programs are written entirely in C. No assembler is required. The commented source code may be customized to fit programmers' needs.

WHAT YOU WILL NEED TO USE THIS BOOK

1. A C compiler. Borland's Turbo C compiler was used to produce the examples in this book. The source code is also totally compatible with Microsoft's QuickC.
2. An IBM PC or compatible computer with enough memory to run the compiler.
3. IBM- or MS-DOS.
4. Experience programming with C. Advanced knowledge is not necessary.

WHAT OTHERS WILL NEED TO RUN YOUR SOFTWARE

1. An IBM PC or compatible.
2. 64K of available RAM. More may be needed if your applications are large.
3. IBM or MS DOS.

THE BOOK LAYOUT

This book is divided into seven chapters.

1. The first chapter is a review of video adapters, memory layout and access, and the use of pointers and BIOS interrupts.
2. The second chapter deals with the creation of a window-based screen function library. Topics covered include creating, removing, and writing to windows; creation of a flexible screen writing routine; and screen buffer "paging" techniques. We also discuss virtual screens and DESQview compatibility.
3. In Chapter 3 we will discuss menu systems. We will build Lotus 1-2-3 style menu bars, multilevel menu bars, pop-up menus, dialogue boxes, and pull-down menus. Of particular importance is the section on pop-up menus; here we establish the data structures, calling conventions, and menu design philosophies that will be used in all our menus.
4. Chapter 4 deals with data entry. We will build a field editor and will use it to construct a dBase style input screen, complete with color-coded fields and data verification.
5. In Chapter 5 we will build a list-select function that will allow the user to select from a virtually unlimited number of options, using point-and-shoot and speed search techniques.
6. In Chapter 6 we will create a function for selecting files from a directory, using the list-select function we created earlier.

7. In Chapter 7 we will build a help screen designer and will show how to add context-specific help to our programs.

Each major topic is subdivided into four categories:

- **Goals:** We discuss the general goals and features we wish to implement in our code. This discussion describes the overall "look and feel" of the product.
- **Application:** This is the practical part of the book. We discuss the individual functions and how they would be used within a program. Sample programs are presented as illustrations. A few tricks for getting the most out of the functions are described.
- **Techniques:** Within this section we discuss the design considerations and techniques used to produce the code. We look at possible programming approaches, pitfalls, and solutions. We place emphasis on aspects of the code that would not be intuitively obvious from examining the source code.
- **Source Code:** The code is highly commented. Every effort has been made to produce readable, useful code and comments. Meaningful variable names are used when possible (e.g., top = 1 instead of t = 1).

This modular approach should allow you to concentrate on the aspects of the book you find most useful. If you are interested in having a set of screen and menu tools, then you will probably prefer the Applications section. If you are interested in finding out how the code works, see the sections on Techniques and Source Code.

OBTAINING SOURCE CODE

Please see Appendix A for instructions for obtaining the source code from this book.

ACKNOWLEDGMENTS

I wish to thank Ed Yourdon for encouraging me to start this project. Constuctive critiques by two anonymous reviewers greatly improved the text, and John Hopkins and Steve Spencer helped test the code. I greatly appreciate the efforts of Paul Becker, Harriet Tellem, Noreen Regina, Robyn Goodale, and all the other helpful professionals at Prentice Hall.

Special thanks go to my wife Chantal, for all her encouragement, suggestions, editing, and proofreading. This book would never have been written without her.

Chapter 1

Accessing
the Display Adapter

In this chapter we will review:

- The types of display adapters.
- The video buffer memory map.
- The use of pointers for accessing video memory.
- Default pointer types for compiler memory models.
- BIOS interrupts.
- The ANSI console driver.

In the first section we will discuss the display adapter, giving particular attention to the video buffer and the techniques used to access it.

DISPLAY ADAPTERS

The wide variety of monitors and text/graphic cards currently available for the IBM PC falls into two major groups, monochrome and color.

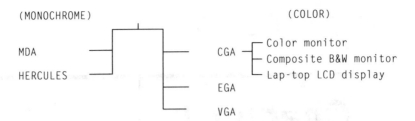

Figure 1–1   Evolution of major display adapters

An evolutionary tree would look somewhat like that in Figure 1–1. The major display adapters are described as follows:

MDA = Monochrome Display Adapter. This card was intended primarily for business applications. It displays very well-defined text characters and is not capable of displaying graphics. The text is displayed in an 80 × 25 format (80 columns with 25 rows). This card requires the use of a monochrome monitor.

Hercules = This card was designed to provide compatibility with the MDA, but is also capable of displaying proprietary high-resolution graphics. This card also requires a monochrome monitor.

CGA = Color Graphics Adapter. This card is capable of displaying both text and graphics in color. The text display is limited to 80 × 25 (maximum).

EGA = Enhanced Graphics Adapter. This card is compatible with the CGA but has increased text and graphics resolution. It supports text modes greater than 80 × 25.

VGA = Video Graphics Adapter. Compatible with the EGA, but with still more text and graphic modes.

LCD = Liquid Crystal Display. Used on laptop computers, this card is usually equivalent to a CGA adapter.

The newer, more advanced cards support the functions and modes found in the earlier ones. For example, VGA cards can run programs written for the CGA, and the Hercules card emulates the MGA. If we write our software so that it is compatible with the CGA and MDA, we gain compatibility with the newer adapters.

COMPOSITE DISPLAYS

Note that the CGA works with two display monitors: color and black-and-white (B&W). The black-and-white composite display tries to show color as shades of grey, with only limited success.

Color characters displayed on composite monitors are often unreadable. The LCD found on many laptops can be grouped with the composite displays since most LCD monitors use grey levels instead of colors.

Users of such B&W displays often use the DOS "mode" command to disable color, allowing only normal or intense text, which is more legible. Entering "mode bw80" at the DOS command line sets the mode to B&W with 80 columns.

Well-written software should check the mode via a BIOS call to ascertain the current mode the user has selected. Based on that mode, the software can select the proper text attributes (e.g., color or not) for that monitor. Unfortunately, if an application writes directly to the video buffer, it bypasses the BIOS and is not affected by the "mode" command, and therefore may write text with color attributes even though it is not appropriate for the user's monitor.

Although software may be enabled to detect what type of display adapter is present, it cannot "know" whether the type of monitor attached to the adapter is color or composite. The software can only ascertain whether the B&W mode has been set.

Later on, we will explore techniques and code for ascertaining the type of display adapter and the currently selected display mode. This information will be essential for producing a legible display.

THE VIDEO BUFFER

The IBM PC uses a section of memory as a video buffer. CGA and CGA compatibles use a buffer beginning at memory segment b800. Monochrome cards (MGA, Hercules and others) use a buffer beginning at b000. The first memory location contains the first character shown on the display, and the next location contains the attribute for that character. This arrangement is known as a *memory mapped display*, and any change made to the video buffer is immediately visible on the video monitor.

If you printed "hello" in the upper left corner of a CGA display, the memory map would appear as in Figure 1–2. The entire display on an 80-column, 25-line display would consist of 2000 (80 × 25) characters plus 2000 attributes. Using a column, row (x, y) screen-based numbering system, the upper left corner of such a display would be 1, 1 and the bottom right corner would be 25, 80. Knowledge of the video memory map will be essential later on as we develop our screen writing techniques.

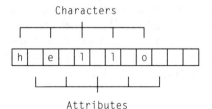

Figure 1–2 Memory map

TEXT ATTRIBUTES

Text attributes vary according to the type of video card in use. Attributes which may be used on monochrome systems include normal, intense, reverse, and underline. Our programs use the header file mylib.h which defines these attributes for us.

```
#define UNDERLINE 1 /* ATTRIBUTES FOR MONOCHROME CARDS
*/
#define NORMAL    7
#define HI_INTEN  15
#define REVERSE   112
```

On a color adapter the attribute byte can be used to set the foreground/ background colors as well as the foreground intensity and blinking characteristics. The color attribute is mapped as in Figure 1–3.

The three primary additive colors—which are red, blue, and green—may be combined to create the so-called "subtractive" colors. For example, red and blue may be added to create magenta; red and green to create yellow. The colors magenta, cyan, and yellow can likewise be combined (subtracted, in this case) to form the primary colors. Cyan and yellow, for example, produce green. The "subtractive" color system is used in photographic enlargers. The relationship is shown in Figure 1–4 in the color wheel.

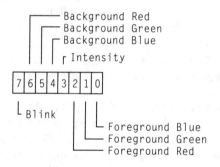

Figure 1–3   Bit map of color attributes

Figure 1–4   The color wheel

The color wheel is only a guide. The actual colors produced depend on the combination of red, blue, green, and intensity. For example, red and green produce brown if the intensity is not set. With intensity set ON, the result is yellow. Table 1–1 shows a bit map naming the colors that result when the primary color bits are turned on (intensity is set to OFF). To simplify the use of color attributes, the following definition is found in mydef.h:

```
#define BLACK     0   /* THESE ARE FOR COLOR CARDS */
#define BLUE      1
#define GREEN     2
#define CYAN      3
#define RED       4
#define MAGENTA   5
#define BROWN     6
#define WHITE     7
#define YELLOW   14   /* intensity set on */
```

The following function-like macro sets the foreground/background colors:

```
#define set_color(foreground,background)\

(((background)<<4) | (foreground))
```

Notice how the macro shifts the background 4 bits to the left, then combines it (bitwise 'or') with the foreground.

For example, using this macro, the variable **attribute** can be set to a foreground color of BLUE and a background color of BLACK with the call:

```
attribute=set_color(BLUE,BLACK);
```

The intensity is set HIGH for any attribute when its fourth bit is set ON (set to a 1). We may force this bit to be set ON for any attribute by use of the macro **set_intense( )** which performs a bitwise 'or' with the decimal number 8 (which equals 00001000 in binary). This forces the bit to become a 1.

```
#define set_intense(attribute) ((attribute) |8)
```

TABLE 1–1. BIT MAP OF PRINCIPAL COLORS

R	G	B	Color	Attribute (decimal)
0	0	0	Black	0
0	0	1	Blue	1
0	1	0	Green	2
0	1	1	Cyan	3
1	0	0	Red	4
1	0	1	Magenta	5
1	1	0	Brown	6
1	1	1	White	7

COLOR TEXT PAGES

The CGA allows for up to four text pages to be displayed in the 80-column mode. By using video interrupts, it is possible to display any of the pages on the computer screen.

I mentioned earlier that the screen buffer for an 80 × 25 display occupies 4000 bytes. The memory offset within the screen buffer is not 4000 as you might expect, but rather 4096. This may not seem reasonable until we look at the numbers in hex. As you can see from Table 1–2 and Figure 1–5, the pages begin in hex increments of 1000, with small blocks of unused memory for each page. Starting the page boundaries on these segments makes it easier to do the calculations required to access the buffer.

TABLE 1–2. BYTES ACTUALLY OCCUPIED BY TEXT PAGES

	Decimal	Hex
Page 0	0 to 3999	0 to f9f
Page 1	4096 to 8095	1000 to 1f9f
Page 2	8192 to 12191	2000 to 2f9f
Page 3	12288 to 16287	3000 to 3f9f

Initially, the computer reads and writes to page 0. A trick that some programmers use is text page flipping; that is, writing to one page while displaying another. This makes screen updates appear to be almost instantaneous. Figure 1–6 shows an example. Of course, it takes just as long to write to the alternate page, but the user does not see the line-by-line writing that normally occurs. A completed page which instantly "pops" onto the screen gives the user the illusion of speed.

A word processor might use the text pages to store the current document page, as well as the next and previous page. When the user touches a paging key, the appropriate text page is displayed. While the user is reading the new page,

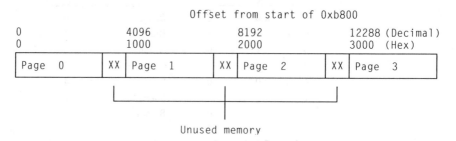

Figure 1–5   Screen buffer

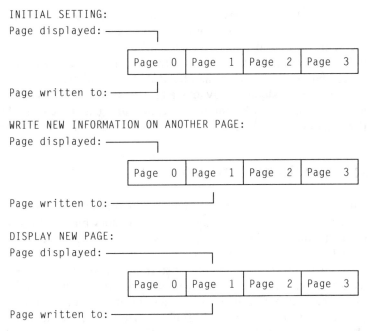

Figure 1–6 Example of page flipping

the other pages are being rewritten. The software is making use of the "idle" time that occurs when we slow humans are deciding what to do next. The user is unaware of the off-screen activity.

If you have a word processor which appears to instantly page through the document, it may be using this technique. You can test this by overloading it. Hold down the page down key (PgDn) and see if the updates are still instantaneous. If the program does not have time to draw the next page between keypresses, there will be a pause while the next page is drawn.

Although text page flipping is very useful, we will not use it in our code for two reasons:

1. Our code must support monochrome displays, which are unable to use this technique.

2. In some cases, more than four pages may be required.

Instead of paging, we will use a technique called *virtual screens*.

VIRTUAL SCREENS

Virtual means "imaginary" or "fake" in computerese. For example, a RAM disk drive is also known as a virtual drive.

Virtual screens may be used to accomplish the same effect as page flipping. A virtual screen is a contiguous section of allocated memory which generally has the same size as the physical screen buffer. Screen writing is directed to this buffer instead of to the screen buffer. When the writing is complete, the virtual screen buffer is copied to the physical screen buffer.

There is a slight disadvantage in the use of virtual screens in that some extra memory and time are required to create and manipulate the buffers. However, the "snappy" screen updates more than make up for the extra overhead.

POINTERS AND MEMORY MODELS

Direct manipulation of the memory buffer provides the optimum in performance for screen functions. To manipulate the memory buffer, it is critical to have a full understanding of the use of pointers and how they relate to compiler memory models.

There are special 16-bit registers designed to specify which segments are used for code and data. The segment registers are shown in Table 1–3.

The segment registers are generally of more concern to assembly language programmers than to C programmers. However, we do need to be concerned about how segments affect our selection of compiler memory models. Turbo C has 6 models: tiny, small, medium, compact, large, and huge. The model you select determines how the segments are used.

Tiny models use the same starting address for all four segments; your code and data occupy the same 64K range. This means that the tiny model can use what is known as a *near* pointer for accessing data. All data are in the same 64K segment which is known to the program. The near pointer need only contain the offset to the data.

A large memory model uses *far* pointers for data. The far pointer must contain both the segment and offset, and is therefore larger than the near pointer. The large model can access 1 megabyte of data.

The tiny, small, and medium models use near pointers for data while the compact, large, and huge models use far pointers. Unless your program requires a lot of data space, you are better off using smaller memory models because they take up less memory and are faster.

TABLE 1–3. SEGMENT REGISTERS

Register	Name	Usage
CS	Code segment	Program code
DS	Data segment	Data storage
SS	Stack segment	Stack location
ES	Extra segment	As needed, usually for more data

With certain C applications there is no need to be concerned with the type of default pointer. The default pointer, which is specific to the memory model, is usually quite adequate for allocating memory, or pointing to variables. When dealing with the video buffer, however, it is quite a different story.

DIRECTLY ACCESSING THE VIDEO BUFFER

The video buffer must be accessed via a far pointer. We must be certain that a far pointer is actually being used. In the following program the default pointer is used to write a character to the screen:

```
main()
{
 char   *screen;
 char ch;

    screen=0xb0000000; /* Monochrome screen address */
    ch='a';

    *screen=ch;
}
```

This program will compile and run under a large memory model because the default pointer for a large model size is far. The program will not work under a small model because small models use near pointers and cannot reach outside the defined data segment.

We can make the program work properly for any model size by changing the declaration of the screen pointer as follows:

```
        char far *screen;
```

The far modifier is not a standard part of the C language, but it is supported by many compilers, including Turbo C and QuickC.

Another area in which we must use caution is in the use of C library functions. Some of these functions use the default memory model pointer and may not operate as expected. Take, for example, the function **movmem( )**, which is used to move bytes from one memory location to another. It takes three parameters:

- A pointer to the source,
- A pointer to the destination, and
- The number of bytes to move.

A library function such as **movmem( )** could be used to move a large chunk of data at once (e.g., to copy the video buffer to another location). Such routines,

which are written in efficient assembler language, are faster than accessing the
bytes one by one in a C program loop. The function **movmem( )** could also be
used to move a single character to the video buffer. For example,

```
#include "mem.h"      /* header file for movmem */

main( )
{
 char *screen;
 char ch;

    screen=0xb0000000;   /* Monochrome screen address */
    ch = 'a';

 movmem(&ch,screen,1);

}
```

This program works well under the large model, but not under a small model.
Unlike the previous example, changing the pointer to *far* will not help. The
movmem( ) function will only accept a pointer of the default size. *This function
should not be used* to access the video buffer unless you are willing to *only* use
larger memory models.

A better choice for moving a large chunk of data to the video buffer would
be the **movedata( )** function. It is given the source segment and offset, the destination segment and offset, and the number of bytes to move. A call to **move-
data( )** might look like this:

```
movedata(source_seg,source_off, dest_seg, des_off,size);
```

You might think we could easily use the **movedata( )** function to move a string
directly to the video buffer. The problem is that the video buffer requires that the
characters in the buffer be separated by attribute bytes. Any string sent to the
screen via **movedata( )** must first be padded with the attribute bytes. Routines
which copy the screen buffer to another location need no padding. An example
of this is copying a virtual screen to the screen buffer.

BIOS INTERRUPTS

The IBM PC and its clones have a number of useful functions stored in ROM.
Known as the Basic Input-Output Services, or BIOS, these functions handle most
of the details of reading the keyboard and controlling screen output.

Included in the BIOS are routines to clear the screen, move the cursor, and
write text to the screen. The purpose of the BIOS is to free the programmer from
needing to know the details of the hardware. For example, the BIOS routine for

moving the cursor will work for any type of monitor card, be it monochrome, color graphics, EGA, or VGA. The programmer simply uses that BIOS routine without worrying about how it works internally. BIOS routines are updated in new computers to handle the newer hardware. Considerable effort goes into making the new BIOS compatible with the older version. A program "written to the BIOS" should, in theory, be compatible with new computers. BIOS routines are accessed via the 8088 interrupts. Each BIOS function has an associated interrupt number. Instead of knowing the physical location of the routine, and making a call to that location, the programmer only needs to know the interrupt number. Newer IBM computers and clones have been freed to move the physical location of the routines anywhere they like, as long as the interrupt number for each function remains the same.

The actual location of the BIOS routines is stored in an interrupt vector table. Each location in the table contains the address of the corresponding routine. When a software interrupt is performed, the BIOS routine number is specified. The 8088 finds the address of the routine in the interrupt table, and calls the routine.

Using BIOS interrupts is a good way to assure compatibility with multitasking systems and future versions of DOS. For example, a multitasking, window-based system such as DESQview can "steal" (redirect) the BIOS interrupt and handle the interrupts according to its own needs. BIOS calls to print text to the screen could be modified so the output is directed to DESQview virtual screens. Applications which write via the BIOS can therefore be controlled and confined to a DESQview window, and can operate in the background.

If the application wrote to the screen directly, instead of using the interrupt, it would "bleed" through into other windows. DESQview cannot intercept text written directly to the video buffer as it does with BIOS calls. In Chapter 2 we will see how to use direct memory access of the DESQview buffers.

PERFORMING AN INTERRUPT

Now let's take a look at the techniques used to utilize the BIOS interrupts from within a C program.

The standard C language contains no provision for DOS interrupts. Fortunately, most C compilers designed for the IBM PC have a special function to perform that task. In Turbo C and QuickC, that function is **int86( )**, which is one of the MS-DOS extensions provided by many MS-DOS-specific compilers.

Prior to calling a BIOS routine, the 8088 general purpose registers must be loaded with values that indicate which particular function is to be invoked, and what parameters to use for that function. We inform **int86( )** how to load the registers by passing it a data structure which is analogous to the 8088 register. Let's look at the registers in detail so we can better understand their structure.

TABLE 1–4. BIOS REGISTERS

16-Bit (word)	8-Bit (byte)	
	MSB High	LSB Low
ax	ah	al
bx	bh	bl
cx	ch	cl
dx	dh	dl

Each general purpose register is 16 bits wide (one word), and can be subdivided into two 8-bit "bytes." The leftmost byte is known as the *high* byte and the rightmost byte is known as the *low* byte. The high and low bytes are sometimes referred to as the MSB (most significant byte) and LSB (least significant byte), respectively. For example, the hex word 22ffH has an MSB of 22 and an LSB of ff.

The registers we need for performing BIOS interrupts are (as words) ax, bx, cx, dx. They are shown in Table 1–4, subdivided into bytes. The register **ah** stands for a-high and **al** stands for a-low.

Both Turbo C and QuickC have structures defining the word and byte representations of these registers. The structures are combined as a union in REGS. Turbo C, for example, defines the union this way:

```
struct WORDREGS {
    unsigned int      ax, bx, cx, dx, si, di, cflag, flags;
};
struct BYTEREGS {
    unsigned char     al, ah, bl, bh, cl, ch, dl, dh;
};
union      REGS   {
    struct      WORDREGS x;
    struct      BYTEREGS h;
};
```

The union REGS can be applied to the variable **regs** within a program with the declaration "union REGS regs;". This union provides a way of looking at the same data as both words and bytes. In the following examples, we see the registers loaded as bytes and as words.

Examples:

  1. Within a program, we could load the low part of the **a** register with the constant 5 using the statement "regs.h.ah = 5;". We could also say "regs.h.ah = (unsigned char)5;" since an unsigned char equals a byte.

2. The word structure for **ax** would be designated as regs.x.ax. We could treat the register as a word and load both bytes with the statement "regs.x.cx = 5;".

The **int86( )** function requires three parameters: the interrupt number, the values to be placed in the registers, and a place to store the register values returned by the interrupt. Some functions, such as the one which reads the cursor position, return the values via the registers. After loading the registers, the call is made to perform the function:

```
int86(0x10, &regs, &regs);
```

Let's look at a very simple program which moves the cursor via a BIOS call. The BIOS routine which moves the cursor is the video interrupt number 10H. The video interrupt accesses an entire class of functions, all related to the video screen. The specific function is specified by the value stored in register **ah.** The cursor-moving function is called by setting ah = 2.

The cursor function must also know the row and column location to which the cursor is to be moved. That is accomplished by loading the register **dh** with the row, and **dl** with the column. The register **bh** is loaded with the text page number, which we will assume is '0'.

The BIOS counts rows and columns starting at 0; whereas we will use a system starting at 1. The upper left corner is 0, 0 to the BIOS, and 1, 1 under our system.

The use of a number system based on 1 is strictly a personal preference. I was a Turbo Pascal programmer before moving to C, and that language has a function called gotoxy which used a 1-based system. Being familiar with that convention, I imitated it.

The function **gotoxy( )** will perform the translation from our numbering system to that used by the BIOS.

```
void gotoxy(int x, int y)
{
union REGS regs;

  regs.h.ah=2;      /* ah=2, the cursor position function */
  regs.h.dh=y-1;    /* row */
  regs.h.dl=x-1;    /* column */
  regs.h.bh=0;      /* assume page 0 */

int86(0x10, &regs, &regs):  /* do interrupt */
}
```

Note that the video interrupt, 10H, is the first parameter passed to the function **int86( ).**

We will develop a more sophisticated, window-based version of this function in the next chapter.

The BIOS functions are certainly very powerful. Unfortunately, they are also slow. The BIOS is not flexible enough to work on virtual screens, and some of the functions will work only on the active text page. Most of the screen functions, such as clearing, scrolling, and writing, can be performed in a faster and more flexible manner via direct memory access of the video buffer. Most of the screen functions we will develop later will use this direct access.

Cursor-related functions are one area in which the BIOS is indispensable. The routines that we will develop to move the cursor and set its shape, will use BIOS calls. If we did not use the BIOS, we would have to deal with each specific video card at the hardware level. In this case, the BIOS is fast enough for the job, and we can benefit from the device-independent nature of BIOS calls.

THE ANSI CONSOLE DRIVER

The American National Standards Institute (ANSI) has designed specifications for a standard screen (console) driver that allows software to operate with a wide variety of computer systems.

On MS-DOS computers, the ANSI driver is installed by means of the line "DEVICE = ANSI.SYS" in the CONFIG.SYS file. When the ANSI driver is installed, it takes control of all screen and keyboard operations. Instructions, such as those to position the cursor, are sent to the screen as special sequences of text characters. Some ANSI drivers bypass the slow BIOS routines found in certain computers. Screen output may actually be faster with these drivers than without them.

To clear the screen when an ANSI driver is installed, the program need only print the Escape character (hex 1b), followed by "[2J". Such a clear screen function would therefore look like this:

```
void cls(void)
{
puts ("\x1b[2J");
}
```

Use of such a driver can be very attractive to a programmer. The programmer is freed from the task of trying to customize software for many types of computers. Programs written for the ANSI driver can be compiled and run on any system which supports it.

There are some problems with using the ANSI driver. If you write your programs for the ANSI system, you are assuming that everyone using your software will have ANSI installed on their system. If they do not have it on their system, they must install it. It is generally a good idea not to write software which forces users to alter their computer system too much. If a program is inconvenient to use, it will often be left on the shelf. I have frequenctly observed users of a software package complain "This program doesn't work, it prints gibberish," when they ran an ANSI-based program without the driver.

It is actually quite easy for a program to check for the presence of the ANSI driver on an IBM PC and print a warning message if it has not loaded. The program can move the cursor to a given position (say 1,1) via the BIOS. The program then prints the ANSI command to move the cursor to another location and checks cursor position via the BIOS. If the cursor has moved correctly, the ANSI driver is present; if not, the driver is absent. In addition to the burden of loading the driver, the ANSI driver also reduces the amount of free memory available to programs.

In keeping with our stated goal of not being dependent on any special drivers or equipment, we will not require use of the ANSI driver with our software. However, our code will work well with an ANSI driver if it is installed.

SUMMARY

We have discussed display adapters, screen buffers, and techniques for controlling the screen display. Two methods of screen control, the BIOS interrupts and ANSI drivers, were shown to be very versatile in dealing with the diverse array of adapter cards. The fastest method of screen control is undoubtedly direct memory access of the video buffer, and it is that technique we will use for our code.

In the next section, we will discuss the construction of a direct screen writing function. We will see that is it possible to build such a function without sacrificing the versatility of the BIOS and ANSI methods. The techniques that we develop will be powerful enough to access virtual screens, virtual windows, DESQview virtual screens, and nonstandard display adapters.

Chapter 2

Window and Screen Functions

In this chapter we will:

- Learn how to write directly to the video buffer.
- Discuss various types of windowing systems.
- Create a window/screen library which we will use to create, access, move, and delete windows.
- Discuss techniques to make our libraries compatible with multitasking environments.

GOALS

Since the C programming language has no provisions for screen and window functions, we must either create our own functions, or use someone else's. The easiest approach would have been to write this book specifically with one C compiler in mind. Many of the compilers come with their own screen libraries ready to link with program code. Choosing a specific compiler would certainly make our programming tasks easier in some regards.

I personally feel there are some disadvantages to writing programs specifically for one compiler. If the maker of the compiler goes out of business, or radically changes the screen libraries, you face an extensive rewrite of your code. Additionally, you cannot modify the library functions to fit your needs unless you can obtain the library source code. Sometimes source code is available (for a price), but it may not be commented enough to understand.

With this in mind, we will create our own windowing environment and thus maintain greater independence and flexibility.

WHAT IS A WINDOW?

There are about as many definitions of windows as there are writers. Rather than give yet another definition, let us discuss the visual characteristics of windows.

To the user, a window appears as a section of the screen within which output is confined. Basically, it appears as a screen within a screen. Windows are usually boxed or framed with lines which help separate them visually from the rest of the screen. Windows may pop up on top of other text, fully or partially overlapping, or may exist side-by-side with other windows.

Perhaps the best way to view windows is in terms of the *Desktop Metaphor*. The computer screen is the desktop and windows are treated as if they were sheets of paper. Paper can be placed on the desk and moved to any location. Other sheets of paper may be on the desk either next to, or on top of, existing sheets. Sheets of paper may be brought to the top of the stack, or inserted in any location. A sheet of paper may be written on, no matter where it is located. Any sheet may be removed from the desk at any time.

If we are to effectively use the Desktop Metaphor, we need functions to accomplish the following:

- Create a window (framed or unframed) anywhere on the physical screen.
- Move any window in any direction.
- Write to, clear, or scroll any window.
- Insert any window between any other windows (change level).
- Delete any window at any time

All of our windows should be available for access at any time.

APPLICATION

This section provides a practical introduction to the window functions. Sample programs are presented to illustrate the use of each function. Numerous suggestions are presented for getting the most from the functions. We will cover:

- How to link the window functions with your code.
- Advantages of library files.
- Command line switches for customizing the code.

- Selecting the best text attributes for applications.
- Clearing, printing, and scrolling the video screen.
- Creating windows.
- Virtual screens.
- Accessing overlapped windows (clearing, writing, and scrolling).
- Moving windows (up, down, left, and right).
- Reordering windows (changing the sequence).
- Removing windows.
- Optimizing window placement (overlapping versus panel).

SPECIFYING A COMPILER

The code presented in this book compiles successfully under both Turbo C (2.0) and QuickC (2.0). The programs presented within this book use conditional compilation statements to handle compiler differences. We define the type of compiler we are using by means of a #define statement located near the beginning of the header file mydef.h. If you plan to use Borland's Turbo C, this line would read:

```
#define TURBOC
```

If you are compiling with Microsoft's QuickC, the line would read:

```
#define QUICKC
```

These two compilers sometimes use different names for similar functions, or utilize different header files. We can resolve these differences by means of #if defined statements within the code.

```
#if defined  TURBOC
   ... Turbo C-specific code statements...
#endif

#if defined QUICKC
   ... QuickC-specific code statements...
#endif
```

By default, the define statement in mydef.h reads "#define TURBOC". If you plan to use this code with QuickC, please change the line to read "#define QUICKC".

The file mydef.h should be included with *all* modules which are linked with the screen/window library.

FUNCTION PROTOTYPES AND CODING TECHNIQUES

Function prototypes are declarations which specify function names, the types of values received by a function, and the type of value returned by a function. The use of function prototypes is highly encouraged under the new ANSI standard for the C language.

The use of function prototypes assures that the correct type and number of parameters are passed to a function. If a parameter with a different data type is passed to the function, it is coerced (converted) to fit the data type expected. This type checking in some ways allows ANSI C to be more forgiving of programmer errors.

For example, the following function prototype defines the function **sum( )** as accepting two integer values and returning an integer.

```
int sum(int x, int y);
```

Function prototypes are placed external to all functions, usually in the header files. All the library function prototypes used in our programs are defined in the header file mydef.h.

If prototypes are used, a function can work properly even with unexpected parameter types. In the example in Table 2–1 the function prototype successfully coerces (converts) a floating point number to an integer. Note in the example in

TABLE 2–1. FUNCTION PROTOTYPE

This does not work	This works!
	`int sum(int x, int y);`
`main()`	`main()`
`{`	`{`
`float x=1,y=1;`	`float x=1,y=1;`
`float total;`	`float total;`
`total= sum(x,y);`	`total= sum(x,y);`
`}`	`}`
`int sum(x,y)`	`int sum(x,y)`
`int x,y;`	`int x,y;`
`{`	`{`
`return(x+y);`	`return(x+y);`
`}`	`}`

Table 2–1 that the function prototype works, even though we have used the old style of defining variables. We will exclusively use the modern ANSI style of designating functions, as in the following example.

```
Old style           Modern style

int sum(x,y)        int sum(int x,int y)
int x,y;            {
{                   }
}
```

USING THE WINDOW MODULES

The functions we will use in our programs are contained in a group of files prefixed with L. Their names, listed in alphabetical order are:

```
L_BAR.C
L_CHIP.C
L_COPY.C
L_DIR.C
L_GETFLD.C
L_GETKEY.C
L_INPUT.C
L_LIST.C
L_MAIN.C
L_POPUP.C
L_PRINT.C
L_SCRN1.C
L_SCRN2.C
L_SCRN3.C
L_SCRN4.C
L_STRING.C
L_TRIM.C
L_WIN1.C
L_WIN2.C
L_WIN3.C
L_WIN4.C
L_WIN5.3
```

The L prefix makes them easily identifiable, and allows you to operate on them with wildcard commands (e.g., copy a:L*.c c:*.*)

The Lmain.c module contains the function **main( )**, which defines and initializes our external variables and calls **start( )**. The function **start( )** is the starting, or entry, point for all our programs.

For example, the following program hello.c clears the screen and prints "hello" in the upper lefthand corner of the screen:

```
/* the program hello.c */

#include "mydef.h"

start( )
{
cls( );
print(1,1,"hello");
}
```

This program would be compiled and linked with all the modules beginning with L. This modular construction allows us to concentrate on particular sections of code without the distraction of dealing with the support functions.

CREATING A LIBRARY

In the preceding example, all the modules are linked with the program being compiled. Linking all the modules can make the final program unnecessarily large, particularly if some modules are not needed.

Individual modules, compiled as *.obj* files, can be placed into a special library file, which has a *.lib* extension. When a library file is linked with a program, an individual module is linked only if one of its functions is called by the program. The entire module is linked if any function within the module is called.

If your goal is to minimize your compiled program size, each function should be in an individual module. This way you would prevent any undesired code from being linked. Alternately, interconnected functions should be placed together. For example, if function A always calls function B, and function B is *only* called by function A, functions A and B should be placed in the same module.

In the real world, functions are seldom so neatly interconnected, so I have compromised by putting together the functions which are most frequently used together. This may result in some unneeded functions being added to the final compiled application, but the library maintenance is greatly reduced.

The procedure for creating library files differs somewhat among compilers. See your compiler reference manual for details.

EXTERNAL VARIABLES

A number of the screen/window functions make use of external data structures. The screen-related data structure is **scr** and the window-related data structure is **w**. The **w** data structure is used internally by the window related functions, and is discussed in the Techniques section, so it is not covered here.

The screen-related data structure, **scr,** contains important information relating the screen size, video adapter type, and text attributes. *Understanding this structure is essential* for proper use of the screen/window library functions.

If you plan to use any of the external variables within a function, include the following lines within the declaration area.

```
extern struct screen_structure scr;

extern struct window_structure w[];
```

These lines let the compiler know that the values are external, and have specific structure tags applied to them. You should, of course, have included mydef.h at the beginning of the module.

Now let's look at the external variables in detail. The external variable **scr.mode** indicates what text mode is present. It will be set to one of the following:

```
BW_80      Composite (black and white) monitor in use.
COLOR_80   Color monitor in use.
MONOCHROME Monochrome monitor in use.
```

Three text attributes are initialized by the function **main( )** according to the setting of **scr.mode.** They are:

> **scr.current** = The text attribute to use when writing to or clearing the screen.
>
> **scr.normal** = The default normal or standard text attribute (white on black).
>
> **scr.inverse** = The default inverse text attribute (black on white).

The screen print routine always writes text to the screen using the attribute defined by **scr.current.**

If these predefined attributes did not exist, and we wanted to print inverse text, we would be forced to test for each monitor type, as in the following statements:

```
if(scr.mode==BW_80) scr.current= set_color(BLACK,WHITE);
if(scr.mode==COLOR_80) scr.current=set_color(BLACK,WHITE);
if(scr.mode==MONOCHROME) scr.current=(INVERSE);
```

Use of the predefined attributes, dependent on screen mode, eliminates the need to pick text appropriate to the monitor being used. Since the appropriate attributes are already defined for each monitor type, we can set the attribute with one statement:

```
scr.current=scr.inverse;
```

If **scr.mode** is equal to COLOR_80, you may set **scr.normal** and **scr.inverse** to more attractive colors.

```
if(scr.mode==COLOR_80) scr.normal=set_color(WHITE,BLUE);
if(scr.mode==COLOR_80) scr.inverse=set_color(BLUE,WHITE);
```

The only time it would be acceptable to create a new attribute would be if a color monitor were in use. Obviously such an attribute would be meaningless on a monochrome display (**scr.mode** equals MONOCHROME), and unreadable on a B&W or LCD display (**scr.mode** equals BW_80).

The intensity attribute may be set with the statement ''scr.current = set_intense(scr.normal)''. In this case the current attribute is set to the attribute defined in **scr.normal,** with the text attribute set to intense.

Other external variables of interest are:

scr.rows   = The number of rows on the display screen.

scr.columns = The number of columns.

scr.buffer   = The address of the screen buffer (a far pointer). If DESQview is detected, this buffer is automatically set to the application's assigned virtual screen.

scr.snow   = Logical TRUE or FALSE indicating if snow avoidance should be used.

COMMAND LINE SWITCHES

Our code is designed to be very flexible, and can be adapted easily for use with hardware that may not even exist yet. Several of the external variables may be overridden at run-time by use of command line switches (arguments).

   s   Changes segment of the video buffer.

   o   Changes offset of the video buffer.

   r   The number of rows on the display screen.

   c   The number of columns.

   n   No snow avoidance.

   b   Black-and-white mode (no colors displayed).

Please note that *all values are given in decimal.*

As an example of how to override the default external variables settings, let us imagine that the program demo is being run on a PC with a new ACME SEE-MORE Panoramic™ display adapter. Let us assume that this adapter is currently configured to display 50 rows of 100 columns each. The base segment address of the video buffer is b700H (46848 decimal). The offset is 0000H. Most software would need to be rewritten to operate on such a nonstandard card. Our software can handle this situation with ease. Simply override the default segment, offset, row, and column settings by typing in the following command at the DOS prompt, before running our software:

```
demo  s=46848  o=0  r=50  c=100
```

The only assumption is that the card's display buffer is mapped to use the convention of character followed by attribute.

TYPES OF WINDOW FUNCTIONS

It might appear that screen and window functions are separate types of functions. In reality the two are tightly bound. *In our system everything is a window.* All screen output takes place within a window environment.

All of our programs begin with a window already defined. This window is unframed, and of maximum size (**scr.rows*scr.columns**). The initial window is also unique in that it is immovable. It cannot be moved up, down, left, or right on the display screen (it's too big), nor can it change levels. It may not be moved on top of other windows; it is always the bottom of the window stack. Think of the initial window as the desktop in our desktop metaphor. The sheets of paper (windows) may be moved, but not the desktop.

Most of the time a program deals with the current, topmost window. A program might spend quite a bit of time with the initial unframed window before opening a new window. When a new window is opened, the new window receives most of the activity.

With this in mind, we divide the screen and window functions into three logical categories of functions:

Default: Functions which apply to the active (topmost) window only.

Window specific: Functions which create new windows, or access previously created windows. They all begin with **win_**, as in **win_make( )**, **win_delete( )** and so on.

Internal: Functions which are called only by other functions. These functions should not be called directly and have therefore been declared *static* functions, which means they cannot be accessed outside the module in which they were compiled.

Default Window Functions

The default functions come the closest to being general screen functions. The fact that you can use them directly on the initial screen adds to this impression. An example of a default function is **cls( )**, which is the clear-screen function. It requires no parameter to indicate the specific window to act upon, because it operates on the default (active) top window only.

`void alt_screen(int action);`
Creates a virtual screen which is not seen by the user (see the Techniques section of this chapter for more information). The contents of the video buffer are copied to the alternate buffer. All screen output (printing, creating windows, and so on) is then routed to this buffer until it is turned off. When the alternate buffer is turned off, the contents are copied to the true video buffer. The screen updates made while the alternate screen was turned on will appear instantly. Use of this technique gives the illusion of great speed.

Example: alt_screen(ON);   Turns the alternate screen on.
                     alt_screen(OFF);   Turns the alternate screen off.

`void ceol(int x, int y);`
Clear from screen coordinate x, y to the **End Of the Line** of the active window.

Example: ceol(3,4);

`void cls(void);`
Just like the DOS command, this clears the current window and moves the cursor to the upper left corner of the active window.

Example: cls( );

`void cursor(int size);`
Sets the cursor size for the active window to one of three predefined values. The variable **size** may be one of the following:

```
BIG_CURSOR=      Largest possible cursor.
NORMAL_CURSOR=   Standard underline cursor.
NO_CURSOR=       Cursor invisible.
```

Example: cursor(NO_CURSOR); Makes the cursor invisible.

Also see **void set_cursor( );.**

`void gotoxy(int x,int y);`
Positions the cursor in the column and row indicated by x, y. The location is relative to the current window.

Example: gotoxy(1,3); Puts the cursor in the first column of the third row.

```
void print(int x,int y,char *string);
```
Prints the text string at the x, y location indicated. The position is relative to the active window. The text is wrapped to stay within the active window. The window is scrolled up when the end of the window is reached. The string is printed with the text attribute specified by the external variable **scr.current.** The cursor is moved one space beyond the last character printed.

   If the external variable **scr.bold_caps** is set TRUE, then all uppercase letters are printed with the intensity set ON (useful for highlighting hot keys with menus).

Example: print(1,1,"options: Sort, Print, Quit"); Would print the following at location 1,1.

"options: **Sort, Print, Quit**" (scr.bold/caps set to TRUE)

"options: Sort, Print, Quit" (scr.bold/caps set to FALSE)


```
void print_here(char *string);
```
Works like **print( )** except that the string is printed at the current cursor location.

Example: print_here("Here I am");


```
void readxy(char *ch, char *attr);
```
Reads the character and attribute at the current cursor location, and sets ch = character and attr = attribute.

Example: readxy(&ch,&attr);


```
void scroll_down(int lines);
```
Scrolls the active window down the number of lines specified. The top lines are cleared. The cursor is also moved in the direction indicated so that it maintains the correct position relative to any existing text. If the number of lines requested is greater than the height of the window, the entire window is cleared.

Example: scroll_down(1);


```
void scroll_up(int lines);
```
Just like scroll_down, but the movement is up.

Example: scroll_up(2);

`set_color(char foreground, char background);`
This is actually a function-like macro defined in mydef.h. It returns the text attribute with the foreground/background attributes requested.

Example: attribute = set_color(BLACK,BLUE);

The predefined colors are BLACK, BLUE, GREEN, CYAN, RED, MAGENTA, BROWN, YELLOW, and WHITE.

`void set_cursor(int start, int end);`
This function sets the cursor starting and ending scan lines. This defines which row of pixels in a character the cursor highlights. The lines are counted from the top to the bottom of a character. On a CGA display for example, the cursor range is 0 through 7 with the normal setting being 6 to 7. On a MDA, the range is 0 through 13 with the normal setting being 11 to 12. If a CGA cursor were set to the 0 through 7 range, the cursor would be large and would highlight the entire character.

Example: set_cursor(0,7);

`set_intense (char attribute);`
A function-like macro defined in mydef.h. It returns the attribute with the intensity bit turned ON.

Example: scr.current = set_intense(scr.normal); Sets the default current attribute to the predefined normal attribute with intensity set ON.

`void set_mode(int mode);`
Calls the BIOS routine to set the mode. The external variable **scr.mode** is updated to reflect the change.

Example: set_mode(BW_80);

`void what_cursor(int *start, int *end);`
Reads the status of the cursor start/end lines. Sets the variables **start** and **end** to the starting/ending scan lines of the cursor.

Example: what_cursor(&start,&end);

`void what_mode(int *mode,int *page);`
Reads the current mode and page (page valid for CGA only). Sets the variable **mode** to the current value of the screen mode, as known to the BIOS. The variable **page** is set to the current text page (color adapters only).

`void wherexy(int *x,int *y);`
Reads the cursor location. Sets x and y to the column and row on which the cursor is located. The position indicated is relative to the current window.

Example: wherexy(&x,&y);

Window-Specific Functions

The window-specific functions require an extra parameter (the handle) to indicate which window is to be used. For example, the window-specific equivalent of **cls( )** is **win_cls(handle).** The handle is an integer number by which the window is accessed. Window-specific functions may be used on the top (default) window as well as on any overlapped window. These functions create new windows, or act on previously created windows. The majority of the functions automatically update the screen to reflect the changes made.

A few of the functions require a call to **win_redraw_all( )** to update (redraw) all the windows on the screen. The functions which require manual redraws are clearly identified. They include the printing, scrolling, and window-clearing functions. All the rest call **win_redraw_all( )** automatically. See the Techniques section for a more detailed discussion.

`void win_ceol(int handle, int x, int y);`
Clears from the cursor position x, y to the end of the line for the window specified by **handle.** Call **win_redraw_all( )** to update the screen.

Example: win_ceol(2,1,1); /* clear the line */
            win_redraw(all); /* update the screen */

This call clears from 1, 1 to the end of the line of window 2.

`void win_cls(int handle);`
Clears the screen of the window indicated by **handle.** The window is cleared with the attribute defined for that window. See the function **win_make( ).** Call **win_redraw_all( )** to update the screen.

Example: win_cls(2);   /* clear the line */
            win_redraw_(all);   /* update the screen */

```
void win_delete(int handle);
```
Deletes the window indicated by **handle.**

Example: win_delete(3);


```
void win_delete_top(void);
```
Deletes the top window on the screen.

Example: win_delete_top( );


```
void win_down(int handle, int amount);
```
Moves the window indicated by **handle** down the number of lines indicated by **amount.**

Example: win_down(1,3); Moves window 1 down 3 lines.


```
void win_gotoxy(int handle,int x,int y);
```
Moves the cursor to x, y in the window specified by **handle.** Since the cursor is visible only in the active window, the move will not be visible until the window is topmost (active).


```
void win_insert(int handle, int position);
```
This function changes the level of the window in the window stack. This move is valid only if several windows are open on the screen.

Example: win_inset(4,1); Moves window 4 to relative position 1.

Moving the window to position 1 would make it appear as the first window above the initial window (the desktop).


```
void win_left(int handle, int amount);
```
Move the window indicated by **handle** left the number of lines indicated by **amount.**

Example: win_left(1,3); Moves window 1 left three columns.


```
int win_make(int x,int y,int width,int height,
             char *array,char *title,
             char frame_attr, char win_attr);
```
Makes a new window and returns the window handle, an integer value that is used by window-specific functions when accessing the window. This new window

is the topmost, or active, window. The parameters are:

x, y   = Upper left corner (column, row) of the INTERIOR of the window.

width   = Width of the window interior.

height   = Height of the window interior.

array   = A string whose elements contain the characters used to build the frame. These elements are upper left, upper right, bottom left, bottom right, horizontal, and vertical. Several frame arrays that are defined in mydef.h are shown in Figure 2–1.

title   = The title to appear in the upper left corner of the window frame. Use " " if no title is required.

frame_att = The attribute to use when drawing the frame.

win_attr   = The default attribute to use for the window interior. This is the attribute used when clearing or scrolling the screen.

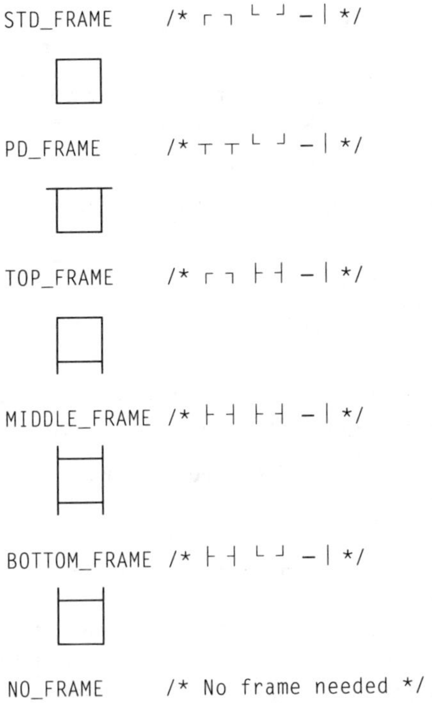

Figure 2–1 Frame arrays and their appearance

When a window is created, the interior of the window is automatically cleared and the cursor moved to the upper left corner. If an attempt is made to create a window which is too large to fit within the physical screen, the window size is adjusted so that it will fit. Likewise, if the window location is such that the edges of the window would extend past the borders of the screen, the window is moved so that it fits within the screen boundaries.

Example: int demo_win;
demo_win = win_make(1,1,10,5,STD_BOX,"Win1",scr.normal,scr.normal);

The window that would be created is shown in Figure 2–2.

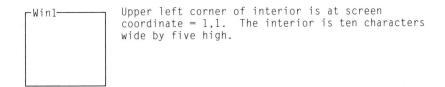

Upper left corner of interior is at screen coordinate = 1,1. The interior is ten characters wide by five high.

Figure 2–2 Sample window

```
void win_pop_top(int handle);
```
Moves the window indicated by **handle** to the top of the window stack. It automatically becomes the active window.

Example: win_pop_top(2);

```
void win_print( int handle, int x,int y, char *string);
```
Prints the text string at position x, y of window indicated by **handle.** Text is printed using the attribute indicated by **scr.current.** This function works just like **print( ),** except that a window handle must be specified.

Example: win_print(2,1,1,"hello");
        win_redraw_all( );

This example prints "hello" in the upper left corner of window 2. A call is made to **win_redraw_all( )** to update the screen. If several **win_print( )** statements are required, it is better to wait until all the statements have been issued, then update the screen with a call to **win_redraw_all( ).** This saves time which would be wasted updating the screen unnecessarily.

```
void win_redraw_all(void);
```
Updates the physical screen to reflect any changes made to the virtual windows. The redraw is done in a virtual screen that is invisible to the user, and which is copied to the screen buffer. The redraw appears to be instantaneous.

Example: win_redraw_all( );

```
void win_right(int handle, int amount);
```
Moves the window indicated by **handle to** the right the number of columns indicated by **amount.** The window is not moved if there is insufficient space on the screen.

Example: win_right(handle,2); Moves window indicated by **handle** to the right two columns.

```
void win_scroll_down(int handle,int lines);
```
Scrolls the contents, including the cursor, of the window indicated by **handle** down the number of lines indicated by **lines.** The top lines are cleared according to the text attribute which was specified for the window when it was created. If the number of lines is greater than the height of the window, the window is cleared.

Example: win_scroll_down (handle,3); Scrolls the window indicated by **handle** down three lines.

```
void win_scroll_up(int handle,int lines);
```
Works like **win_scroll_down( )**, except the direction is up.

```
void win_set_attr(int handle, char attribute);
```
Sets the default text attribute for the window specified.

```
void win_up(int handle, int lines);
```
The window indicated by **handle** is moved up the number of lines indicated by **lines.**

```
char win_what_attr(int handle);
```
Returns the text attribute which was defined for the window specified by **handle.**

Internal Functions

These functions are intended to be called by other functions. Directly calling these functions may result in strange and wonderful displays. Several of the functions are defined as *static* and therefore are unaccessible outside the module within which they were compiled.

```
void display_cursor(void);
```
Updates the cursor position and size to reflect the values stored in the active window definition. This function is generally intended for internal use, but may be called directly.

```
void dma_print(int *x, int *y,char *string);
```
This function is called by **print( )**. It does not physically move the cursor to the end of the line after printing the text, but it does change the values of **x** and **y** to indicate where the cursor should go. This function is especially useful when you wish to print text but do not want the cursor jumping about the screen. Note that **dma_print( )** is passed pointers to **x** and **y** so that they may be updated to indicate where the cursor would have been moved to.

```
void draw_frame (int x,int y,int width,int height,
char *array,char *title,int attribute);
```
Draws a window frame. The parameters have the same meaning as those used by the function **win_make( )**.

```
static void init_window(void);
```
Initializes internal arrays used by the window routines. This function is used by the function **main( )** as part of the initialization process.

```
void move_scr_mem (char far *string,char far *video,int
                          number);
```
Moves memory from ***string** to ***video**. The variable **number** indicates the number of bytes to move. If the external variable **scr.snow** is set to TRUE, steps are taken to avoid screen snow.

```
static void set_screen_attr(void);
```
Checks the equipment and initializes external screen (**scr**) variables. This is called by the function **main( )**.

```
static void test_dv(void);
```
Tests for the presence of DESQview or Windows and sets the external variable **scr.buffer** to the application buffer.

```
void update_margins(void);
```
Used to reset the active window margins to the values stored in the window definition.

```
static void win_point(int handle);
```
Used by many of the window functions to route output to a specific window.

```
static void win_redraw(int handle);
```
Redraws a specific window on-screen and would make it appear to be on top of all other windows. This function is called by **win_redraw_all( )** to redraw the windows in the proper order.

```
void win_save(void);
```
Saves the contents of the top window. This function is called by **win_make( )**.

```
int win_validate (int handle);
```
Verifies that a window specified by **handle** is part of the current window stack. A -1 is returned if the window does not exist. If the window does exist, the relative position of the window in the stack is returned.

USING THE FUNCTIONS

It is perhaps easiest to illustrate the use of the functions with a sample program. The following program, windemo.c, prints a background of dots on the initial screen, then creates and moves several windows. There is an interesting display of window animation, in which a window moves over and under other windows. Virtual screens are utilized, as well as default and window-specific functions.

```
/******************* WINDEMO.C *************************/

#include "mydef.h"    /* always include this */
#include <stddef.h>   /* we need the definition of NULL from here  */

/* function prototype */
void fill_win(void);
```

```
int start(void)        /* start is the entry point */
{
extern struct screen_structure scr;
extern struct window_structure w[];

char string[255];
int i;
char frame_attr, window_attr;
int w1,w2,w3,message;      /* variables to hold window handles */

/* clear the screen */
        cls();
/* fill the screen with dots '.'*/
/* make up a string of '.' wide enough to fill each row */

   /* build the string */
   for(i=0;i<scr.columns;i++) string[i]='.';
   string[i]= '\0';             /* terminate it*/

/*turn on alternate (virtual) screen so the printing is not seen*/

   alt_screen(ON);

/* now fill each row of the screen with the string of '.' */

   for (i=1;i<=scr.rows;i++) print(1,i,string);

/* make the newly drawn screen visible */
   alt_screen(OFF);

/* make window 1, and print to it */

   w1=win_make (1,1,35,6,STD_FRAME,"Window1",scr.normal,scr.normal);

   print(1,1,"This window is framed.");
   print(1,2,"The frame attribute is normal.");
   print(1,3,"The interior attribute is normal.");
   print(1,4,"The cursor is of normal size.");
   print(1,6,"TOUCH ANY KEY TO CONTINUE:");

   getch();

/* make window 2 */
   w2= win_make (4,4,35,6,NO_FRAME,"",scr.normal,scr.inverse);

   cursor(BIG_CURSOR);   /* set the cursor to large */

   print(1,1,"This window is unframed.");
   print(1,3,"The interior attribute is inverse.");
   print(1,4,"The cursor is of large size.");
   print(1,6,"TOUCH ANY KEY TO CONTINUE:");

   getch();
```

```
/* make window 3 */
  w3=win_make (8,8,40,9,STD_FRAME,"Window3",scr.normal,scr.normal);

  cursor(NO_CURSOR);  /* hide the cursor */

/* demonstrate the use of attributes */

  print(1,1," Here are the predefined text attributes:");
  scr.current=scr.normal;
   print(1,2,"NORMAL");
  scr.current=set_intense(scr.current);
   print(1,3,"intense");
  scr.current=scr.inverse;
   print(1,4,"INVERSE");
  scr.current=scr.normal;

/* demonstrate bold caps */

  scr.bold_caps=TRUE;  /* set bold caps flag */
   print(1,5,"Demo of Bold Caps.");
  scr.bold_caps=FALSE; /* turn off flag */

  print(1,7,"The cursor is hidden.");
  print(1,9,"TOUCH ANY KEY TO CONTINUE:");

    getch();

/* make a message window */
/* if color mode, set color attributes */

  if(scr.mode==COLOR_80){
    window_attr=set_color(WHITE,BLUE);
    frame_attr=set_color(YELLOW,BLACK);
  }
   else {    /* if not color then use predefined attributes */
    frame_attr= scr.normal;
    window_attr=scr.normal;
  }

  message=win_make (10,20,47,5,STD_FRAME," message window",
                    frame_attr,window_attr);

  print(1,1,"Touch a key several times ");
  print(1,2,"to pop windows 1-3 to the top.");
  print(1,3,"The correct cursor appears for each window");
  print(1,5,"TOUCH ANY KEY TO CONTINUE:");

  getch();

/* now pop the windows to the top, one by one */
```

```
  win_pop_top(w1);     /* pop window one to the top */
   getch();
  win_pop_top(w2):     /* pop window two */
   getch();
  win_pop_top(w3);     /* pop window three */

/* pop the message window */
  win_pop_top(message);

  /* get the window attribute */
  scr.current=win_what_attr(message);
   cls();
  print(1,1,"Touch any key to see window movement");

   getch();

/* now move window 2 around the screen */

  for(i=0;i<4;i++) win_up(w2,1);       /* move it up */
  win_insert(w2,3);                    /* insert at level 3 */
  for(i=0;i<17;i++) win_down(w2,1);    /* move it down */
     win_insert(w2,2);                 /* move it to level 2 */
  for(i=0;i<14;i++) win_up(w2,1);      /* move it up */

/* give a demonstration of clearing and writing to overlapped
windows */

   cls();
  print(1,1,"Touch any key to see the windows cleared");
  print(1,2,"and new text written");
   getch();

/* do window 1 */
/* we will not do a win_redraw_all() until all the windows are done */

  win_cls(w1);                    /* clear window 1 */
  scr.current=win_what_attr(w1);  /* get the attribute */
  win_print(w1,1,1,"Window 1");   /* print with the correct attribute
                                     for window 1 */

/* do window 2 */

  win_cls(w2);                     /* clear window 2 */
  scr.current=win_what_attr(w2);   /* get the attribute */
  win_print(w2,1,1,"Window 2");    /* print */

/* do window 3 */

  win_cls(w3):                     /* clear window 3 */
  scr.current=win_what_attr(w3);   /* get the attribute */
  win_print(w3,1,1,"Window 3");    /* print */
```

```
/* now that all the virtual windows have been updated,
   we will display the changes */

  win_redraw_all();

/* note: the active window is still the message window */

  cls();
  /* get attribute for window */
  scr.current =win_what_attr(message);

  print(1,1,"Touch any key to delete the windows");
   getch();
  for(i=0;i<4;i++) win_delete_top();    /* delete the window */

return(0);
}
```

OPTIMUM WINDOW PLACEMENT

Careful consideration should be given to the style and placement of windows in an application. Windows are sometimes overdone, with too many windows popping in and out of existence in a confusing manner. The window functions give us the ability to access partially overlapped windows. This looks snazzy on a demo, but may be impractical or irritating to the enduser.

Take, for example, the hypothetical application displayed in Figure 2–3, which accesses a number of remote weather stations. The local information is in the background window, while a pop-up window informs us that the program is currently polling the other sites. In theory this program could update the background window while scanning the other sites. Unfortunately, since most of the information is obscured, the updates are of little use. At best, the update would give assurance that local data was still available.

The layout of this application is much improved by the use of nonoverlapping windows. We will refer to these nonoverlapping windows as *panels* although they

```
 ┌─Local──────────────┐          ┌─Local────────────────┐
 │Time:  10:23        │          │Time:   10:23         │
 │Temp┌───────────────┴┐         │Temp:  65  F          │
 │    │Standby:        │         │                      │
 │Toda│Polling remote  │         │Today:                │
 │Tot │sites.        00│         │  Total Rainfall:  0.00│
 │Ozo │Site count:  15 │         │  Ozone:              │
 │Hum └────────────────┘         │  Humidity:  55%      │
 │Spore count: 458 / c│          │  Spore count:  458 /cc│
 └────────────────────┘          └──────────────────────┘

                                  ┌──────────────────────┐
                                  │Polling:    Site count 15│
                                  └──────────────────────┘
```

Figure 2–3 Overlapping windows   **Figure 2–4** Two-panel layout example

```
┌─────────────────────────────────────────────┐
│ File: myfile    Size: 2258    Free:254089    │
└─────────────────────────────────────────────┘

┌─────────────────────────────────────────────┐
│ Last name:                                    │
│ First name:                                   │
│                                               │
│ Street:                                       │
│ City:                                         │
│ State:                                        │
│                                               │
│ Phone:                                        │
└─────────────────────────────────────────────┘

┌─────────────────────────────────────────────┐
│ Options:   Edit   Next   Print   Quit         │
└─────────────────────────────────────────────┘
```

Figure 2–5 Three-panel layout example

are also known as *tiled* windows. "Nonoverlapping" refers to the contents of the windows themselves. The frames may or may not overlap. Figure 2–4 is an example of a panel layout of the weather station data. With the panel layout, none of the information is obscured, and each panel may be freely updated.

Panels allow us to group related data on the screen. The user knows exactly where to look to find specific information. In Figure 2–5, information relating to the file in use is shown at the top of the screen, the menu is at the bottom, and the input screen is in the middle.

One disadvantage of panels is the space occupied by the window frame. In Figure 2–5, six rows of screen space are wasted by the frame lines. We can improve this by drawing the windows so that the frames overlap. The frame types may be selected so that the lines appear to merge, as shown in Figure 2–6. These are then positioned so that the frames overlap (bottom over middle, middle over top). Now, in Figure 2–7, the frames occupy only four rows instead of six.

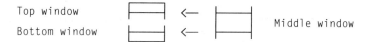

Figure 2–6 Example of merging frames to save space

```
┌─────────────────────────────────────────────┐
│ File: myfile    Size: 2258    Free:254089    │
├─────────────────────────────────────────────┤
│ Last name:                                    │
│ First name:                                   │
│                                               │
│ Street:                                       │
│ City:                                         │
│ State:                                        │
│                                               │
│ Phone:                                        │
├─────────────────────────────────────────────┤
│ Options:   Edit   Next   Print   Quit         │
└─────────────────────────────────────────────┘
```

Figure 2–7 Efficient panel layout

Listed next is a sample program which creates three panels. Note that the program does not assume an 80 × 25 display. Instead, it checks the external variables **scr.rows** and **scr.columns.**

```
/********************     PANEL1.C     **************************/

/* demonstrate the creation of three window panels */

#include "mydef.h"    /* always include this */
#include <stddef.h>   /* we need the definition of NULL from here */

int start(void)
{
extern struct screen_structure scr;
extern struct window_structure w[];

int top, middle,bottom;

cls();             /* clear initial window */

alt_screen(ON);    /* Let's draw the windows off screen */

/* calculate the window sizes to fit true column and row */
/* don't assume 80x25 */

top=win_make(2,2,scr.columns-2,1,TOP_FRAME,"",scr.normal,
             scr.normal);
print(1,1,"test panel 1");

middle=win_make(2,4,scr.columns-2,scr.rows-6,MIDDLE_FRAME,"",
             scr.normal,scr.normal);
print(1,1,"test panel 2");

bottom=win_make(2,scr.rows-1,scr.columns-2,1,BOTTOM_FRAME,"",
             scr.normal,scr.normal);
print(1,1,"test panel 3");

win_pop_top(middle);  /* make middle window topmost */

alt_screen(OFF); /* show the finished screen */

return (0);
}
```

We can even further increase the amount of screen space available for writing data by using unframed windows to create our panels. Without frames, the panels would not be distinct, so it is necessary to use text attributes to set off each window. In this situation, we can make the top and bottom panels inverse, and the middle panel normal.

Here is the program rewritten to create panels offset by their attributes:

```
/********************   PANEL2.C   **************************/

/*
Demonstrate the creation of three window panels.
The panels are unframed with the upper and lower panels
displayed in inverse.
The upper and lower panels occupy one line.
*/

#include "mydef.h"  /* always include this */
#include <stddef.h> /* we need the definition of NULL from here */

int start(void)
{
extern struct screen_structure scr;
external struct window_structure w[];

int top, middle, bottom;

   cls();           /* clear initial window */
   alt_screen(ON);  /* Let's draw the windows off screen */

     /* calculate the window sizes to fit true column and row */
     /* don't assume 80x25 */

     top=win_make(1,1,scr.columns,1,NO_FRAME,"",scr.normal,
                  scr.inverse);
        print(1,1,"test panel 1");

     middle=win_make(1,2,scr.columns,scr.rows-2,"","",scr.normal,
                  scr.normal);
        print(1,1,"test panel 2");

     bottom=win_make(2,scr.rows,scr.columns,1,"","",scr.normal,
                  scr.inverse);
        print(1,1,"test panel 3");

     win_pop_top(middle);  /* make middle window topmost */

   alt_screen(OFF); /* show the finished screen */

return(0);
}
```

This panel effect could be produced without using windows. The **print( )** function could be used to produce an identical screen. But there are very distinct advantages to the windows:

1. We can easily clear the middle panel with a **win_cls( )** call.

2. The top and bottom panels may be accessed without as many column,row calculations as would be needed otherwise, because they each begin at 1, 1 relative to their window.

The panel layout gives the impression that the panels all exist at the same level, but in reality they are windows in a stack. In the case just shown, we have a four-level window stack consisting of the initial window plus the top, middle, and bottom panels.

A panel may be accessed either by popping that panel to the top with **win_pop_top( )** and using the default window functions, or by using the window-specific functions directly on the window. If you intend to access a window for a period of time, such as for data entry, use the **win_pop_top( )** function. Access to the active topmost window is faster since it is unbuffered.

The cursor is only visible in the topmost window. The cursor may be used to indicate which window or panel is active. In the case just shown, the middle window is the data input window, and it would be essential that the middle window be on top so that the user could see the cursor. Accessing the other windows could still be accomplished by using the window-specific functions.

It is possible to turn off the cursor for any given window. When the window is first created, issue the statement "cursor(NO_CURSOR);". The screen functions remember the location and shape of the cursor when the window is popped to the top. The cursor will stay off for that window until it is turned back on by issuing another **cursor( )** call.

MISCELLANEOUS TRICKS

Saving the Initial Screen

When exiting to DOS, some applications restore the text that existed on the screen prior to the program's execution. Some users find this a useful feature, as it reminds them of what they were doing before running the application.

We can easily accomplish similar screen restorations with our programs. The initial screen, which is actually an unframed full-screen window, is not automatically cleared when the program executes. Normally, the screen is overwritten by the application's output.

We can prevent this overwriting by creating a new full-sized window, framed or unframed, which completely covers the initial screen. This window can then be treated as though it were the desktop, which provides the backdrop for the other windows.

Before the application exits, all the windows (other than the original window) are deleted, and the initial screen is restored.

The slight disadvantages of using this technique are that it uses more memory and slows down the **win_redraw_all( )** function because it has an additional window to redraw each time we redraw all the windows.

Hiding Windows

If a second full-sized window is created to serve as the desktop, as just described, it may be used to conceal other windows. For example, suppose we have three windows—the initial desktop, a second full-screen window, and a smaller window—as shown in Table 2-2. The variables **newdesk** and **small** contain the handles for the two movable windows (the initial window can't be moved). The initial window needs no variable to store its handle; it is always 0. The window in position 2 in the stack may be moved to the first position with the command "win_insert(small,1);". After the movement, the stack is arranged as in Table 2-3. Since window "small" is underneath the larger full-screen window, it is not visible. Later, when needed, it could be popped back to the top, or inserted in a more visible position.

This technique could be used to hide numerous windows, which could be popped up as needed. Once again, there is a memory and speed disadvantage to having numerous windows open at once.

TABLE 2-2.   ORIGINAL WINDOW SEQUENCE

Position	Window	Handle
0	Initial window (Un-movable).	0
1	Second full-screen window.	newdesk
2	Small window.	small

TABLE 2-3.   NEW WINDOW SEQUENCE

Position	Window	Handle
0	Initial window (Un-movable).	0
1	Small window	small
2	Second full-screen window.	newdesk

TECHNIQUES

In this section we take a more in-depth look at the screen function library. We will discuss design considerations, techniques, and any aspect of the screen and window system which would not be intuitively obvious from the source code. We will cover:

- Types of window systems (simple, virtual, and our hybrid).
- The data structures and variables used to implement the system.
- Window stack list, and how to keep track of window sequences.

- Changing the order of the window (altering the window stack).
- Vertical and horizontal movements of windows on screen.
- Printing to active and overlapped windows.
- Accessing overlapped windows.
- Removing windows.
- Cursor shape and positioning.
- Screen snow and techniques to avoid it.
- The DESQview environment, detection, and compatibility.

TYPES OF WINDOWS

There are multiple approaches to windowing systems. We will discuss simple, virtual, and a hybrid "sliding virtual" system. While the outward appearance of these systems may be similar, the programming approaches vary greatly.

Simple Windows

If only one pop-up window were needed on the screen, the task could be easily accomplished as follows:

- Copy the screen display buffer to a memory buffer.
- Draw a box on the screen and write text within it.
- When finished with the window, restore the original screen by copying the memory buffer back to the screen display buffer.

The user sees a window appear on top of existing text, then disappear. The window could be moved by repeatedly restoring the original screen and redrawing the window at another location.

Multiple windows could be created by repeating the process for each window that appears. A structure would be needed to keep track of the screen images that were saved, and the images would need to be restored in the proper order. The cursor location and size would need to be saved for each screen image so that they could be restored properly.

A more efficient use of memory could be made by saving only the portion of the screen that is being overwritten, rather than the entire screen buffer. On the other hand, more calculations would be required to calculate the memory map offsets of the saved window area, and the time required would be greater.

There is a certain attractiveness to the simple window system. It is very fast, easy to program, and requires very little memory. Although simple window systems are quite adequate for the production of menus, they are too limited for more advanced applications.

Virtual Windows

At the other end of the spectrum we have virtual windows. With simple windows, the window contents exist on screen physically within the window boundaries. With virtual windows, the window contents actually exist off the screen in RAM. A "copy" of the virtual window is displayed on the video display.

In the example in Figure 2–8, a window named Win1 has been created on the video screen. The contents of its virtual buffer remain intact, even though the screen representation shows its text clipped to fit within the window frame.

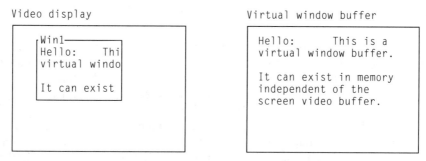

Figure 2–8   Video display and contents of virtual window buffer

Similarly, the contents of a virtual window remain intact even if its image on the screen is overwritten by other windows. To illustrate this, two virtual windows shown in Figure 2–9 are clipped and overlapped when displayed on the computer screen, as in Figure 2–10. However, window 1's buffer is still intact even though its screen image has been overwritten by window 2. As you can imagine, the task of managing virtual windows becomes quite complex.

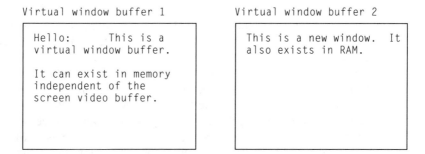

Figure 2–9   Two virtual window buffers

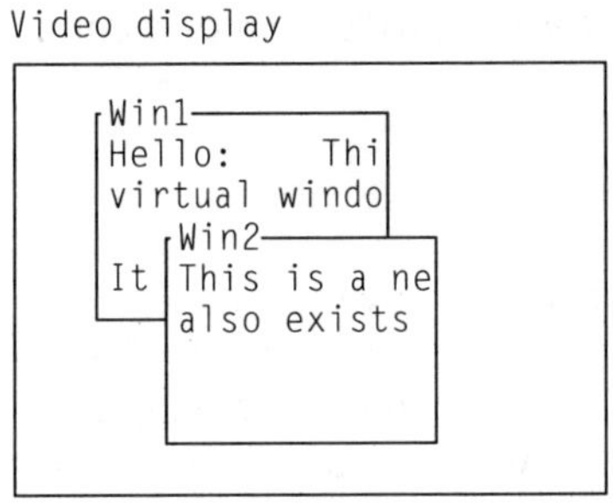

Video display

```
┌─────────────────────────────┐
│ ┌Win1──────────┐            │
│ │Hello:    Thi │            │
│ │virtual windo │            │
│ │ ┌Win2──────────┐          │
│ │It│This is a ne│          │
│ └──│also exists  │          │
│    │             │          │
│    └─────────────┘          │
│                             │
└─────────────────────────────┘
```

Figure 2–10 Two virtual windows as
displayed on screen

UPDATING WINDOWS

This brings up the problem of how to write to window 1 and update its screen image without covering up window 2, which is on top. With virtual windows, text is always written first to the window buffer, then the screen image is updated. There are several approaches used for screen updating. The two most common techniques are screen mapping and redrawing.

In the screen mapping system, a map is kept of every screen character location. The map shows which window "owns" each character. This technique is much like the File Allocation Table (FAT) used by DOS to map the use of disk sectors. This map will be referred to as a Screen Allocation Table (SAT).

If window 1 were updated using this technique, each character in window 1 would be compared against the SAT. If a character was still owned by window 1, it would be updated. The characters owned by window 2 would be left alone.

The second technique is to redraw each window in the order in which it appears on the screen. Redrawing the windows would leave the finished screen with the windows overlapping correctly. Such redrawing is often done in a second "virtual" screen. When the redraw is finished, the virtual screen is then copied to the video buffer. The user does not see the redraw and the window update appears to be instantaneous.

Each technique has advantages. The screen mapping SAT technique is perhaps faster if large numbers of windows are open. However, the redraw technique is easier to program.

The virtual window method is a very attractive windowing method which might fulfill our requirements. The primary disadvantage is that it is slower and far more complex to program than the simple window system. Most of the time we are dealing with the top window. Only occasionally do we need to access a covered window. Yet the virtual system would still require us to first write to the buffer and then update the screen, even if we were only using the top window.

THE SLIDING VIRTUAL WINDOW

The system we will build combines aspects of both simple and virtual windows. This system starts out as a simple window. A frame is drawn and text is written to the window area. At this point there is no memory buffer for the window. Text is written directly to the screen.

One difference between our system and the simple windows is that the screen image beneath the window is not saved before creating the window. The window area is saved only when another window is created. Just before creating a new window, the current window—frame and all—is copied to a memory buffer. At that point it becomes a virtual window. I call it a *sliding virtual window* because the image "slides" from the screen to a virtual buffer. The original contents of the window are still shown on the screen, and they may be overwritten.

The top window (the last one created) is always simple; all others are virtual. The top window usually receives the most output, and the unbuffered access is very fast. The virtual windows may still be accessed, but not as quickly. Virtual windows are updated using the redraw technique.

The initial window is predefined as an unframed full-screen (**scr.rows*scr.columns**) window. This window may be thought of as our desktop. It is unique in that its order in the stack may not be changed (it is always the bottom window), and it may not be deleted.

Detailed information must be maintained on each window. We must know each window's location, width, cursor size and location, as well as the logical sequence (i.e., which window goes first). Information is also required about the video screen, the segment and offset of the video buffer, and the number of rows and columns displayed, the text attributes, and so on.

Before we can proceed with a more detailed discussion of how the window system works, we need to examine the structures used to store screen and window information. The structures are defined in the file mydef.h and are included in the Source Code section of this chapter. The variables are initialized in the function **main( )**.

EXTERNAL PARAMETERS (DATA STRUCTURES)

We briefly looked at a few external parameters in the Application section. Now let's take a closer look. Of particular interest are the variables **scr** and **w** which define the screen and window parameters. Our screen/window functions are closely linked, because everything operates within a window. Likewise, our screen and window variables are tightly linked.

The structure **screen_structure** is listed next. This structure is applied to the external screen data structure **scr** in the module L_main.c.

```
struct screen_structure{
 /* Screen buffer related variables */

 char far *buffer:  /* pointer to screen buffer */
 int rows;     /* number of rows the monitor can display */
 int columns; /* number of columns the monitor can display */
  int top;     /* the top margin of active screen area (row) */
  int bottom; /* the bottom margin of active screen area(row) */
  int left;    /* the left margin of active screen area(column) */
  int right;  /* the right margin of active screen area(column) */
 int mode;     /* screen mode (as reported by BIOS) */
 int page;     /* the text page in use (color cards only) */
 int snow;     /* flag to indicate if snow avoidance ia used */

 /* Attribute related variables */

 char current;   /* current text attribute used when printing text*/
 char inverse;   /* default inverse attribute (predefined for mode) */
 char normal;    /* default normal attribute (predefined for mode) */
 int bold_caps; /* flag to indicate if upper case letters are
                    printed with intensity set high */

 /* window related variables */

 int active;     /* the handle (number) of the active window */
 int ptr;        /* pointer to the window list (how many windows) */
 int list[MAX_WINDOW+1];  /* the list of windows (sequence) */
 int update;     /* flag to indicate if cursor should be updated */
};
```

The variables within **scr** are grouped into three categories: screen buffer, attribute, and window.

The screen buffer group shows us where the screen buffer is located (**scr.buffer**), and the number of rows and columns that can be displayed (**scr.rows** and **scr.columns**).

The variables **scr.top, scr.bottom, scr.left,** and **scr.right** refer to the area within the video buffer to which the output must be confined. These values will be referred to as *margins*. The top and bottom margins are measured from the top of the screen, and the left and right margins are measured from the left. For example, the margins are initially set to **scr.top** = 1, **scr.bottom** = 25, **scr.left** = 1 and **scr.right** = 80 for an 80 × 25 display.

If a framed window (with a size of 5 * 5) were created in the upper left corner of the screen, then ouput would need to be confined to that area. The window and the new margins are shown in Figure 2–11. The elements of the screen variable **scr** which we term *window-related* are closely linked with the external window variable **w[ ]**.

At any given time, there may be from 1 to MAX_WINDOW windows open. MAX_WINDOW is defined in mydef.h as 20 but may be set to any reasonable

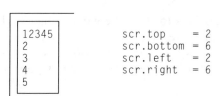

```
12345        scr.top    = 2
2            scr.bottom = 6
3            scr.left   = 2
4            scr.right  = 6
5
```

Figure 2–11 A window and its corresponding margins

size. These windows may be stacked, overlapped, and moved about the screen by the various functions. The complete description of each window is stored as an element in the separate variable array **w**. The data element **w[0]** represents the initial screen, and the first new window created is stored in **w[1]**.

When a window is created with **win_make( )**, the integer **handle** which is returned by the function is actually the position in the array **w** where the window data are stored.

Therefore, the first window created on top of the initial window has a handle of 1 and is stored in **w[1]**, the second has a handle of 2 and is stored in **w[2]**, and so on. If window 1 were deleted, the handle 1 and the corresponding array element **w[1]** would be made available for use the next time a window was created.

Although the location of a given window in the **w** array does not change for the life of the window, the relative position of the window on the screen may change relative to the other windows. The variable element **scr.list** is a list of the relative positions of the windows as they appear on the screen (the window stack). The data structure **scr.list** is an array which is initially set to:

```
scr.list= [0,1,2,3,4,5...,MAX_WINDOW].
```

The elements of **scr.list** form an index to the storage locations in **w** and indicate which absolute location within **w** is associated with each relative window position on the screen. For example, the number found in **scr.list[0]** is actually an index number which tells us where to find the storage space for the window 0. Because the value stored in **scr.list[0]** is a 0, we know that the first window on the screen is actually stored in **w[0]**. The initial window cannot change levels, so it is always a 0. Other windows can change levels on the screen, as we will now discuss.

The function **win_redraw_all( )**, which updates the screen by redrawing the windows, draws the windows in the order in which they are stored in **scr.list.**

Let's imagine that five new windows have been opened on the screen. Including the initial window, this gives a total of six windows. The data element **scr.ptr** indicates the number of windows currently in existence.

```
scr.ptr=5
scr.list= [0,1,2,3,4,5,6,7,8,..MAX_WINDOW]
                       ^
```

We would normally use variables to store the window handle; but for simplicity in these examples, we use the integer constants directly.

At this point window 1, whose handle is also 1, is popped to the top with the command ''win_pop_top(1);''. When the window is popped, the array must be updated.

```
scr.ptr=5
scr.list= [0,2,3,4,5,1,6,7,8,..MAX_WINDOW]
                    ^
```

Window 1 is now on top of the stack. The absolute storage location for it is still **w[1]**. The **win_pop_top( )** function calls **win_redraw_all( )** to redraw the windows. The windows are redrawn in the sequence found in **scr.list.**

Now let's pop window 3 to the top with the command ''win_pop_top(3)''.

```
scr.ptr=5
scr.list= [0,2,4,5,1,3,6,7,8,..MAX_WINDOW]
                    ^
```

If we now delete window 3 with the command ''win_delete_top();'', the storage space in **w[3]** is freed, and the **scr.ptr** is reduced by 1.

```
scr.ptr=4
scr.list= [0,2,4,5,1,3,6,7,8,..MAX_WINDOW]
                  ^
```

If a new window were created at this point, it would get handle 3.

If a window is to be deleted but is not currently on top, it must first be moved to the top. More precisely, the list is rearranged; the on-screen window is not visually moved. For example, let us delete window 4 with the command ''win_delete(4);''.

Step 1: move window 4 to the top.

```
scr.ptr=4
scr.list= [0,2,5,1,4,3,6,7,8,..MAX_WINDOW]
                  ^
```

Step 2: delete the window.

```
scr.ptr=3
scr.list= [0,2,5,1,4,3,6,7,8,..MAX_WINDOW]
                ^
```

The handle, or physical location of the top window, could be expressed as **scr.list[ptr].** To simplify matters, the handle number of the top window is stored in the external variable **scr.active.** In the preceding sample, scr.active = 1. This saves us a calculation step, although it is slightly wasteful of memory.

The logical position of any window within **scr.list[ ]** can be found by making the call:

```
win_validate(handle);
```

This function returns the integer value of the location if it is a valid window, and a −1 if it is invalid. In the list just shown, the valid windows are 0, 2, 5, and 1 since those windows have been created. Therefore, the call "win_validate(5);" would return a 2, since window 5 occupies location 2. The call "win_validate(6);" would return a −1, because window 6 is not in use.

The process of updating **scr.list** is somewhat more difficult when we wish to insert a window into a given position in the stack. For this we use the function **win_insert(handle,location).** This function allows us to move the window in either direction, above or below its current location. Let us look at both situations.

First we move a window above its current location. Window 5, which occupies position 2, is moved to position 6 with the command "win_insert(5,6);".

```
scr.ptr=7
scr.list= [0,2,5,1,4,3,6,7,8,9,10,..MAX_WINDOW]
                 ^
```

Window 5 is removed from the list, and everything from its position (2) to its target position (6) is moved down one position. The list looks like this:

```
scr.ptr=7
scr.list= [0,2,1,4,3,6, ,7,8,9,10,..MAX_WINDOW]
                      ^
```

Next, window 5 is inserted into position 6, which is now vacant.

```
scr.ptr=7
scr.list= [0,2,1,4,3,6,5,7,8,9,10,..MAX_WINDOW]
                      ^
```

If a window is moved down, the same process occurs but in the opposite direction. Suppose we issue the command "win_insert(5,2);", then window 5 is moved back to location 2. The first step is to remove window 5 from the list, and move the windows between the target position and the empty slot up one slot. After the move, a slot is now available in position 2.

```
scr.ptr=7
scr.list= [0,2, ,1,4,3,6,7,8,9,10,..MAX_WINDOW]
                ^
```

Window 5 is inserted in the vacant slot, and we obtain this list:

```
scr.ptr=7
scr.list= [0,2,5,1,4,3,6,7,8,9,10,..MAX_WINDOW]
                ^
```

Listed next is the code which determines the direction of the move and reorders **scr.list.** The variable **location** is the logical location of the window being moved, and the variable **position** is the logical position to which it is being moved.

```
if(position>location)      /* the window is moved up */
  for(i=location;i<position;i++) scr.list[i]=scr.list[i+1];
else                       /* the window is moved down */
  for(i=location;i>position;i--) scr.list[i]=scr.list[i-1];
```

We have seen how **scr.list** points to the location in **w[ ]** where the specific windows are stored. Now let's look at the structure of **w[ ]**.

THE WINDOW STRUCTURE

The structure window_structure is defined in mydef.h and is applied to the external variable **w[ ]** in the module **1_main( ).**

```
struct window_structure{
  int frame; /* flag to indicate if window is framed
               or unframed */
  int x,y;        /*cursor position (column,row) */
  char attribute; /* The attribute specified for the window */
  int start, end; /* cursor scan lines */
  int top,bottom,left,right; /* window margins */
  char  *buffer;            /* buffer to store image */
};
```

When a window is first created, the window variables are initialized. Functions that change the window status automatically update the window variables. Take, for example, the window movement function **win_right( ),** which moves an entire window on the screen. The function **win_right( )** changes the window margin values stored in **w[ ]** to reflect the new location of the window. If the function **win_right( )** is used to move the top window, it must also update the screen variables **scr.top, scr.bottom, scr.left,** and **scr.right** to reflect the new screen margins. The function **win_right( )** then calls **win_redraw_all( )** to redraw the windows.

The function **win_redraw_all( )** draws the windows in the sequence found in **scr.list.** The screen location for each window is based on the information found in **w[ ].**

Now that we have examined the external screen and window variables, let's see how we write to the screen.

SCREEN WRITING

Screen writing is not as simple as it might seem to be. First of all, a window always exists on the screen, and output must be confined to a window. The updates must be fast, and yet not cause snow on CGA adapters. Writing routines must be versatile enough to write to virtual screens and DESQview video buffers, as well as to any window, active or virtual.

The only method fast and flexible enough to accomplish all this is to write directly to the video buffer. The highly compatible ROM BIOS screen function calls are simply too slow. In addition, the BIOS is not capable of working with virtual screens or virtual windows, and can only deal with the true video buffers.

There are actually several interrelated functions in our code which control screen output. The lowest level work is done by the internal function **move_scr_mem( )**, which directly handles all screen output. This function also is responsible for avoiding screen snow. Nothing gets to or from the screen without going through **move_scr_mem( )**.

Higher level functions that we are interested in are **print( )** and **dma_print( )**. The real workhorse is **dma_print( )**. It does all the calculations, and in turn calls **move_scr_mem( )**. The function **print( )** is actually a front end which calls **dma_print( )** and then updates the cursor position.

Therefore, when we discuss the function **print( )**, we are actually describing a process which includes **print( )**, **dma_print( )**, and **move_scr_mem( )**. Writing to the screen requires that we know the following:

- The segment and offset of the video buffer.
- The number of rows and columns displayed on the video screen.
- The current active window parameters (the top, bottom, left, and right margins of the window).

Because we will need this information for writing to the screen, let's see how simple screen-relative x, y locations can be converted to an offset within the video buffer. We must be cautious not to assume an 80×25 display (that can be overridden at run-time). Instead we will use the variables **scr.columns** and **scr.rows**.

Assume that we want to know the offset within the screen buffer which corresponds to a screen coordinate of $x = 2$, $y = 2$. The buffer offset can be calculated as:

```
(y-1)*scr.columns*2 + (x-1)*2
or
( (y-1)*scr.columns + (x-1) )*2
```

If scr.rows = 80 we have:

```
((2-1)*80 + (2-1))*2 = (80+1)*2 = 162
```

In reality the situation is more complicated, because we always have at least one window open on the screen (i.e., the initial window). A window is rather like a screen within a screen, and has its own window-relative coordinate system. In the window-relative number system, the upper left corner of the window is 1,1.

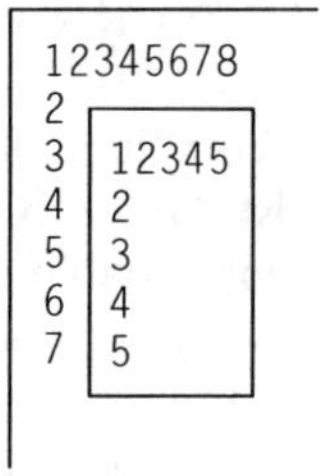

```
                       Interior
 12345678              Window limits:| x,y         Margins
2
3  12345               upper left   = | 3,3        left=     3   x
4  2                   upper right  = | 7,3        right=    7   x
5  3                   bottom left  = | 3,7        top=      3   y
6  4                   bottom right   | 7,7        bottom=   7   y
7  5
```

Figure 2–12 Window with margins

If we wish to access 1,1 within the window, we must translate that to the screen-relative coordinate. From there it may be transformed to a screen buffer offset.

Suppose there is a window, as in Figure 2–12, which is five characters wide and five characters high. This window is the top or active window, and the upper left corner of the interior is located at screen position 3,3. As you may recall from the earlier discussion, the left and right margins refer to the left and right limits of the window expressed as a screen-based x coordinate. In Figure 2–12, the left side of the window begins at x = 3 and the right side of the window ends at x = 7. The top and bottom margins are the window limits based on the screen y coordinate. These margins are stored in the external data structure **w[ ]**. Since this window is the topmost window, the screen margin values (**scr.top, scr.bottom, scr.left,** and **scr.right**) are identical.

If we wished to convert the window-relative location x = 2, y = 3 to the screen-based coordinate system, we would take the following steps.

```
assume scr_x== screen x
       scr_y== screen y

scr_x= (x-1)+left = (2-1)+3 = 4
scr_y= (y-1)+top  = (3-1)+3 = 5
```

Next, convert the screen coordinates to an offset.

```
( (scr_y-1)*scr.columns + (scr_x-1) )*2
= ( ( 5-1)*80 + (4-1) )*2/(substitute 80 for scr.columns)
= (320 +3)*2
= 646
```

If we are attempting to write text to the video screen, finding the location within the screen buffer which corresponds to a given window-relative coordinate is only the beginning. The string must be moved onto the screen in such a way that it does not spill outside the window boundaries. When a line of characters reaches the end of a line, it must wrap to the next line within the window. When the end of the last line is reached, the window must be scrolled up to make room at the bottom of the window for more text.

One way of doing this would be to output the text, character by character, checking each location to assure that the text is placed correctly. Unfortunately, this would be extremely time-consuming and the screen performance would suffer.

It is far more efficient to give a chunk of text to one of the built-in C functions such as **movedata( )** which can move it all at once to the screen. The function **movedata( )** is extremely fast. It can move blocks of text much more quickly than we could with a character-by-character C function. The function **movedata( )** is called from the function **move_scr_mem( )**. Remember that our screen printing process requires three functions: **print( )**, **dma_print( )**, and **move_scr_mem( )**.

Several steps must be taken before text can be passed to the function **movedata( )**. First, a string must be created which contains the original text padded with the attribute bytes. The attribute that we use is the value stored in **scr.current.** If the variable **scr.bold_caps** is set to TRUE, the attributes associated with uppercase letters have the intensity bit set ON.

Next, the text must be broken into chunks, which are sent one at a time to **movedata( )**. Each chunk must be of the correct size to fill one line of the window.

Look at this example. The following statement is issued while a 10 × 4 window is active on the screen:

```
print(4,1,"hello out there: this is a test.");
```

The text is padded with attributes, then broken into chunks and sent to the screen. The attributes are not actually shown in the example in Figure 2–13. The first line must be printed at the window-relative coordinate 4, 1. As before, the window-relative coordinate is converted into screen coordinates. The width of the first segment is adjusted so it will fit within the window.

The second and third segments are written to the screen offsets which correspond to the start of that window line. They are long enough to fit exactly within the window. The last line is shorter because there is less text to print. If the text had extended beyond the bottom of the window, the window contents would be scrolled up. We will discuss the scroll functions shortly.

The key facts to remember are:

- The printing routine writes to the buffer whose address is pointed to by **scr.buffer.** This buffer is used by a screen display whose size is **scr.columns** wide, and **scr.rows** high.
- Within this screen buffer, the writing is confined to the values stored in the margins values (**scr.top, scr.bottom, scr.left,** and **scr.right**). These values

```
String segments:            Window
                                              Width=10
"hello o"      ──→      ┌──────────┐ Height=4
"ut there:  "  ──→      │  Hello o │
"this is a  "  ──→      │ ut there:│
"test."        ──→      │ this is a│
                        │ test.    │
                        └──────────┘
```

Figure 2–13 String segments sent to the screen

respond to the window margin of the topmost window, and they are stored in the **w[ ]** array.

These external variables define where the printing functions output text. By changing these values, we can trick the printing routine into writing text anywhere we wish. An example of such a trick would be virtual screens.

VIRTUAL SCREENS

The virtual screen is turned on by the statement:

```
alt_screen(ON);
```

The function **alt_screen( )** does the following:

- Allocates memory of the size scr.rows*scr.columns*sizeof(unsigned char)*2, which is the size of the current screen buffer.
- Copies the contents of the screen buffer to the newly allocated memory. At this point the virtual screen is an exact duplicate of the true screen buffer.
- Changes the external variable **scr.buffer,** which is a pointer to the true screen buffer, so that it points to the virtual screen buffer.

At this point, the screen still shows the same image that it did before the virtual screen was activated. The printing functions will now send all output to the virtual screen instead of to the true buffer.

When the virtual screen is turned off with the statement "alt_screen(OFF);", the following occurs:

- The contents of the virtual screen buffer are copied to the true screen buffer.
- The screen buffer pointer **scr.buffer** is reset to its original value.
- The cursor is moved to reflect any changes made while the virtual screen was active.
- The memory allocated for the virtual screen is de-allocated.

Rerouting text output to the virtual screen is fairly simple. Now, let's look at a more difficult task.

WRITING TO A VIRTUAL WINDOW

When a window is overwritten by another window, it is saved, frame and all, to a memory buffer. This buffer is allocated as needed, and is pointed to by the variable **w[handle].buffer.** The window is now in virtual mode, and is protected from alteration by screen writing routines.

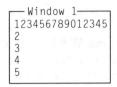

Figure 2–14   A virtual window

Shown in Figure 2–14 is a virtual window as it might appear in memory. Of course the memory is actually contiguous (one-dimensional), but we may visualize it in two dimensions, as we do the screen buffer. We could think of this virtual window buffer as though it were a tiny video screen buffer. The entire buffer is 17 columns wide (15 interior + 2 frame elements) and 7 rows high (5 + 2). Displayed on this tiny screen is a full-screen window which is framed and has an interior size of 15 × 5. If this is the case, the external variables which define it are:

SCREEN VARIABLES: (in scr.)
scr.buffer   = (address of the virtual window)
scr.rows   = 7
scr.columns = 17

WINDOW MARGINS: (in w[ ].)
top   = 2
bottom = 6
left   = 2
right   = 16

As you may have guessed by now, the routines which access the virtual windows change the external variables so that they point to the virtual windows. For example, the function **win_print( )** which can print to any window, sets the external variables to point to the desired window. The variables **scr.buffer, scr.columns, scr.rows, scr.top, scr.bottom, scr.left,** and **scr.right** are altered to point to the virtual window. The function **win_print( )** then calls the function **print( )** to do the actual output.

It is the same with **win_cls( )**. This function changes the variables, then calls **cls( )** to actually clear the screen. Each of the other window-specific functions does the same thing: point to the desired window, then call the default function to do the work (see Types of Functions in the Applications section of this chapter).

Rather than have each window-specific function do the pointing, which would be a duplication of code, a call is made to **win_point( )**. The function **win_point( )** alters the external variables so that they point to the desired virtual window. For example, the call **win_point(1)** points to window 1. A second call to **win_point( )** resets the external variables to the original values.

As you can see, the alteration of the external variables is a powerful tool for accessing any area of memory. There is one other case in which we alter the external variables, and that is with multitasking environments.

COMPATIBILITY WITH MULTITASKING ENVIRONMENTS

We discussed DESQview and Windows briefly in the Chapter 1. We will use DESQview as an example of a multitasking environment which is capable of running several applications at once. Some principles we discuss work for Microsoft Windows and other environments as well.

Multitasking is much easier for operating systems which utilize the newer processor chips such as the Intel 80386. Microsoft Windows 3, for example, can run multiple DOS applications simultaneously. Each application thinks that it is in possession of an entire PC, and memory and screen conflicts are minimized.

However, because we are developing applications which can run on PCs using the 8088 chip, we will concentrate more on the text-based DESQview environment. DESQview can easily run our applications on standard PCs.

Within DESQview, applications may operate in the foreground, taking up the entire screen, or in the background, where they are not seen but continue to operate. Some applications may operate within on-screen windows, where they appear to operate concurrently with other applications. The user may jump from application to application using the DESQview hot key.

Multitasking does not mean that separate applications are truly operating concurrently. The 8088 processor can only do one task at a time. Actually, DESQview gives each application a tiny bit of time to work, then jumps to the next application. The time slicing approach operates so fast that it appears that all applications are working concurrently. Since the processor time may be split between several applications, each application operates more slowly than it would if it were working alone.

One difficult task for DESQview-type environments is confining an application to an on-screen window. DESQview handles the problem by assigning each application to a virtual window. In addition, DESQview "steals" the BIOS interrupts. By stealing, we mean that it modifies the BIOS vector table so that it points to DESQview functions. If an application writes to the screen via BIOS calls, DESQview knows about it, and sends the output to the application's virtual screen. DESQview can then update the on-screen display.

A special problem occurs with applications which write directly to the screen buffer. Multitasking environments such as DESQview have no way to redirect the output from such an application. This type of application cannot be confined to an on-screen window. The only way DESQview can deal with such an application is to only allow it to run in the foreground. Foreground applications take over the screen completely, and therefore no other application window can be seen. When the user switches to another application, the foreground application is suspended to prevent it from overwriting the screen.

There is a way, however, that applications can use the fast direct memory access and still operate within a DESQview environment. The application can ask DESQview to tell it the address of the virtual screen. The application can then write directly to that buffer instead of to the screen. Such applications are said to be *DESQview-aware*.

Applications can inquire about the virtual screen by using a BIOS interrupt. The interrupt is 10H, function OfeH. This interrupt was originally used by IBM's TopView, an early multitasking environment. The interrupt is called with:

ah   = OfeH.
es:di = segment:offset of the assumed video buffer.

After execution of the interrupt, the registers are set with **es:di** equal to the segment:offset of the virtual screen. In other words, we put the segment:offset of **scr.buffer** (where we assume the buffer to be) in **es:di,** and do the interrupt. If the value has changed, then DESQview is present. If **scr.buffer** is set to the value returned in **es:di,** then our application will work quite well in the DESQview environment.

Performing this particular interrupt is more difficult than the interrupts we discussed in Chapter 1. The problem is that we must load the **es:di** registers. The **int86( )** function which is supported by Turbo C and QuickC uses a structure called REGS to define the general purpose registers. What we need is a function and structure to support **es** (which is a segment register) and **di** (which is a special purpose register). Unfortunately, I could not find identical functions in the two compilers to do this. Each compiler does have a function that will do the job. For Turbo C, the function is **intr( ),** and for QuickC the function is **int86x( ).**

The function we use to test for DESQview is called **test_dv( ),** and is found in Lmain. The complete listing is found in the Source Code section of this chapter. The function **test_dv( )** takes the general form:

```
#if defined TURBOC
  void test_dv(void)
  {

    .  .  .

    intr( )

    .  .  .

  }
#endif
#if defined QUICKC
  void test_dv(void)
  {

    .  .  .

    int86x( )

    .  .  .

  }
#endif
```

If you are using a compiler other than Turbo C or QuickC, you may need to add another conditional #if statement.

We must do one more thing before our application can operate successfully under DESQview, and that is tell DESQview how our application works. Before an application is run the first time under DESQview, a set-up screen must be filled in. This lets DESQview know if the application writes directly to the screen and whether it must therefore operate only in the foreground. This screen should be filled in, therefore, to indicate that our application does *not* write directly to the screen. After this is done, our applications will operate successfully in the foreground, background, or within a DESQview window.

One problem that DESQview or any window-based application must deal with is what to do with the cursor.

CURSOR MANAGEMENT

Even though there may be several windows on the screen at one time, there is only one cursor. The cursor is found within the active, topmost window. If there are several nonoverlapping windows (panels) on the screen, the user can look for the cursor to indicate which window is active. Some windowing environments use additional visual clues, such as putting a double line frame around the active window, with the other windows having single line frames.

The cursor can be a problem when we are dealing with virtual screens or virtual windows. Suppose that a program has turned on the virtual screen with the statement "alt_screen(ON);", and screen output is redirected. The user will not see the text being written because it is going directly to the virtual screen. But what about the cursor?

The **print( )** function automatically moves the cursor to the end of the line when it finishes writing. Likewise, the **cls( )** function moves the cursor to the Home position in the upper left corner of the screen. If these functions directly called the BIOS to move the cursor, the user would see the cursor jumping madly about the screen for no apparent reason.

The solution to this problem is the external variable **scr.update,** which is a flag that indicates whether or not the cursor should be moved. When the virtual screen is turned on, the flag is set to FALSE, and the cursor is not moved.

Even though the cursor is not physically moved, the location of the cursor must be saved. For example, when the virtual screen is turned off, and its contents copied to the true screen buffer, the cursor must be shown in its correct new location (reflecting the changes made). Therefore, when **gotoxy( )** is called to move the cursor, it always updates the cursor location for the window, which is stored as x, y in the data structure **w[ ].** The function **gotoxy( )** physically moves the cursor only if **scr.update** equals TRUE.

Likewise, when text is written to an overlapped virtual window, the new cursor location is saved in the window definition. Later, when the window is uncovered by a function such as **pop_top( )**, the cursor is moved to the correct location.

SNOW REMOVAL

Snow is the annoying interference which occurs when direct access is made of the CGA screen buffer at the same time the electron beam is turned on and is "painting" the video screen. Visually, snow looks very much like the interference seen on a TV screen when a vacuum cleaner is running nearby. Snow does not occur when writing to the screen via BIOS calls.

The problem may or may not occur with CGA clones; very close clones often have the problems, some do not. Snow does not occur in Monochrome (MDA), Hercules, VGA, or EGA display adapters. The CGA adapter sweeps an electron beam across the Cathode Ray Tube (CRT) from left to right. When the beam reaches the right side of the CRT, the beam is turned off and is repositioned on the left side of the display. This period when the electron beam is off is known as the *horizontal retrace*.

There is another delay when the beam reaches the lower right end of the display. This delay occurs as the beam is reset to the top of the display. This delay is known as the *vertical retrace*.

During these delays when the beam is turned off, it is safe to write directly to the video buffer. One method of avoiding snow is to watch the CGA port and detect these periods of inactivity. Blocks of text can be written while the display is turned off. The delay lasts longer during the vertical retrace and a larger block of text can be written. A smaller block of text can be written during the horizontal retrace.

The periods of time during which text may be written are quite brief, and this task is better suited to assembler programming. In Chapter 1 we stated that we would not use any assembler; therefore, we will use a slightly different approach.

Another method of avoiding screen snow is to turn off the electron beam during the periods that we are writing to the display. It might seem that this approach would be distracting, but in practice it is not. The display is turned off for such brief periods that the user often does not notice any change. The normal printing of text with **print( )** does not cause a noticeable change in the display. Functions which do massive screen updates, such as **win_redraw_all( ),** cause a slight blink. The blink only appears on CGA monitors; other display adapters are not affected.

The function which turns off the display is **move_scr_mem( )**, which is the low level function that ultimately handles all screen output.

The first step in avoiding snow is detecting the CGA adapter. The BIOS mode setting, which is called to set the external variable **scr.mode,** lets us know a color display adapter is in use. We must take other steps to ascertain which

adapter it is. There are specific interrupt calls which may be used to access
the EGA and its descendent, the VGA. If we know from the mode setting that
we have a color display adapter, we can issue one of these interrupts and see
if we get a response. If we do, then we know that there is an EGA or VGA. If
not, we can assume the card present is a CGA.

After these tests, which are conducted in the 1_main.c module, we set the
variable **scr.snow** to TRUE if the CGA is present, and FALSE if the CGA is not
present. If the software is run on a computer with a CGA clone which does not
cause snow, the variable **scr.snow** may be set to FALSE with the command line
argument "n" (as in "filename n").

When the function **move_scr_mem( )** is called to output a block of text to
the screen, it first checks **scr.snow**. If **scr.snow** is TRUE the function turns off
the display. Unfortunately, the display can not be turned off at just any time. If
the display is switched off in mid-sweep, say halfway down the screen, and back
on when it is at a totally different location, a strobing effect occurs. This strobing
looks like large bars of light that appear at various locations on the screen. The
bars apparently correspond to points at which the beam is turned off and on. It
is therefore necessary to wait until the beam reaches the bottom of the screen
and begins its vertical retrace, before we turn it off.

This is similar to the technique we discussed earlier; both techniques require
that writing wait until the beginning of the vertical retrace. They differ in that the
screen blanking technique can write everything at once. Since the electron beam
is turned off, there is no need to squeeze text in between retraces. The timing is
not as critical, and we do not need assembler to do the task.

It is necessary to access the CGA port register in order to watch the retrace
periods and to turn off the display. The register at location 3daH is a 4-bit read-
only register which shows the retrace and light pen status. Bit 3 indicates the
status of the vertical retrace. When it changes from a 0 to a 1, it marks the
beginning of the vertical retrace.

The display is turned off and on by writing to the CGA register at location
3d8H (the mode register). When bit 3 of this register is set to 0, the display is
turned off; when it is set to 1 the display is turned on. We must take care not to
disturb the other bits in the register; therefore we must preserve the contents of
the register before altering its contents. This register is write-only, so we can't
read its contents directly. Fortunately, the BIOS stores a copy of the register in
memory location 0:465H. We read this location, modify the third bit, and write
the resulting value to register 3d8H.

Following is the program loop which reads the memory location, watches
for the vertical retrace, and turns off the display.

```
if (scr.snow==TRUE){

/* save the mode setting */
ptr=MAKE_FP(0 ,0x465);   /* point to BIOS location for mode */
regval=*ptr;             /* read the mode */
origval=regval;          /* save the original value */
regval=regval&0x37;      /* mask bit 3 off */
```

```
/* wait for the CGA status register (bit 3) to go from 0 to 1 */
for(;;){
 vert =inp(0x3da);        /* read the CGA status register */
 if ((vert&8)==0) break; /* is bit three equal 0? if so, break */
}

for(;;){
 vert=inp(0x3da);         /* read the status register again */
 if((vert&8)==8) break;   /* exit when bit three equals 1   */
}
outp (0x3d8,regval);    /* send new mode to CGA controller */
}
```

After the text has been written, the controller is turned back on by writing the original value back to the register.

```
if (scr.snow==TRUE)
      outp(0x3d8,origval); /* set controller to original value */
```

Unfortunately, both techniques for avoiding snow involve waiting for retraces, and the performance suffers. This is unavoidable if we wish to avoid snow. However, we must not let the snow avoidance slow down nonscreen writing.

SNOW AND NONSCREEN OUTPUT

All screen output is routed through **move_scr_mem( )**, which waits for vertical retrace periods when **scr.snow** is set to TRUE. This could cause a noticeable performance loss when writing to virtual screens and windows. Neither virtual screens nor virtual windows exist within the video buffer; therefore there is no reason to use snow avoidance when writing to them. Any routine which writes to those buffers first saves the **scr.snow** variable, then resets **scr.snow** to FALSE. When the output is finished, **scr.snow** is reset to its original value.

MAXIMUM PERFORMANCE DURING SCREEN UPDATES

Many of the functions which operate on virtual windows automatically update the screen with a call to **win_redraw_all( )**. In some cases it may not be appropriate to update the screen immediately.

Take for example the function **win_print( )** which is a window-specific writing routine. Functions which write to windows are often called repeatedly. If a data input screen were being created, numerous calls would be made to **win_print( )** to prepare the screen.

Imagine that there are five windows open, and we need to prepare window number 1 for data input by writing to ten different locations. If **win_print( )** automatically redraws all the windows, we would have ten different calls to

win_redraw_all( ), for a total of 50 individual redraws. The updates would be much too sluggish.

For this reason, **win_print( )** does not automatically call **win_redraw_all( )**. Instead, we make the ten calls to **win_print( )**, then call **win_redraw_all( )** to show the changes.

The functions which don't automatically update the screen are the window clearing, scrolling, and printing functions. These functions are often called during a major window update. The other functions, which are not used as extensively, automatically update the screen. The function descriptions, found in the applications section, indicate which functions require a call to **win_redraw_all( )**.

SUMMARY

We have examined the concepts, data structures, and approaches used in the construction of our screen/window library. The following code section will reveal the step-by-step process of constructing the library.

This library is not an end unto itself. It is merely a foundation, the environment in which we will build our menus and data input screens.

SOURCE CODE

MYDEF.H

```
/******************** MYDEF.H  *************************/

/*
Set the following define statement of "#define TURBOC" if you are
using Borland "Turbo C", set it to "#define QUICKC" if you are using
Microsoft "QuickC".
*/

#define TURBOC

#define MAX_WINDOW 20

#define MAX_STRING 500    /* maximum length of strings.
                            (includes '\0') */

#define MAKE_FP(seg,off) \
      ((char far *) (((unsigned long)(seg) << 16)!(unsigned)(off)))

#define set_color(foreground,background)\
             (((background)<<4)!(foreground))
#define set_intense(attribute)((attribute)!8)

/* Screen mode definitions (the most common)*/
```

```
#define BW_40        0   /* 40 column B&W */
#define COLOR_40     1   /* 40 column color */
#define BW_80        2   /* 80 column B&W */
#define COLOR_80     3   /* 80 column color */
#define MED_COLOR    4   /* 320x200 4 color graphics mode */
#define MED_BW       5   /* 320x200 4 shade levels */
#define HI_RES       6   /* 640x200 B&W */
#define MONOCHROME   7   /* monochrome display */

#define FALSE 0          /* logic values */
#define TRUE  1

#define ON  1
#define OFF 0

#define BLACK      0          /* text attributes for color cards */
#define BLUE       1
#define GREEN      2
#define CYAN       3
#define RED        4
#define MAGENTA    5
#define BROWN      6
#define WHITE      7
#define YELLOW  14   /* intensity set on */

/* definitions of box types */

#define STD_FRAME      "\xda\xbf\xc0\xd9\xc4\xb3"  /* ┌┐ └┘ ─ │ */
#define PD_FRAME       "\xc2\xc2\xc0\xd9\xc4\xb3"  /* ┬┬ └┘ ─ │ */
#define TOP_FRAME      "\xda\xbf\xc3\xb4\xc4\xb3"  /* ┌┐ ├┤ ─ │ */
#define MIDDLE_FRAME   "\xc3\xb4\xc3\xb4\xc4\xb3"  /* ├┤ ├┤ ─ │ */
#define BOTTOM_FRAME   "\xc3\xb4\xc0\xd9\xc4\xb3"  /* ├┤ └┘ ─ │ */
#define NO_FRAME       ""

#define UP        0x48
#define DOWN      0x50
#define LEFT      0x4b
#define RIGHT     0x4d
#define HOME      0x47
#define END       0x4f
#define INSERT    0x52
#define DELETE    0x53
#define PGDN      0x51
#define PGUP      0x49
#define ESCAPE    0x1b
#define RETURN    0x0d
#define BACKSPACE 0x08
#define BELL      0x07
#define F1        0x3b

#if defined QUICKC
 #include <stddef.h>    /* for NULL definition */
#endif
```

```
#define UNDERLINE 1      /* ATTRIBUTES FOR MONOCHROME CARDS */
#define NORMAL    7
#define BOLD      15
#define INVERSE   112

/* cursor types */
#define BIG_CURSOR     2
#define NORMAL_CURSOR 1
#define NO_CURSOR      0

/* for input screens */

#define OK     0
#define REDO   1
#define REDRAW 2

/* window structure */

struct screen_structure{
 /* Screen buffer related variables */

  char far *buffer;   /* pointer to screen buffer */
  int rows;     /* number of rows the monitor can display */
  int columns; /* number of columns the monitor can display */
   int top;     /* the top margin of active screen area (row) */
   int bottom; /* the bottom margin of active screen area(row) */
   int left;    /* the left margin of active screen area(column) */
   int right;   /* the right margin of active screen area(column) */
  int mode;     /* screen mode (as reported by BIOS) */
  int page;     /* the text page in use (color cards only) */
  int snow;     /* flag to indicate if snow avoidance is used */

 /* Attribute related variables */

  char current; /* current text attribute used when printing text*/
  char inverse; /* default inverse attribute (predefined for mode) */
  char normal;  /* default normal attribute (predefined for mode */
  int bold_caps; /* flag to indicate if upper case letters are
                    printed with intensity set high */

 /* window related variables */

  int active;      /* the handle (number) of the active window */
  int ptr;         /* pointer to the window list (how many windows) */
  int list[MAX_WINDOW+1]; /* the list of windows (sequence) */
  int update;      /* flag to indicate if cursor should be updated */
};

struct window_structure{
  int frame; /* flag to indicate if window is framed or unframed */
  int x,y;          /*cursor position (column,row) */
  char attribute;  /* The attribute specified for the window */
```

```
  int start, end;  /* cursor scan lines */
  int top,bottom,left,right; /* window margins */
  char  *buffer;              /* buffer to store image */
};


/* information for menus */

#define MAX_BAR 10  /* The maximum number of options in the */
                     /* moving light bar menu. */


/* menu structure for the pop-up menu */

struct pop_struc{
 char *name;          /* the menu option */
 int (*fun)();        /* the pointer to function */
 int select_id;       /* the list-select return code */
};


/* menu structure for moving light bar menu */

struct bar_struc{
 char *name;          /* the name of the function */
 char *info;          /* the info line appearing under options */
 int (*fun)();        /* the pointer to function */
 int select_id;       /* the list-select return code */
};


/* menu structure for the pull-down menus */

#define MAIN_OPT    5  /* the actual number of options appearing
                          in the main menu */
#define PD_SUB       3  /* the maximum number of sub-options in the
                          pull-down menus */
#define PD_SUB_ROW 4  /* the row that the pull-down window appears */

#define PD_MAIN_FRAME STD_FRAME /* frame used for the main menu
                                    window */
#define PD_SUB_FRAME  PD_FRAME  /* frame used for the pull-down
                                    menu window */

struct pd_str{
 char *main;            /* option to appear in main menu */
 char *sub[PD_SUB];     /* array of options to appear in Pull-down*/
 int (*fun[PD_SUB])();  /* array of function pointers for pull-down*/
 int select_id[PD_SUB]; /* array of list-select return code */
};

struct window_colors{
 char main_frame;       /* attribute used for main menu frame */
 char main_interior;    /* " " " " menu interior */
 char main_inverse;     /* " " " " menu highlighter */
```

```
 char pd_frame;            /* " " " pull-down frame */
 char pd_interior;         /* " " " pull-down interior */
 char pd_inverse;          /* " " " pull-down highlighter */
};

/* structure for help files */

struct help_structure{
     char filename[80]; /* the current help file */
     char message[80];  /* the window title */
     int x;             /* the column for the upper left corner of
                           the help window */
     int y;             /* the row for the upper left corner of
                           the help window */
     int  page;         /* page within file to use */
     char frame_attr;   /* character attribute for help interior */
     char interior_attr;/* character attribute for help frame */
     };

/* structure for input screens */
struct in_struc {
 int  x;       /* x position for data input field (start of label)*/
 int  y;       /* y position for data input field (start of label)*/

 char *prompt;/* the prompt for the field */
 char *ptr;   /* pointer to string to edit */
 int  length; /* the maximum length of the field */

 unsigned int label_f,label_b;  /* label foreground,background
                                   color */
 unsigned int input_f,input_b;  /* input field foreground,background
                                   color */
 };

/* function prototypes */

int start(void);   /* for start function */

/***********      l_main.c      ***********/

int main(int argc,char *argv[]);
static void init_window(void);
static void set_screen_attr(void);
static void test_dv(void);
void update_margins(void);

/***********      l_scrn1.c      ***********/

void ceol(int x, int y);
void cls(void);
void gotoxy(int x,int y);
void scroll_up(int lines);
```

```
void scroll_down(int lines);
void set_mode(int mode);
void what_mode(int *mode,int *page);


/**********      l_scrn2.c      **********/

void wherexy(int *x,int *y);
void readxy(char *ch,char *attr);
void what_cursor(int *start, int *end);


/**********      l_scrn3.c      **********/

void cursor(int size);
void set_cursor(int start, int end):


/**********      l_scrn4.c      **********/

void alt_screen(int action);


/**********      l_win1.c      **********/

int win_make(int x,int y,int width,int height,char *array,\
             char *title, char frame_attr, char win_attr);
void win_save(void);
void win_delete(int handle);
int win_validate (int handle);
void win_delete_top(void);
void draw_frame (int x,int y, int width,int height,\
             char *array,char *title,char attribute);
int win_center(int width,int height,char *array,char *title,\
             char frame_attr, char win_attr);


/**********      l_win2.c      **********/

void win_pop_top(int handle);
void display_cursor(void);
static void win_redraw(int handle);
void win_redraw_all(void);


/**********      l_win3.c      **********/

void win_ceol(int handle, int x, int y);
void win_cls(int handle);
void win_scroll_up(int handle,int lines);
void win_scroll_down(int handle,int lines);
void win_gotoxy(int handle,int x,int y);
void win_print( int handle, int x,int y, char *string);
static void win_point(int handle);
```

```
/**********       l_win4.c       **********/

void win_up(int handle, int amount);
void win_right(int handle, int amount);
void win_left(int handle, int amount);
void win_down(int handle, int amount);
void win_insert(int handle, int position);

/**********       l_win5.c       **********/

char win_what_attr(int handle);
void win_set_attr(int handle, char attribute);

/**********       l_print.c       **********/

void print(int x,int y,char *string);
void print_here(char *string);
void dma_print(int *x, int *y,char *string);
void move_scr_mem (char far *string,char far *video,int number);

/**********       l_getkey.c       **********/

void get_key(char *ch, char *ext);

/**********       l_popup.c   **********/

int pop_up(struct pop_struc pop_menu[],int x,int y,\
          char normal, char inverse);

/**********       l_bar.c    **********/

int bar_menu(struct bar_struc menu[], char normal, char inverse);

/**********       l_chip.c    **********/

void chip_left(char *chip,char *block,int number);
void chip_right(char *chip,char *block, int number);

/**********       l_copy.c    **********/

void copy (char *from,char *to,int first,int length);

/**********       l_getfld.c    **********/

char getfield(char *string, int inlength, int start, char attribute);
void hilight_field(int x, int y, int length, char attribute);

/**********       l_input.c    **********/

int input(struct in_struc in_scrn[]);
```

```
/**********      l_string.c     **********/

int pos(char *string,char *pattern);
void caps(char *string);

/**********      l_list.c     **********/

int list_select(char *ptr[]);

/**********      l_dir.c     **********/

int dir(char *filespec, char  *selection);
int file_count(char *filespec);

/**********      pd.c     **********/

int pull_down (struct pd_str m_menu[], struct window_colors color);
static int pull_down_sub(struct pd_str m_menu[],struct window_colors\
                         color,int option, char *ext, int *expert);
```

L_MAIN.C

```
/*********************      L_MAIN.C      *************************/

#include "mydef.h"
#define <dos.h>
#include <string.h>

/* define our external variables */
/* window definitions */

struct screen_structure scr;
struct window_structure w[MAX_WINDOW+1];
struct help_structure hlp;

int main(int argc,char *argv[])
{
extern struct screen_structure scr;
extern struct window_structure w[];
extern struct help_structure hlp;

   int i;
   unsigned int seg,off;
   long l;
   char string[10];
   int return_code;

set_screen_attr();        /* set screen attributes */
test_dv();                /* check for DesqView */
```

```
/* extract segment and offset of screen buffer */
seg=FP_SEG(scr.buffer); off=FP_OFF(scr.buffer);

/* check command line values for override values */
 if(argc>1)
 for(i=1;i<=argc;i++){

    copy(argv[i],string,2,4); /* copy any values. i.e. r=30 */
                              /* note: copy() is found in l_copy.c */
    /* check for segment override */
    if ( toupper (argv[i] [0])=='S') if(atoi(string)) seg=atoi(string);

    /* check for offset override */
    if ( toupper(argv[i] [0])=='O') if(atoi(string)) off=atoi(string);

    /* check for row override */
    if ( toupper(argv[i] [0])=='R')
     if(atoi(string)) scr.rows=atoi(string);

    /* check for column override */
    if ( toupper(argv[i] [0])=='C')
     if(atoi(string)) scr.columns=atoi(string);

    /* check for black & white override */
    if ( toupper(argv[i] [0])=='B') set_mode(BW_80);

    /* check for snow override (turn off snow avoidance)  */
    if ( toupper(argv[i] [0])=='N') scr.snow=FALSE;
 }

scr.buffer=MAKE_FP(seg,off);

init_window();             /* initialize window structure */
update_margins();
                           /* initialize help structure */
hlp.filename[0]='\0';  /* empty string (no current help file) */

/* set text which appears in window frame */
strcpy(hlp.message,"Esc: to exit ");
hlp.page=0;                    /* page zero */
hlp.x=1;                       /* upper left column of help window */
hlp.y=1;                       /* upper left row of help window */
hlp.interior_attr=scr.normal; /* set window interior to normal */
hlp.frame_attr=scr.normal;    /* set window frame to normal */

return_code=start();
return(return_code);
}

static void init_window(void)
{
extern struct screen_structure scr;
```

```
extern struct window_structure w[];
int i;

/* initialize initial window (desk top) */
  w[0].frame=FALSE;
  wherexy(&w[0].x,&w[0].y); /* save current cursor location*/
  what_cursor(&w[0].start,&w[0].end);
  w[0].left=1;w[0].right=scr.columns;
  w[0].top=1;w[0].bottom=scr.rows;
  w[0].attribute=scr.normal; /* assume default normal attribute */

/* initialize window pointer array */

for(i=0;i<=MAX_WINDOW;i++){
 scr.list[i]=i;
 }
}


/******************************************************************

 Usage: static void set_screen_attr(void);

 Ascertains what type of graphics card is in use, sets external
 text attributes and screen buffer address recording.

 ******************************************************************/

static void set_screen_attr(void)
{
extern struct  screen_structure scr;
extern struct window_structure w[];

 what_mode(&scr.mode,&scr.page);  /*set current textmode and page */

 if(scr.mode==MONOCHROME) scr.mode = MONOCHROME;

 if(scr.mode==BW_40){        /* if 40 column BW set to 80 column */
  set_mode(BW_80);
  scr.mode =BW_80;
 }

 if(scr.mode==COLOR_40){    /* if 40 column color, set to 80 column */
       set_mode(COLOR_80);
       scr.mode=COLOR_80;
 }

/* set character attributes */

 if (scr.mode==BW_80){               /* set attributes for BW */
   scr.normal=  set_color(WHITE,BLACK);
   scr.inverse= set_color(BLACK,WHITE);
   }
```

```
    if (scr.mode==COLOR_80){              /* set attributes for COLOR */
      scr.normal=  set_color(WHITE,BLACK);
      scr.inverse= set_color(BLACK,WHITE);
     }

    if (scr.mode==MONOCHROME){     /* set attributes for MONOCHROME */
     scr.normal = NORMAL;
     scr.inverse = INVERSE;
     }

     scr.current = scr.normal;     /* set screen attribute to normal */
  /* set screen buffer address */
  if(scr.mode==MONOCHROME)
     scr.buffer= (char far *)0xb0000000;      /* monochrome address */
    else
      scr.buffer=(char far *)0xb8000000;     /* color address */

   scr.rows=25;scr.columns=80;   /* assume standard values for now */
   scr.update=TRUE;
   scr.bold_caps=FALSE;
   scr.ptr=0;scr.active=0;

   /* set snow flag if not ega and not monochrome */
   scr.snow= (!test_ega() && (scr.mode!=MONOCHROME));

   /* set screen margins */
   scr.top=1;
   scr.bottom=scr.rows;
   scr.left=1;
   scr.right=scr.columns;

}


#if defined TURBOC

static void test_dv(void)
{
extern struct  screen_structure scr;
int seg,off;

   struct REGPACK regs;

   seg = FP_SEG(scr.buffer);
   off = FP_OFF(scr.buffer);

   regs.r_ax=0xfe00;

   regs.r_es= seg;
   regs.r_di= off;
```

```
     intr(0x10, &regs);

  if(regs.r_es != seg || regs.r_di != off)
   scr.buffer=MAKE_FP(regs.r_es,regs.r_di);
}

#endif

#if defined QUICKC

static void test_dv(void)
{
extern struct  screen_structure scr;
int seg,off;

union REGS inregs,outregs;
struct SREGS segregs;

  seg = FP_SEG(scr.buffer);
  off = FP_OFF(scr.buffer);

   inregs.h.ah=0xfe;
   segregs.es= seg;
   inregs.x.di= off;

   int86x(0x10, &inregs,&outregs,&segregs);

  if(segregs.es != seg || inregs.x.di != off)
   scr.buffer=MAKE_FP(segregs.es,inregs.x.di);

}
#endif

int test_ega(void)
{
 union REGS reg;

 reg.h.ah = 0X12;              /* call an ega function */
 reg.h.bl = 0X10;
 reg.x.cx = 0Xffff;            /* stuff the register */

 int86(0X10, &reg, &reg);
  if (reg.x.cx==0Xffff) return (0);  /* if it isn't changed, no ega */
    else
     return(1);  /* contents changed, there is a ega */
}

void update_margins(void)
{
extern struct  screen_structure scr;
extern struct window_structure w[];
```

```
scr.top= w[scr.active].top;
scr.bottom= w[scr.active].bottom;
scr.left= w[scr.active].left;
scr.right= w[scr.active].right;
}
```

L_SCRN1.C

```
/********************     L_SCRN1.C     *************************/

#include "mydef.h"
#include <dos.h>

/*****************************************************************

  Usage: void ceol(int x, int y);

  x= column.
  y= row.

  Clears the active window from the x-y coordinate to the end
  of the line.

  *****************************************************************/

void ceol( int x, int y)
{
extern struct  screen_structure scr;
extern struct window_structure w[];

int i;
char string[255];
int width;
char old_current =scr.current;
  if(x>(scr.right-scr.left+1))  return;   /* out of bounds */
  if(y>(scr.bottom-scr.top+1))  return;

  scr.current=w[scr.active].attribute;    /* set scr.current to window
                                             attribute */
  width=scr.right-scr.left -x +2;         /* figure width to clear */

  for(i=0;i<width;i++) string[i]=' ';     /* build a string of blanks */
  string[i]='\0';                         /* terminate it */
  dma_print (&x,&y,string);               /* print the string but
                                             don't move cursor */
  scr.current= old_current;       /* restore the current attribute */
}
```

```
/******************************************************************

 Usage; void cls();

 Clears active window.

 ******************************************************************/


void cls()
{
extern struct  screen_structure scr;
extern struct window_structure w[];
int height;

 height=scr.bottom-scr.top +1;
   scroll_up(height+1); /* scrolling up more lines than possible
                           clears the screen */
   gotoxy(1,1):          /* move cursor to "home" position */
}



/******************************************************************

 Usage: void gotoxy(int x, int y);

 x= column (x coordinate)
 y= row    (y coordinate)

 Moves cursor to position indicated by x,y. Movement relative
 to active window.

 Numbering starts at 1,1. ie gotoxy(1,1) moves cursor to upper
 left corner of active window.

 ******************************************************************/


void gotoxy(int x,int y)
{
extern struct  screen_structure scr;
extern struct window_structure w[];

union REGS regs;

  /* store new cursor in window array */
  w[scr.active].x=x; w[scr.active].y=y;

  if(scr.update!= TRUE ) return; /* return if update flag == FALSE */
```

```
     x=(x-1)+scr.left; /* adjust relative  x,y position */
     y=(y-1)+scr.top;  /* to true "physical screen" co-ordinate */

     /* if outside window boundaries, correct */
     if (x<scr.left) x=scr.left;
     if (x>scr.right)
          x=scr.right;
     if (y<scr.top)
          y=scr.top;
     if (y>scr.bottom) y=scr.bottom;

      /* perform interrupt */

      y--;x--;                    /* adjust to BIOS numbering system */

     regs.h.ah=2;                /* ah=2, the cursor position function */
     regs.h.dh=y;                /* row */
     regs.h.dl=x;                /* column */
     regs.h.bh=scr.page;         /* page number */

     int86(0x10, &regs, &regs);     /* do interrupt */
}


/*******************************************************************

  Usage: void scroll_up (int lines);

  n= number of lines to scroll up.

  Scrolls the active window up n number of lines.

 *******************************************************************/


void scroll_up(int lines)
{
extern struct  screen_structure scr;
extern struct window_structure w[];

int width, height;
int offset;
char far *from;char far *to;
int i,j;
int abs_x,abs_y;
char string[401];    /* big enough for 200-column display */

 width=scr.right-scr.left+1;
 height=scr.bottom-scr.top +1;

 if(lines<1)return;
```

```
abs_x=scr.left-1;     /* figure absolute start of window */
abs_y=scr.top-1;

    offset=( abs_x*2+(abs_y*scr.columns*2) );

    /* build a string (with attributes) = width */
    for(i=0;i<=width*2;i+=2){
     string[i]=' ';
     string[i+1]=w[scr.active].attribute;
    }
    string[i-2]='\0';

     j=0;                   /* starting line */

if(lines<height){

/*
The following code sets the j pointer to first line of the window
the second pointer "i" is set equal the number indicated by "lines"
each line of the window is moved from "i" to "j". This is repeated
for each line in the window with "i" and "j" incrementing.
If the call "scroll_up(3); " were made, line 4 would be
moved to line 1, line 5 to line 2 etc */

    for(i=lines;i<=height-1;i++){
     from=scr.buffer+offset+i*scr.columns*2;
     to=scr.buffer+offset+j*scr.columns*2;
       move_scr_mem(from,to,width*2);
     j++;
    }
}


/* clear the left over lines, (if a scroll of 3 lines were made,
   the bottom 3 lines would need to be cleared) */

 for(i=j;i<height;i++){
  to=scr.buffer+(offset+i*scr.columns*2);
  move_scr_mem(string,to,width*2);
 }

 if(w[scr.active].y >= lines){
  w[scr.active].y=w[scr.active].y-lines;
 } else
  {
   w[scr.active].x=1;
   w[scr.active].y=1;
  }
  display_cursor();
}
```

```
/*****************************************************************


  Usage: void scroll_down (int lines);

  n= number of lines to scroll down.

  Scrolls the active window down n number of lines.

  *****************************************************************/


void scroll_down(int lines)
{
extern struct  screen_structure scr;
extern struct window_structure w[];

int width, height;
int offset;
char far *from;char far *to;
int sourc_line,dest_line;
in i;
int abs_x,abs_y;
char string[401];    /* big enough for 200-column display */

 width=scr.right-scr.left+1;   /* figure width and height of window */
 height=scr.bottom-scr.top+1;

 if(lines<1)return;

 abs_x=scr.left-1;    /* figure absolute start of window */
 abs_y=scr.top-1;

    offset=( abs_x*2+(abs_y*scr.columns*2) );

    /* build a string (with attributes) = width */
    for(i=0;i<=width*2;i+=2){
      string[i]=' ';
      string[i+1]=w[scr.active].attribute;
    }
    string[i-2]='\0';

    /* The following works like the code described in scroll_up(), */
    /* except that index pointers move the lines down */

    dest_line=height-1;
    if(lines<height){

      for(sourc_line=height-1-lines;sourc_line>=0;sourc_line--){
       from=scr.buffer+offset+sourc_line*scr.columns*2;
       to=scr.buffer+offset+dest_line*scr.columns*2;
        move_scr_mem(from,to,width*2);
```

```
      dest_line--;
    }
   }

 for(sourc_line=dest_line;sourc_line>=0;sourc_line--){
  to=scr.buffer+(offset+sourc_line*scr.columns*2);

  move_scr_mem(string,to,width*2);
 }

 if(w[scr.active].y >= lines){
  w[scr.active].y+= lines;              /* =w[scr.active].y-lines;*/
 } else
  {
   w[scr.active].y=height;
  }
   display_cursor();
}


/****************************************************************

 Usage: void set_mode(int mode)

 Sets video mode.

 ****************************************************************/

void set_mode(int mode)
{
extern struct  screen_structure scr;
extern struct window_structure w[];

   union REGS regs;

   regs.h.ah= 0;           /* set video state function */
   regs.h.al=mode;         /* mode to set */

    int86(0x10, &regs,&regs);  /* do interrupt */
    scr.mode=mode;                /* update external variable */
}


/****************************************************************

 Usage: void what_mode(int *mode,int *page);

 Call with address of mode and page "what_mode(&mode,&page);"

 Sets mode and page variables to actual mode and page.

 Defines for mode are found in "mydef.h".

 ****************************************************************/
```

```
void what_mode(int *mode,int *page)
{
   union REGS regs;

   regs.h.ah= 15;              /* return video state function */

    int86(0x10, &regs,&regs);  /* do interrupt */

   *mode= regs.h.al;   /* set mode */
   *page= regs.h.bh;   /* set page */
}
```

L_SCRN2.C

```
/********************     L_SCRN2.C     **************************/

#include "mydef.h"
#include <dos.h>

/***************************************************************

 Usage: void wherexy(int *x,int *y);

 Call with address of x and y "wherexy(&x,&y);"

 Returns the current address of the cursor. x=column y=row
 Value is relative to active window. 1,1 is upper left corner.

 ***************************************************************/


void wherexy(int *x,int *y)
{
extern struct  screen_structure scr;
extern struct window_structure w[];

   union REGs regs;

   regs.h.ah = 3;  /* read cursor  function */

   regs.h.bh = scr.page;        /* page to read */

   int86(0x10, &regs,&regs);  /* do interrupt */

   /* get x from dl and adjust for window */
   *x=( regs.h.dl +2-scr.left);

   /* get y from dh and adjust for window */
   *y= (regs.h.dh +2-scr.top);
}
```

```
/*********************************************************************

  Usage: void readxy(char *ch,char *attr);

  Call with address of ch and attr "readxy(&ch,&attr);"

  Returns with ch= the character under the cursor.
  attr= text attribute under the cursor.

 *********************************************************************/


void readxy(char *ch,char *attr)
{
extern struct screen_structure scr;

   union REGS regs;

   regs.h.ah = 8;          /* read char function */
   regs.h.bh = scr.page;   /* page number to read */

   int86(0x10, &regs,&reg); /* do interrupt */

   *ch = regs.h.al;         /* get character from al */
   *attr = regs.h.ah;       /* get attribute from ah */
}



/*********************************************************************

  Uage: void what_cursor(int *start,int *end);

  Call with address of start and end "What_cursor(&start,&end);"

  Returns the starting and ending scan lines for the cursor.

 *********************************************************************/


void what_cursor(int *start, int *end)
{
extern struct screen_structure scr;

union REGS regs;

  regs.h.ah=0x3;         /* read cursor */
  regs.h.bh=scr.page;    /* must tell it what page for color systems */

  int86(0x10,&regs,&regs);  /* do interrupt */

  /* starting line in ch, ending line in cl */
  *start=regs.h.ch; *end=regs.h.cl;
}
```

L_SCRN3.C

```
/********************    L_SCRN3.C    *************************/
#include "mydef.h"
#include <dos.h>

/*******************************************************************


   Usage: int cursor(int size);

   Sets the size of the cursor.

   Uses the following definitions found in "mydef.h":

   BIG_CURSOR    = 2      Full-sized cursor.
   NORMAL_CURSOR = 1      Normal underline cursor.
   NO_CURSOR     = 0      Cursor invisible.

*******************************************************************/


void cursor(int size)
{
extern struct screen_structure scr;
int start,end;

    /* set cursor for color graphic type cards */

    if (scr.mode == COLOR_80 || scr.mode == BW_80){
        if (size == NO_CURSOR){
            start=16; end=0;
        }
        if (size == NORMAL_CURSOR){
            start=6; end=7;
        }
        if (size == BIG_CURSOR){
            start=0,end=7;
        }
    }

    /* set cursor for monochrome cards */

    if (scr.mode == MONOCHROME ){
        if (size == NO_CURSOR){
            start=16;end=0;
        }
        if (size == NORMAL_CURSOR){
            start=11;end = 12;
        }
```

```
        if (size == BIG_CURSOR){
            start=0;end=14;
        }
    }

    set_cursor(start,end);
}


/***********************************************************************

 Usage: void set_cursor(int start, int end);

 Sets the size of the cursor based on start and end scan lines.

 Gives more control than cursor(size);

 ***********************************************************************/


void set_cursor (int start, int end)
{
extern struct screen_structure scr;
extern struct window_structure w[];

 union REGS regs;

 if(scr.update==TRUE){      /* if update ok then set cursor */

  regs.h.ah=0x01;           /* set cursor function */

  regs.h.ch=start;          /* starting line in ch */
  regs.h.cl=end;            /* ending line in cl   */

  int86(0x10,&regs,&regs);  /* do interrupt */
 }

/* save cursor information */
w[scr.active].start=start;
w[scr.active].end=end;

}
```

L_SCRN4.C

```
/********************   L_SCRN4.C   *************************/

#include "mydef.h"
#include <dos.h>

#if defined QUICKC
```

```
#include "malloc.h"
#include "memory.h"

#endif

#if defined TURBOC

#include "alloc.h"    /* Turbo C header file */
#include "mem.h"
#include "string.h"
#include "stdlib.h"

#endif


/*********************************************************************

 Usage: void alt_screen(int action);

 int action = ON or OFF.

 Turns on the alternate virtual screen. The true video buffer is
 copied to the alternate screen. All output (screen writing,
 window creation etc.) is routed to the alternate screen until
 the command "alt_screen(OFF);" is issued. The alternate screen
 is then copied to the video buffer where it may be seen.

 *******************************************************************/


void alt_screen(int action)
{
extern struct  screen_structure scr;
extern struct window_structure w[];

static char far *v_screen;
static char far *orig_screen;
static int old_snow;
static int old_update;
int buffsize=scr.rows*scr.columns*sizeof(unsigned char)*2;

  if (action==1){    /* open alternate (virtual) screen */
   if (orig_screen!=NULL)return;   /* screen already set */
   old_update=scr.update;    /* save old update info */
   scr.update=FALSE;    /* don't update cursor until done */

   old_snow=scr.snow;

   orig_screen=scr.buffer;    /* save original screen */
   v_screen=(char far *)malloc(buffsize);   /* alloc new screen */
   if(v_screen==NULL)return;   /* exit if allocation not made */
    move_scr_mem(scr.buffer,v_screen,buffsize);
```

```
    scr.snow=FALSE;
    scr.buffer=v_screen;
  }

  if (action==0){   /* close alternate screen */

   if(orig_screen==NULL)return;   /* not open */
    scr.buffer=orig_screen;    /* reset buffer */
    scr.snow=old_snow;
      move_scr_mem(v_screen,scr.buffer,buffsize);

      scr.update=old_update;   /* we can update cursor now */
      set_cursor(w[scr.active].start,w[scr.active].end);
      gotoxy(w[scr.active].x,w[scr.active].y);

   /*release v_screen memory */
   free((void *)v_screen); v_screen=NULL;
   orig_screen=NULL;
  }
}
```

L_WIN1.C

```
/******************** L_WIN1.C ***********************/

#include "mydef.h"
#include <dos.h>

#if defined QUICKC

#include "malloc.h"
#include "memory.h"

#endif

#if defined TURBOC

#include "alloc.h"
#include "mem.h"
#include "string.h"
#include "stdlib.h"

#endif


/***************************************************************

  Usage: int win_make(int x, int y, int width,int height \
            char *array, char *title, char frame_attr,char win_attr):
```

```
int x,y = column,row of upper left corner of active window area
          (not upper left frame corner);
int width= width of window (interior).
int height= height of window (interior).

char *array= pointer to string containing frame elements
          (macros defined in mydef.h).
char *title= title to appear in upper left corner
          of frame.
char frame_attr= attribute to use when drawing frame.
char win_attr= default attribute for window.

Creates a window, returns a "handle" (integer) which is used
to access the window in later operations. The newly created
window is placed on top of all existing windows, and is the
default active window. The newly created window is cleared.
A -1 is returned if too many windows are opened.

The window created will be resized and repositioned if necessary
to fit the screen.

****************************************************************/


int win_make(int x,int y,int width,int height,char *array,
          char *title, char frame_attr, char win_attr)
{
extern struct screen_structure scr;
extern struct window_structure w[];

 int t,b,l,r;   /* hold calculated values of top,bottom,left,right */

   /* check parameters and correct if necessary */

   if(scr.ptr==MAX_WINDOW)return(-1);

   /* adjust x,y,width & height to fit screen */

  if(array[0]=='\0'){                           /* no frame */

    if(x<1)x=1;                                      /* too far left? */
    if(y<1)y=1;                                      /* too far up? */
    if(width>scr.columns) width=scr.columns;         /* too wide? */
    if(height>scr.rows) height=scr.rows;             /* too high? */
    if(x+width>scr.columns) x=scr.columns-width+1;   /* too far right?*/
    if(y+height>scr.rows) y=scr.rows-height+1;       /* too far down?*/

  }
  else{
   if(x<2)x=2;                                   /* frame present */
   if(y<2)y=2;                                   /* allow for frame */
   if(width+2>scr.columns) width=scr.columns-2;  /* too wide? */
   if(height+2>scr.rows) height=scr.rows-2;      /* too high? */
```

```
   if(x+width+2>scr.columns) x=scr.columns-width;   /* too far right */
   if(y+height+1>scr.rows) y=scr.rows-height;        /* too far down */
   }

 if (array[0]=='\0')                         /* no frame */
   w[scr.list[scr.ptr+1]].frame=FALSE;
 else                                        /* frame present */
   w[scr.list[scr.ptr+1]].frame=TRUE;

    t=y;b=y+height-1;l=x;r=x+width-1;/* calc. window coordinates*/

    win_save();      /* save window (include frame) */
    scr.ptr++;       /* increment screen pointer */

    /* make new window the active window */
    scr.active=scr.list[scr.ptr];

/* release window so we can write anywhere
   (the printing routines can't write outside existing window
   so we temporarily expand window so we can draw frame)     */
 scr.top=1;
 scr.bottom=scr.rows;
 scr.right=scr.columns;
 scr.left=1;

 if (array[0]!='\0'){    /* if frame requested */

  draw_frame(x-1,y-1,width,height,array,title,frame_attr);

 }

/* set current attribute to window attribute */
scr.current = win_attr;

w[scr.active].attribute=win_attr;   /* save the window attribute */

/* set active window values */

w[scr.active].top=t;w[scr.active].bottom=b; /* save top and bottom */
w[scr.active].left=l;w[scr.active].right=r; /* save left and right */

update_margins():

    /* set default "underscore" cursor for new window */

    if (scr.mode == COLOR_80 || scr.mode == BW_80){
           w[scr.active].start=6; w[scr.active].end=7;
    }

    if (scr.mode == MONOCHROME ){
           w[scr.active].start=11;w[scr.active].end = 12;
    }
```

```
        /* save cursor information */
        cursor(NORMAL_CURSOR);  /* change actual cursor */
         cls();

return(scr.active);  /* return the window "handle" */

}

/******************************************************************

  Usage; void win_save(void);

  Saves the screen buffer of the top window.
  Used by other routines when the top window is about to be
  over written or the screen is being redrawn.

  This function should not be called directly.

******************************************************************/


void win_save(void)

{
extern struct screen_structure scr;
extern struct window_structure w[];

  int y;
  char far *dest_ptr;
  char far *scrn_ptr;
  int buff_size;  /* memory size required to hold saved image */
  int t,b,l,r;

/* set t,b,l,r to represent window top,bottom,left and right
   adjust to include frame if necessary */

    if (w[scr.active].frame==TRUE){
      t=scr.top-1;b=scr.bottom+1;l=scr.left-1;r=scr.right+1;
      }
     else{
      t=scr.top;b=scr.bottom;l=scr.left;r=scr.right;
      }
    /* copy external screen pointer to local pointer */
    scrn_ptr=scr.buffer;

     if (scr.ptr > MAX_WINDOW){
       cls();puts("too many windows ");exit(1);
       return;
     }

    /* calculate memory required to hold screen image */
    buff_size=( (r-l+1)*(b-t+1) )*2;
```

```
    if (w[scr.active].buffer==NULL)   /* if no memory is allocated */
    w[scr.active].buffer =
      (char *)malloc  (buff_size*sizeof(unsigned char));

                /* set up destination pointer (dest_ptr) and
                   screen pointer (scrn_ptr */

                dest_ptr=w[scr.active].buffer;

                /* initialize pointers */
                scrn_ptr=scr.buffer;
                scrn_ptr=scrn_ptr+((t-1)*(scr.columns*2))+(2*(l-1));
                dest_ptr=w[scr.active].buffer;

    /* move each row from screen to buffer */
    for(y=1 ;y<=b-t+1;y++){
      move_scr_mem(scrn_ptr,dest_ptr,2*(r-l+1));
      scrn_ptr=scrn_ptr +(2*scr.columns); /* update screen pointer */
      dest_ptr=dest_ptr+ (2*(r-l+1));/* update destination pointer */
    }

}  /* end function */

/*****************************************************************

 Usage: void win_delete(int handle);

 Deletes the window indicated.
 Rearranges window list to reflect change.

 *****************************************************************/


void win_delete(int handle)
{
extern struct screen_structure scr;
extern struct window_structure w[];

int location,i;

if (handle==0) return;  /* can't delete initial window */

/*if it is the top window call win_delete_top */
if (handle==scr.active) {
     win_delete_top();
     return;
}

location=win_validate(handle);
if(location==-1) return;              /* not a window */

win_save();  /* save top window */
```

```
/* Deleting a window requires that the window list be
   rearranged. We shift all values after the window
   being deleted forward one, then put the deleted
   window at the end        */

for(i=location;i<scr.ptr+1;i++) scr.list[i]=scr.list[i+1];

scr.list[scr.ptr]=handle;  /* move window to top of list */

if (w[handle].buffer!=NULL){
 free(w[handle].buffer);  /* free buffer of deleted window */
 w[handle].buffer=NULL;  /* NULL pointer */
}
scr.ptr--;   /* point down one level (we have one less window) */

win_redraw_all();
}


/*****************************************************************

  Usage: int win_validate(int handle);

  Checks the list of allocated windows to see if the
  Window handle indicated is valid.

  Returns a -1 if not valid, else returns the location
  of the window in the list.

*****************************************************************/

int win_validate(handle)
{
extern struct  screen_structure scr;
extern struct window_structure w[];

int i,location=-1;
 for(i=0;i<=scr.ptr;i++){   /* find if handle is allocated window */
  if (scr.list[i]==handle){
   location=i;
   break;
  }
 }
 return location;
}


/*****************************************************************

  Usage: void win_delete_top(void);

  deletes the top window.

*****************************************************************/
```

```
void win_delete_top(void)
{
extern struct  screen_structure scr;

if (scr.ptr==0)return;  /* can't delete initial window */

scr.ptr--;                  /* set the window pointer down one level */
scr.active=scr.list[scr.ptr];

update_margins();
win_redraw_all();         /* redraw all windows */

/* win_redraw will free buffer of top window when done
   we do not need to do it here */
}


/*****************************************************************

  Usage: void draw_frame(int x,int y,int width,int height,char *array,
                       char *title, char attribute)

  int x,y = Upper left corner of frame.
  int width,height= Width and height of interior of frame.
  char *array= Array of characters used to build frame. (see mydef.h)
  char *title= Title to use in upper left corner of frame
  int attribute= Text attribute to use for frame.

  *****************************************************************/


void draw_frame (int x,int y,int width,int height,char *array,\
                char *title,char attribute)
{
extern struct screen_structure scr;

 int old_attribute;
 int i,j,ctr,u_right,u_left;
 int x2,y2;
 char string[255];

 old_attribute=scr.current;  /* save current attribute */
 scr.current=attribute;
    /* draw first line of frame */
    string[0]= array[0];                          /* left corner */
    for(i=1;i<=width;i++) string[i]=array[4]; /* horizontal part */
    string[i++]=array[1]; string[i]='\0';              /* right corner and
                                                          terminator */
     x2=x;y2=y;
     dma_print(&x2,&y2,&string[0]);                /* print string */

     if (title!=NULL)           /*is there a title ? */
       if (strlen (title)<= width) {  /* will it fit? */
        x2=x+1;y2=y;
        dma_print(&x2,&y2,title );
        }
```

```
    y++;    /* move to next line */

      for (i=0; i<height;i++){          /* print vertical border */
       string[0]=array[5];string[1]='\0';  /* left border */
       x2=x;y2=y;
       dma_print(&x2,&y2,string);
       x2=x+width+1;y2=y++;             /* right border */
       dma_print(&x2,&y2,string);
      }
         string[0]=array[2];          /* draw bottom line of frame */
         for(i=1;i<=width;i++) string[i]=array[4];
         string[i++]=array[3];string[i]='\0';
         x2=x;y2=y++;
         dma_print(&x2,&y2,&string[0]);

         scr.current=old_attribute;      /* restore old attribute */
}



/*********************************************************************

  Usage: int win_center(int width,int height,char *array
                   char *title, char frame_attr,char win_attr);

   int width= width of window (interior).
   int height= height of window (interior).

   char *array= pointer to string containing frame elements
             (macros defined in mydef.h).
   char *title= title to appear in upper left corner
             of frame.
   char frame_attr= attribute to use when drawing frame.
   char win_attr= default attribute for window.

   Creates a window which is centered in the middle of the
   computer screen. It is called just like win_make(), except
   that no row and column is specified.

*********************************************************************/


int win_center(int width,int height,char *array,char *title,
              char frame_attr, char win_attr)
{
extern struct screen_structure scr;
extern struct window_structure w[];

 int x,y;

 x=(scr.columns/2)-(width/2); /* calculate window's column location*/
 y=(scr.rows/2)-(height/2);   /* calculate window's row location */
```

```
/* call win make to create centered window */

return(win_make(x,y,width,height,array,title,frame_attr,win_attr));

}
```

L_WIN2.C

```
/********************** L_WIN2.C *************************/

#include "mydef.h"
#include <dos.h>

#if defined QUICKC

#include "malloc.h"
#include "memory.h"

#endif

# if defined TURBOC

#include "alloc.h"       /* Turbo C header file */
#include "mem.h"
#include "string.h"
#include "stdlib.h"

#endif

/****************************************************************

 Usage: void win_pop_top(int handle);

 int handle = window handle.

 Moves the window indicated by "handle" to the top of the stack.
 Updates the window list and redraws the screen.

 ****************************************************************/

void win_pop_top(int handle)
{
extern struct screen_structure scr;
extern struct window_structure w[];

int location, i;

 if (handle==0) return;  /* can't delete initial window */
 if(handle==scr.active)return;  /* already on top */

 /* get location of window(handle) in list */
 location=win_validate(handle);
```

```
if(location==-1)return;   /* invalid handle */
win_save(); /* save current window, it is about to be overdrawn */

/* Popping a window to the top requires that the window list be
   rearranged. We shift all values after the window being popped
   (handle) forward one, then put the popped window at the end  */

for(i=location;i<scr.ptr+1;i++)
    scr.list[i]=scr.list[i+1];  /* shuffle */
scr.list[scr.ptr]=handle;   /* move window to top of list */

win_redraw(handle); /* redraw the window to make it appear on top */

scr.active=scr.list[scr.ptr];/* reset pointer to reflect new list */

 /* do if window has allocated memory */
 if (w[scr.active].buffer !=NULL){
  free(w[scr.active].buffer);       /* free buffer of new top window */
  w[scr.active].buffer=NULL;        /* null the pointer */
 }
 update_margins(); /* a new window is on top,
                      update screen margins */

 display_cursor(); /* display cursor for new window */

}


/********************************************************************

 Usage: void display_cursor(void);

 Moves the cursor to the location indicated by the variables for
 the active window. Also resets the cursor starting/ending
 scan lines.

 Mostly used when a window redraw occurs.

 ********************************************************************/

void display_cursor(void)
{
extern struct screen_structure scr;
extern struct window_structure w[];

gotoxy(w[scr.active].x,w[scr.active].y);   /* position cursor */

/* set cursor shape */
set_cursor(w[scr.active].start,w[scr.active].end);
}
```

```
/*********************************************************************

  Usage; void win_redraw(int handle);

  int handle = handle of window to redraw.

  Redraws the specified window. Does not rearrange the list.

 *********************************************************************/

static void win_redraw(int handle)
{
extern struct screen_structure scr;
extern struct window_structure w[];

int t,b,l,r;
char far *source_ptr;
char far *scrn_ptr;

int i;

  if(w[handle].buffer==NULL) return; /* window is not virtual,
                                        cannot redraw */
 /* is handle requested in list? */
 if(win_validate(handle)==-1 ) return;

   /* if the window is framed, the margins must be adjusted */

  if(w[handle].frame==TRUE){
    t=w[handle].top-1;b=w[handle].bottom+1;
    l=w[handle].left-1;r=w[handle].right+1;
  } else{
    t=w[handle].top;b=w[handle].bottom;
    l=w[handle].left;r=w[handle].right;
    }

    /* initialize pointers */
    scrn_ptr=scr.buffer;
    scrn_ptr=scrn_ptr+((t-1)*scr.columns*2)+(2*(l-1));

    source_ptr=w[handle].buffer;

 for(i=1 ;i<=b-t+1;i++){  /*do for each row in window*/
   move_scr_mem((char far *)source_ptr,
     (char far *)scrn_ptr,2*(r-l+1));
   /* update screen and destination pointer */
   scrn_ptr=scrn_ptr +(2*scr.columns);
   source_ptr=source_ptr+ (2*(r-l+1));
 }
}
```

```
/*********************************************************************

  Usage: void win_redraw_all(void);

  Redraws all the windows.
  The redraw is done on a virtual screen which is then copied to
  the true screen buffer.

  *********************************************************************/
void win_redraw_all(void)
{
extern struct screen_structure scr;
extern struct window_structure w[];

char far *hold_buffer;
char *new_buffer;
int i,loc,buffsize;
int oldsnow=scr.snow;
hold_buffer=scr.buffer;

buffsize=scr.rows*scr.columns*2;  /* calc size of buffer */

new_buffer= NULL;

  /* save top window as all will be redrawn */
   loc=scr.list[scr.ptr];   /* loc= top window */

  if(w[loc].buffer==NULL)  /* save only if it is not virtual */
    win_save();

/* allocate memory */
new_buffer= malloc (buffsize*sizeof(unsigned char));

/* if we got a new buffer set external screen pointer to it */
/* write routine will now write to new buffer */

if (new_buffer!=NULL) scr.buffer=(char far *)new_buffer;

/* turn of snow flag, we are not writing to screen buffer */
scr.snow=FALSE;

/* redraw all windows */
for(i=0;i<scr.ptr+1;i++)
    win_redraw(scr.list[i]);

scr.snow=oldsnow; /* turn snow flag back on */

/* free up buffer of top window */

  if(w[loc].buffer!=NULL){  /* be sure it is allocated */
    free(w[loc].buffer);    /* free it */
    w[loc].buffer=NULL:     /* mark it as freed */
  }
```

```
/* if we did get a new buffer, move it to screen */

  if(new_buffer!=NULL){
   scr.buffer =hold_buffer;    /* restore original screen buffer */
   move_scr_mem((char far *)new_buffer,scr.buffer,buffsize);
   free(new_buffer);   /*free memory */
   new_buffer=NULL;    /* mark it */
   display_cursor();   /* redisplay cursor */
  }
}
```

L_WIN3.C

```
/******************* L_WIN3.C   *************************/

#include "mydef.h"
#include <dos.h>

#if defined QUICKC

#include "malloc.h"
#include "memory.h"

#endif

#if defined TURBOC

#include "alloc.h"    /* Turbo C header file */
#include "mem.h"
#include "string.h"
#include "stdlib.h"

#endif

/****************************************************************

  Usage: void win_ceol(int handle, int x, int y);

  handle= Window handle.
  x= column.
  y= row.

  Clears the window indicated by handle from the x-y coordinate to
  the end of the line.

  ****************************************************************/

void win_ceol(int handle, int x, int y)
{
extern struct screen_structure scr;
extern struct window_structure w[];
```

```
if(w[handle].buffer==NULL){   /* if it is the top window call ceol() */
   ceol(x,y);
   return;
   }


win_point(handle);   /* direct output to handle */
 ceol(x,y);              /* now we can call ceol()   */
win_point(handle);   /* a second call to win_point() redirects
                         output to original values.
                         note: the parameter "handle" is ignored */

}



/*****************************************************************

 Usage: void win_cls(int handle);

 handle= Window handle.

 Clears the screen of the window indicated.

 ****************************************************************/

void win_cls(int handle)
{
extern struct screen_structure scr;
extern struct window_structure w[];

  /* if it is the top window call cls() */
  if(w[handle].buffer==NULL){
    cls();
    return;
   }

  win_point(handle);/* direct output to handle */
   cls();                /* output is redirected, we can call cls() now */
  win_point(handle);/* a second call to win_point() redirects
                        output to original values. */
}



/*****************************************************************

 Usage; void win_scroll_up(int handle, int lines);

 handle= Window handle.

 Scrolls the window indicated by "handle" up by the number
 indicated by "lines".

 ****************************************************************/
```

```
void win_scroll_up(int handle,int lines)
{
extern struct screen_structure scr;
extern struct window_structure w[];

  if(w[handle].buffer==NULL){  /* if the window is not virtual */
   scroll_up(lines);           /* call scroll_up(); */
   return;
   }

  win_point(handle);     /* redirect output to handle */
   scroll_up(lines);     /* now scroll_up */
   win_point(handle);    /* toggle output back to previous value */
}



/******************************************************************

  Usage: void win_scroll_down(int handle, int lines);

  handle= Window handle.

  Scrolls the window indicated by "handle" down by the number
  indicated by "lines".

  ******************************************************************/

void win_scroll_down(int handle,int lines)
{
extern struct screen_structure scr;
extern struct window_structure w[];

  if(w[handle].buffer==NULL){  /* if the window is not virtual */
   scroll_down(lines);         /* call scroll_down(); */
   return;
   }

  win_point(handle);     /* redirect output to handle */
   scroll_down(lines);   /* now scroll_down */
   win_point(handle);    /* toggle output back to previous value */
}



/******************************************************************

  Usage: void win_gotoxy(int handle, int x,int y);

  handle= Window handle.
  x,y   = column and row.

  Moves the cursor to the position x,y relative to window (handle).
  The cursor is visible only in the current active window.
```

If the window (handle) is not active, the change is not seen
until the window is made active (moved to the top).

```
****************************************************************/
void win_gotoxy(int handle,int x,int y)
{
extern struct screen_structure scr;
extern struct window_structure w[];

  if(w[handle].buffer==NULL){  /* if the window is not virtual */
   gotoxy(x,y);                /* call scroll_up(); */
   return;
   }

  win_point(handle);    /* redirect output to handle */
    gotoxy(x,y);        /* move the cursor */
  win_point(handle);    /* toggle output back to previous value */

}



/****************************************************************

  Usage: void win_print(int handle, int x, int y, char *string);

  handle= Window handle.
  x,y= Position (column and row).
  string= String to write.

  Writes string in window indicated by handle.

****************************************************************/
void win_print( int handle, int x,int y, char *string)
{
extern struct screen_structure scr;
extern struct window_structure w[];

  if(w[handle].buffer==NULL){     /* if not virtual */
   print(x,y,string);            /* call print routine */
   return;
   }
  win_point(handle);    /* direct output to window */
    print(x,y,string);  /* call print routine */
  win_point(handle);    /* toggle pointer back to original values */
}


/****************************************************************

  Usage: static win_point(int handle);

  handle= Window handle.
```

This function is used internally by many of the win_ functions.

It saves important values stored in the screen(scr) and window
(w) data structures and replaces them with new values which point
to the window indicated. It in essence "tricks" other routines
into acting on the new window. A second call to win_point()
acts as a toggle and restores the original values.

```
***************************************************************/

static void win_point(int handle)
{
extern struct screen_structure scr;
extern struct window_structure w[];

static char far *hold_screen;
static int t,b,l,r;

/*
   We are going to trick the external definitions of the screen
   (scr.buffer, scr.rows, scr.columns, scr.top, scr.bottom, scr.left,
   and scr.right) so they "point" to the virtual window. If the
   window is framed, the margins will show an indention of 1, if
   unframed then no indention. */

/* the following variables are used to store the "true"
   external variables */

static int wt,wb,wl,wr;
static int rows,columns;
static int in_use=FALSE;
static int update;
static int active;
static int snow;

if (w[handle].buffer==NULL) return;  /* return if window is active */

   if(in_use==FALSE){    /* enter here if the function is not already
                             pointing to another window? */

      in_use=TRUE;        /* mark it used */
      update=scr.update; /* store old update info */

      scr.update=FALSE;  /* don't update cursor, window is virtual */

      hold_screen=scr.buffer;  /* save screen buffer */
      snow =scr.snow;          /* save snow info */
      scr.snow= FALSE;  /* window is virtual, we are not writing to
                           screen so we don't need to worry about
                           snow */

      active=scr.active;  /* save old active */
      scr.active=handle;  /* set handle as new active window */
```

```
    t=scr.top,b=scr.bottom,   /* save more values */
    l=scr.left,r=scr.right;

    /* store the old row, columns setting */
    rows=scr.rows;columns=scr.columns;

    /* the following are the margin values of the window.
       save them, and use for calculations of new margins */

    wt=w[handle].top;
    wb=w[handle].bottom;
    wl=w[handle].left;
    wr=w[handle].right;

    /* now make the pointer to the screen buffer
       point to our window buffer */
    scr.buffer=(char far *) w[handle].buffer;

/* now find out if the window has a frame and
   set the window margins accordingly */

    if(w[handle].frame==FALSE){   /* no frame */
     scr.rows=wb-wl+1;            /* set screen rows and columns */
     scr.columns=wr-wl+1;          /* to values of window */

     scr.top=1;              /* set margin values */
     scr.bottom=scr.rows;
     scr.left=1;
     scr.right=scr.columns;
    } else                 /* the window has a frame */
    {
       scr.rows=wb-wt+3;   /* include frame in rows and column count */
       scr. columns=wr-wl+3;

       scr.top=2;              /* set margins so frame not included */
       scr.bottom=scr.rows-1;
       scr.left=2;
       scr.right=scr.columns-1;
    }

  } else             /* active =TRUE */
  {                  /* enter here to restore original values */
   in_use=FALSE;
   scr.update=update;   /* restore update flag */

   /* restore values */

   scr.top=t; scr.bottom=b;
   scr.left=l;scr.right=r;
   scr.rows=rows; scr.columns=columns;
   scr.buffer=hold_screen;
   scr.active=active;
   scr.snow=snow;
  }
}
```

L_WIN4.C

```
/********************    L_WIN4.C    *************************/

#include "mydef.h"
#include <dos.h>

#if defined QUICKC

#include "malloc.h"
#include "memory.h"

#endif

#if defined TURBOC

#include "alloc.h"      /* Turbo C header file */
#include "mem.h"
#include "string.h"
#include "stdlib.h"

#endif


/*******************************************************************

 Usage: void win_up(int handle, int amount);

 int handle = window handle
 int amount = the number of lines to move the window.

 Moves the window indicated up on the screen, the screen is
 updated to show the movement. If there is insufficient space
 to move the requested amount, the window is moved as far as
 possible.

 ******************************************************************/

void win_up(int handle, int amount)
{
extern struct  screen_structure scr;
extern struct window_structure w[];
 int win_top;

 /* if the window selected is on top then save */
 if(scr.active==handle)
    win_save();

    /* calculate true top of window.
       this depends on presence of frame */

    if(w[handle].frame==TRUE) win_top=w[handle].top-1;
     else win_top=w[handle].top;
```

```
    if(win_top==1) return;   /*return if already on top*/

    /* adjust amount of movement if there is not space */
    if(win_top-amount<=0)amount=win_top-1;

    /* change the window margin definitions to show the changes */
    w[handle].top-= amount;
    w[handle].bottom-= amount;

 win_redraw_all(); /* show the changes */

 if(scr.active==handle){        /* if the window is active */
   free(w[handle].buffer) ;   /* free the memory */
   w[handle].buffer=NULL ;
   update_margins();            /* change the screen margins */
                                /* to reflect the new active */
                                /* window area */
   display_cursor();        /* update cursor position */
 }
}


/***************************************************************

 Usage: void win_right(int handle, int amount);

 int handle = window handle
 int amount = the number of lines to move the window.

 Moves the window indicated right on the screen, the screen is
 updated to show the movement. If there is insufficient space
 to move the requested amount, the window is moved as far as
 possible.

 ***************************************************************/

void win_right(int handle, int amount)
{
extern struct screen_structure scr;
extern struct window_structure w[];
 int win_right;

 /* if the window selected is on top then save */
 if(scr.active==handle)
    win_save();

   /* calculate true right edge of window.
      this depends on presence of frame */

   if(w[handle].frame==TRUE) win_right=w[handle].right+1;
    else win_right=w[handle].right;
```

```
     /*return if already on right border */
     if(win_right==scr.columns) return;

     if(win_right+amount>=scr.columns)amount=scr.columns-win_right;

     /* change the window margin definitions to show the changes */
     w[handle].right += amount;
     w[handle].left+=amount;

 win_redraw_all();      /* show the changes */

 if(scr.active==handle){   /* if the window is active */
   free(w[handle].buffer) ; /* free the buffer */
   w[handle].buffer=NULL ;
   update_margins();             /* update screen margins
                                    to reflect new active
                                    window area */

     display_cursor();        /* update cursor position */
 }
}


/*****************************************************************

 Usage: void win_left(int handle, int amount);

 int handle = window handle
 int amount = the number of lines to move the window.

 Moves the window indicated left on the screen, the screen is
 updated to show the movement. If there is insufficient space
 to move the requested amount, the window is moved as far as
 possible.

 *****************************************************************/

void win_left(int handle, int amount)
{
extern struct screen_structure scr;
extern struct window_structure w[];

 int win_left;

 /* if the window selected is on top then save */
 if(scr.active==handle)
    win_save();
    /* calculate true left edge of window.
       this depends on presence of frame */

    if(w[handle].frame==TRUE) win_left=w[handle].left-1;
     else win_left=w[handle].left;
```

```
      if(win_left==0) return;   /*return if already on left border */

      if(win_left-amount<=0)amount=win_left-1;

   /* update the window margins to show the move */
   w[handle].left  -= amount;
   w[handle].right -= amount;
 win_redraw_all();    /* update the screen */
 if(scr.active==handle){   /* if the window is active */
   free(w[handle].buffer) ;
   w[handle].buffer=NULL ;
   update_margins();        /* update the screen margins
                               to reflect changes made to
                               the active window   */

   display_cursor();       /* update cursor position */
 }
}


/*******************************************************************

 Usage: void win_down(int handle, int amount);

 int handle = window handle
 int amount = the number of lines to move the window.

 Moves the window indicated down on the screen, the screen is
 updated to show the movement. If there is insufficient space
 to move the requested amount, the window is moved as far as
 possible.

 ******************************************************************/
void win_down(int handle, int amount)
{
int win_bottom;

extern struct screen_structure scr;
extern struct window_structure w[];

 /* if the window selected is on top then save */
 if(scr.active==handle)
    win_save();

    /* calculate true top of window.
       this depends on presence of frame */

    if(w[handle].frame==TRUE) win_bottom=w[handle].bottom+1;
    else win_bottom=w[handle].bottom;

    if(win_bottom==scr.rows) return;   /*return if already on top*/

    if(win_bottom+amount>=scr.rows)amount=scr.rows-win_bottom;
```

```
        /* update the window margins to reflect change */
        w[handle].top += amount;
        w[handle].bottom +=amount;

   win_redraw_all(); /* update the screen */
   if(scr.active==handle){   /* if the window is active */
     free(w[handle].buffer) ; /* free the buffer */
     w[handle].buffer=NULL ;
     update_margins();              /* update the screen margins
                                       to reflect the new active
                                       window area */
      display_cursor();        /* update cursor position */
   }
}


/**************************************************************

   Usage: void win_insert(int handle, int position);

   int handle = window handle
   int position = relative position within the window stack.

   Places the window indicated by "handle" to the relative screen
   location indicated. Position 1 would be the first window on top
   of the initial "desktop" window. The screen is updated to show
   the move.

   *************************************************************/

void win_insert(int handle, int position)
{
extern struct  screen_structure scr;
extern struct window_structure w[];

int location,i;

if (handle==0) return;  /* can't move initial window */

if(position==scr.ptr) {   /* if it is moved to the top */
  win_pop_top(handle);    /* pop it */
  return;
}

 /* return if move to same location is requested. */
 if (handle==scr.list[position]) return;

   location=win_validate(handle); /* see if window is open */
   if (location==-1) return;          /* exit if not in list */

/* inserting a window requires that the window list be
   rearranged. The direction of the shift depends on whether the
   window is moved up or down in the stack. */
```

```
win_save();  /* save top window before shuffle */

 /* shuffle order */

    /* if the position requested is higher in the stack than the */
    /* actual location, do the following */

     if(position>location)     /* the window is moved up */
       for(i=location;i<position;i++) scr.list[i]=scr.list[i+1];
     else                      /* the window is moved down */
       for(i=location;i>position;i--) scr.list[i]=scr.list[i-1];

  scr.list[position]=handle;
win_redraw_all(); /* redraw the window */
}
```

L_WIN5.C

```
/********************    L_WIN5.C    *************************/

#include "mydef.h"

/*******************************************************************

 Usage: int win_what_attr(int handle);

 Handle= window handle;

 Returns the screen attribute of "handle"

 *******************************************************************/

char win_what_attr(int handle)
{
extern struct screen_structure scr;
extern struct window_structure w[];

return (w[handle].attribute); /* return the attribute */
}

/*******************************************************************

 Usage: void win_set_attr(int handle, char attribute);

 Handle= window handle;
 Attribute = text attribute;

 Sets the default text attribute of the window "handle" to
 "attribute".

 *******************************************************************/
```

```
void win_set_attr(int handle,char attribute)
{
extern struct screen_structure scr;
extern struct window_structure w[];

 w[handle].attribute = attribute;
}
```

L_PRINT.C

```
/********************    L_PRINT.C   **************************/

#include "mydef.h"
#include <dos.h>

#if defined TURBOC
#include <mem.h>
#endif

#include <string.h>

/**********************************************************************

 Usage: void print(int x, int y, char *string);

 int x,y      = column, row at which text is printed.
 char * string = string to print.

 Prints the string at the location indicated for the active window.
 The string is printed with the text attribute stored in scr.current.
 If the external variable scr.bold_caps is set true, uppercase
 letters are printed with the attribute intensity set high.
 Text is wrapped to fit within the window, and the window is scrolled
 up when the bottom of the screen is reached. The cursor position is
 updated.

 Calls dma_write() to do actual work.

 **********************************************************************/

void print(int x,int y,char *string)
{
  int x2,y2;
  x2=x;y2=y;                      /* make copies of x,y, we don't want
                                     original values changed */
  dma_print(&x2,&y2,string);  /* call dma_print to write the text */
  gotoxy(x2,y2);                  /* move the cursor */
}

/**********************************************************************

 Usage: void print_here(char *string);
```

```
char * string = string to print.

Just like print() except that it prints the text at the current
cursor location.

*******************************************************************/

void print_here(char *string)

{
 int  x,y;
 wherexy(&x,&y);      /* find out where the cursor is */
 print(x,y,string); /* print the string */
}


/*****************************************************************

 Usage: void dma_print(int *x, int *y, char *string);

 int *x,*y        = column, row at which text is printed.
 char * string = string to print.

Works like print() except the cursor is not moved. x and y are
set to the location that the cursor should occupy. This function
is useful if you don't actually want the cursor moved.

*******************************************************************/

void dma_print(int *x, int *y,char *string)
{
extern struct  screen_structure scr;
extern struct window_structure w[];

 int i,j,str_index,write_width;
 int abs_x,abs_y;
 int orig_y;
 int width,height;
 unsigned offset;
 char far *video_buffer;
 char string2[MAX_STRING*2];

 orig_y=*y;  /* save the original y */
 width=scr.right-scr.left+1;     /* figure the length of the window */
 height=scr.bottom-scr.top +1;  /* figure the height of the window */

 if(*y> height){  /* if y is beyond last line of window*/
  *y= height;      /* set y = last line of window */
  scroll_up(1);   /* scroll_up window to make space */
 }
  if(*x> width)*x=width; /* if x greater than last column, */
                         /* set equal to last column */

  abs_x=(*x-1)+scr.left;  /* adjust to screen coordinates */
  abs_y=(*y-1)+scr.top;
```

```
/* do final adjustment of coordinates so they fit screen */
   if (abs_x<scr.left) abs_x=scr.left;
   if (abs_x>scr.right) abs_x=scr.right;
   if (abs_y<scr.top) abs_y=scr.top;
   if (abs_y>scr.bottom) abs_y=scr.bottom;

/* the following code creates a new string, padded with attributes */
   i=0;
   while(*string){
      string2[i++]=*string; /*copy char to string2 */

         /* is it an uppercase char ?*/
         if (*string >=65 && *string <=90 && scr.bold_caps==TRUE)
           string2[i++]= set_intense(scr.current); else
           string2[i++]=scr.current;
             string++;
   }
      string2[i]='\0';   /* terminate string */

/* keep index pointer for location within string2, copy sections of
   the string into the screen buffer, staying within the screen
   margins */

      str_index=0;
      j=0;

      for(;;){   /* do for each row of window */
       /* calculate offset */
       offset=(((abs_y-1)*scr.columns)+(abs_x-1))*2;

       /* figure width of sting to write */
       write_width=(scr.right-abs_x+1)*2;

       /* trying to write beyond end of string ? */
       if (str_index+write_width>strlen(string2))
        write_width=strlen(string2)-str_intdex; /* adjust length */
        video_buffer=scr.buffer+offset;       /* set video pointer */

       /* move the string segment */
       move_scr_mem((char far *)&string2[str_index],
                    video_buffer,write_width);

      abs_x=scr.left;
      abs_y++; j++;   /* update index to new location */
      str_index=str_index+write_width; /* increment string index */

      if(str_index>=strlen(string2)) break;  /* end of string */
      if(abs_y>scr.bottom){   /* past bottom of window */
        scroll_up(1);
        abs_y--;
        }
    }

    /* update cursor location */
```

```
      *y=*y+j-1;
      if(*y>orig_y)
       *x=(write_width/2)+1;
      else
       *x=*x+(write_width/2);
      /* if last char printed on border */
      if((*x>width) && *y< height){
       (*y)++; *x=1;                          /* move cursor down */
      }
}
```

```
/*******************************************************************

  Usage: void move_scr_mem(char far *string,char far *video,
                           int number)

  char far *string = string to print.
  char far *video  = address within screen buffer to which text is
                     written.
  int number       = the number of bytes to write.

  Copies the string to the video buffer. The pointers are far,
  so the string could be copied any where in conventional memory.
  Can also copy from screen to another location. Avoids screen
  snow on CGA display adapters when the external variable scr.snow
  is set to TRUE.

  *******************************************************************/

void move_scr_mem (char far *string,char far *video,int number)
{
unsigned int sseg,soff,dseg,doff;
int regval;
int origval;
int vert;
char far *ptr;

sseg=FP_SEG(string);soff=FP_OFF(string);
dseg=FP_SEG(video);doff=FP_OFF(video);

  if (scr.snow==TRUE){

     /* save the mode setting */
     ptr=MAKE_FP(0 ,0x465);  /* point to BIOS location for mode */
     regval=*ptr;            /* read the mode */
     origval=regval;         /* save the original value */
     regval=regval&0x37;     /* mask bit 3 off */

     /* wait for the CGA status register (bit 3) to go from 0 to 1 */
     for(;;){
      vert =inp(0x3da);       /* read the CGA status register */
      if ((vert&8)==0) break; /* is bit three equal 0? if so, break */
     }
```

```
   for(;;){
    vert=inp(0x3da);           /* read the status register again */
    if((vert&8)==8) break;   /* exit when bit three equals 1   */
    }
   outp (0x3d8,regval);    /* send new mode to CGA controller */
 }

 movedata(sseg,soff,deseg,doff,number);  /* move the data */

 if (scr.snow==TRUE)
     outp(0x3d8,origval); /* set controller to original value */
 }
```

Chapter 3

Menu Design

In this chapter we will review the following topics:

- Command line menus.
- Point-and-shoot techniques.
- Quick keys.
- Pop-up menus.
- Full versus partial menus.
- Horizontal moving light bar menus.
- Stacked (multilevel) light bar menus.
- Pull-down menus.

INTRODUCTION

We will survey several steps in the evolution of what are now "standard" user interfaces. We will discuss design considerations, first from the user's and then from the programmer's point of view.

116

User Viewpoint

Two of the most popular methods for communicating with an application are the "command line" interface and the menu-based system.

An example of a command line interface is provided by the program command.com. The user communicates with the computer via a series of commands that can be entered at the DOS prompt. For example, the DOS command "copy myfile.doc myfile.bak" translates to the English "copy the file myfile.doc to the file myfile.bak".

A disadvantage of the command line interface is the lack of guidance provided to the user by the program. The user must essentially learn a new language— both commands and syntax. Although the command line interface is quite powerful in the hands of an expert, the novice may find command lines cryptic and difficult to use.

An advantage of menu-based applications is that the options are displayed on-screen. In many menu-based systems, the user may select an option with a single keystroke, instead of typing out commands as would be required by command line interfaces. Some menu systems even provide pop-up *dialogue boxes* that inform the user about such things as the status of a job to be executed or the appropriateness of a keystroke.

In complex applications there are more options than can be displayed on a single screen. In such cases, a hierarchical series of menus is created, which leads the user from more general to increasingly specific options.

The simplest type of menu, which many of us have created at one time or another, might look like Figure 3–1. Although this menu is not very glamorous, it does its job adequately. The options are presented, and the user is informed how to make the selection.

One slight problem with this menu is its use of numbers to represent options. The user must read the list of options, find the corresponding number, and then enter it. Because it is easier to remember letters that are logically associated with

```
Options:

1)  Sort a data file.
2)  Print a file.
3)  Delete a file.
4)  Copy a file.
5)  Quit program and return to DOS.

Please enter a number (1-5), then press Enter or Return
to select an option:_
```

Figure 3–1 Simple menu with options identified by number

menu options (mnemonics) than it is to remember numbers, the menu is improved by using the first letter of each option to select it, as in Figure 3–2. This menu requires two steps to make a selection: pressing the proper key, then pressing Enter. It would be faster if the program read each keystroke from the keyboard and immediately executed the chosen option.

Although single-key selection would definitely speed up the process of choosing an option, inexperienced users might not want to have an accidental keypress send the program off and running. The slow, deliberate action of entering a letter, seeing it on the screen, then finalizing the selection by touching the Enter key can be very reassuring.

Even more reassuring to the new user is the "point-and-shoot" concept. The user points to a selection by highlighting the desired option using the cursor keys, then selects that option by pressing the Enter key. The highlighted option usually appears as inverse text. The point-and-shoot technique is particularly desirable if the user is not a touch typist. No time is wasted hunting for the keys.

Another popular point-and-shoot technique involves the use of a *mouse* to move the cursor to an item and select by pressing a button on the mouse. However, we stated in the introduction to this book that our software would avoid reliance on any hardware which is not universally found on IBM PCs and their clones. Personally, I feel that most text-based menus can be manipulated as fast, if not faster, using keyboard input as they would using a mouse. I find it is faster to press a single key to select an option than it is to point with a mouse. Although mice and other pointing devices such as light pens are extremely efficient for many graphics-oriented programs, they will not be discussed further here.

Combining the elements of point-and-shoot and single-key selection, we get a menu which looks like that in Figure 3–3 (the highlighter is shown as an under-line.) Now we have a menu supporting single-key selection for power users, and a deliberate point-and-shoot approach for novice users.

All the menus that we will create in this chapter will support both single-key selection and point-and-shoot techniques.

```
Options:

Sort a file.
Print a file.
Delete a file.
Copy a file.
Quit program and return to DOS.

Please enter the letter (S,P,D,C or Q) then press Enter
or Return to select an option.
```

Figure 3–2   Menu using first letters of options

```
Options:

Sort a data file.
Print a file.
Delete a file.
Copy a file.
Quit program and return to DOS.

Please enter the letter (S,P,D,C or Q) or highlight
the selection using the cursor keys and press Enter._
```

Figure 3–3   Point-and-shoot menu

Programmer's Viewpoint

So far we have discussed the menu from the user's viewpoint—that is, the look and feel of the interface. Another important issue, particularly from the programmer's perspective, is the reusability of program code.

In the rush to complete a programming project, many programmers create "quick and dirty" functions which work only with a specific application. In this way a menu system might be created with the options "hard-wired" into the code. If the programmer decides to use a similar menu system in a later project, the entire code must be rewritten.

A more efficient approach is to create versatile functions which require little or no modification for each project. A menu function, for example, could be passed a data structure containing all the information needed to create the menu. Menus containing different options could be created simply by changing the information contained within the data structure.

Very often when a particular menu option is selected, a specific function is called. For example, if the user selects the option "Print" it might be necessary to call the function **printer( )**. A well-designed menu function should allow specific functions to be automatically called.

At other times, we may not want the menu to automatically call a specific function. Instead we might want to know which option was chosen, via a return code.

A versatile menu function should have the capability of automatically calling functions or returning the number of the option selected. With these considerations in mind, all of our menu systems will have the following features:

- The menu function is passed a pointer to a data structure which contains information describing the menu and its options.
- The menu function prints the menu and processes all user input until a selection is made or until the user presses the Escape key to exit the menu.

- Each menu function supports both single-key ("quick key") and point-and-shoot menu selection.
- The quick key used to select an option is represented by the capitalized letter appearing within each option. This letter is automatically displayed on the screen with the intensity set high.
- When a selection is made, the menu can automatically call a specified function or, optionally, can close down the menu and return an integer (indicating the option selected) to the function which called the menu.

We will now examine several menu systems in detail. We will see how each menu presents options, how it behaves for novice and expert users, and how well the menus navigate the user throughout the menu hierarchy.

Each menu system will have a sample program to demonstrate the use of the menu. The sample programs will all use multilevel menus with the menu hierarchy shown in Figure 3–4. In this hypothetical application, selecting the option "Print" will result in the creation of a new menu with the options "Printer" and "Text-file" (print to a standard ASCII text file on disk). If the "Printer" option is selected from the second menu, a third menu appears, giving the options "Lpt1:" and "1Pt2:". Selection of an option from the third menu will perform the hypothetical task of printing and then will return the user to the first menu.

```
Sort, Print, Delete, Copy, Quit
        └─ Printer, Text-file
            └─ Lpt1:, 1Pt2:
```
                           Figure 3–4   Menu hierarchy

GOALS FOR THE POP-UP MENU

Although the pop-up menu is our simplest menu, in some ways it is our most important. Here we establish the data structures, calling conventions, and menu design philosophies which will be used in all future menus. I highly recommend reading this section.

The pop-up menu is designed to appear within a window which "pops" onto the screen. The options appear vertically within the window, and the first option is highlighted with inverse text. The user may select from the menu using quick keys or point-and-shoot techniques.

In Figure 3–5 is a "screen capture" of a pop-up menu which appears on top of a backdrop of dots. *Please note that the quick key highlighting is not visible in screen captures.* When this menu terminates, the menu window is removed, returning the background to its initial state (in this case, dots).

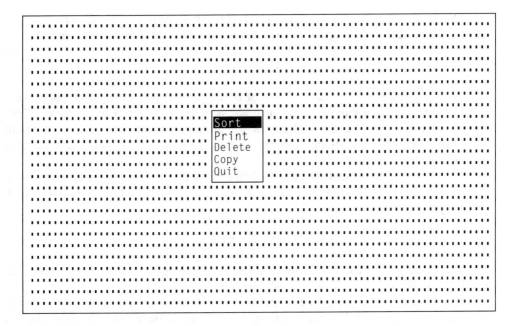

Figure 3–5   Screen capture of pop-up menu

APPLICATION

The pop-up menu is extremely easy to add to an application. As with all our programs, *the header file mydef.h must be included at the beginning of each code module*. The file mydef.h contains define statements and structures for all the menus.

The pop-up menu is created by a call to the function **pop_up( )** which is contained in the library module **1_popup.c.** Prior to calling **pop_up( )**, the menu data structure must be applied and initialized for the specific application.

Variations of this data structure are used for each of our menu systems, so let's examine this structure in more detail. Here is the data structure **pop_struc** as it appears in mydef.h:

```
struct pop_struc{
  char *name;        /* the menu option */
  int (*fun)();      /* the pointer to function */
  int select_id;     /* the list-select return code */
};
```

The elements of this data structure are defined as follows:

```
                         char *name;
```

This is a pointer to a text string which represents each option. If **name** pointed to "Print" for example, the string "Print" would appear as a menu option.

```
int (*fun) ( );
```

This is a pointer to a function. This type of pointer is almost tailor-made for menus. A function pointer can be set to the address of any function. For example, **(*fun)** ( ) may be assigned the address of the function **demo**( ) with the statement "fun = demo;". The function **demo**( ) may then be called with the statement "(*fun) ( );".

If we want a function called when this menu option is selected, we would put that function pointer here. If we don't want a function automatically called, the pointer would be set to NULL.

```
int select_id;
```

This value is returned to the calling function if the function pointer is set to NULL. If the function pointer has a value, **select_id** is ignored.

The structure **pop_struc** is applied to a data array of size n, where n = (number of options + 1). We create this array with one extra element because the last element is used to mark the end of the array. The last element is indicated by setting ***name** to an empty string ("\0").

Each menu option occupies one element of the array, and has a value for **name, (*fun)** ( ), and **select_id.** For example "struct pop_struc pop_menu [3];" would create a menu array large enough for two menu options. Take a look at this example:

```
struct pop_struc pop_menu [3]={

/*  *name          (*fun)()  select_id */

    " Start " ,    demo,      0,
    " Quit  " ,    NULL,      1,
    "\0"      /* mark the end of the options list */

};
```

The preceding data array would instruct **pop_up**( ) to create a menu with two options: "Start" and "Quit". If "Start" was selected, the function **demo**( ) would be called; if "Quit" was selected, the menu would close down and the integer 1 would be returned.

Once the menu data structure is applied and initialized, as just demonstrated, the pop-up menu is created by calling the function **pop_up**( ):

```
int pop_up(struct pop_struc pop_menu[ ],int x,int y,
char normal, char inverse);
```

The parameters passed to **pop_up( )** are defined as follows:

> pop_menu[ ] = The menu data array.
>
> x,y   = The screen coordinates for the upper left corner of the menu window.
>
> normal   = The normal text attribute to use for the menu window.
>
> inverse   = The inverse text attribute (for highlighter).

All the work of creating the pop-up window and processing the user input is done by **pop_up( )**. The width and height of the pop-up window are calculated by **pop_up( )**, based on the number and length of the menu options.

When **pop_up( )** is called, it will remain active until the user selects an option, or touches the Escape key. If the user makes a selection, **pop_up( )** will do one of two things:

- If the option has a function pointer specified, the specified function is called immediately upon selection by the user.
- If the option has a NULL function pointer, the pop-up window is closed, and the value specified by the element **select_id** is returned to the function which called **pop_up( )**.

The menu is also closed by touching the Escape key, in which case the return code is 0.

It is possible to have a menu which consists completely of options with NULL function pointers. In such a case, the menu is actually a simple form of list selection. For example,

```
struct pop_struc pop_menu [6]={
        " Apple      " ,NULL, 1,
        " Banana     " ,NULL, 2,
        " Cherry     " ,NULL, 3,
        " Date       " ,NULL, 4,
        " None       " ,NULL, 5,
        "\0"        /* mark the end of the options list */
};
```

This technique works quite well for user selection from a short list. In Chapter 5, we will create a far more advanced list selection function.

When an option is selected which does have a function pointer specified, **pop_up( )** calls the function and then examines the value returned by the function. All our menu systems expect functions to return an integer value. If the function returns a value of 0, **pop_up( )** keeps the menu open, ready for another selection. If an integer other than 0 is returned, **pop_up( )** closes the menu and the return code is passed to the function which invoked **pop_up( )**.

The menu is closed by **pop_up( )** only under three conditions:

1. The user touches the Escape key, in which case the return code is 0.
2. A called function returns a non-0 value. The value is returned to the function which called **pop_up( )**.
3. A selected option has a NULL function pointer associated with it, in which case the integer **select_id** associated with the option is returned to the calling function.

The most important point to remember is that any function called by **pop_up( )** which returns a value *other than 0* will cause **pop_up( )** to close the menu. The menu will return this return code to the function which defined the menu and invoked **pop_up( )**.

To better illustrate the creation of a pop-up menu, let's look at the program popdemo.c which appears in the Source Code section of this chapter. There are three functions in popdemo.c which interest us:

```
FUNCTION      OPTIONS PRESENTED

start( )      "Sort, Print, Delete, Copy and Quit"
prtdemo( )    "Printer, Text-file"
printer( )    "Lpt1:, 1Pt2:"
```

You may notice a potential problem with the options "Lpt1:" and "Lpt2:", because they both begin with the same letter. In all the previous options the quick key (which is capitalized) has always been the first letter. Since both of these options begin with "L" we must pick a different letter for the second option. We therefore make the options "**L**pt1:" and 1**P**t2:".

The function **start( )** creates and initializes the necessary data structure for the first menu as:

```
struct pop_struc pop_menu [6]={
/*  *name    (*fun)() select_id */

    " Sort   " ,fake,   0,
    " Print  " ,prtdemo,0,
    " Delete " ,fake,   0,
    " Copy   " ,fake,   0,
    " Quit   " ,NULL,   1,  /* returns a 1 when selected */
    "\0"       /* mark the end of the options list */
};
```

Three of the options ("Sort", "Delete", and "Copy") have the function **fake( )** specified. The function **fake( )** does nothing more than create a pop-up dialogue box to inform the user that a particular option was selected. The option "Print" calls the function **prtdemo( )** which is the menu path that we will follow.

The option "Quit" has a NULL function pointer. As just discussed, anytime a selected option has a NULL function pointer, the menu is closed and **select_id** is returned to the calling function. Since this menu is the top level or *parent* menu, selecting "Quit" would remove the initial menu window from the screen, and the program would terminate.

The function **start( )** fills the screen with dots '.' to provide a background for the menu window, and then invokes the menu with the following call:

```
return (pop_up (pop_menu,33,10,scr.normal,scr.inverse));
```

This call generates the sample image that was illustrated in the Goals section of this chapter.

Let's assume the option "Print" is selected, and the function **prtdemo( )** is called. The function **prtdemo( )** creates a new data structure with options for another pop-up menu.

```
struct pop_struc pop_menu [3]={
/* *name          (*fun)()  select_id */

" Printer    " ,printer, 0,
" Text-file " ,text,    0,
"\0"       /* mark the end of the options list */
};

return_code= (pop_up (pop_menu,41,13,scr.normal,scr.inverse));
```

This new data structure instructs **pop_up( )** to create the first *child* menu, illustrated in Figure 3–6. If the option "Printer" is selected from this menu, the function **printer( )** is called and it creates the final menu.

```
 struct pop_struc pop_menu [3]={

/* *name          (*fun)()  select_id */
  " Lpt1: ",   lpt1,    0,
  " lpt2: ",   lpt2,    0,
  "\0"       /* mark the end of the options list */
 };

return (pop_up (pop_menu,53,15,scr.normal,scr.inverse));
```

Figure 3–7 shows a screen capture with all the menus active.

So far, we have discussed the process of creating menus. An equally important topic is the method of closing menus in a multilevel menu system.

Take, for example, the third menu in a three-level menu stack. In this menu system, let us see how menu function 3 can control whether its parent menu (number 2) remains open or closes down. The function which creates the third menu takes the following steps:

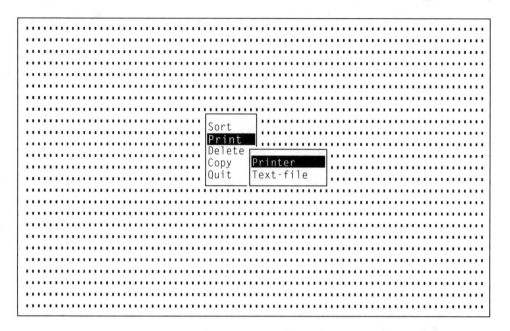

Figure 3–6   Pop-up menu with first child

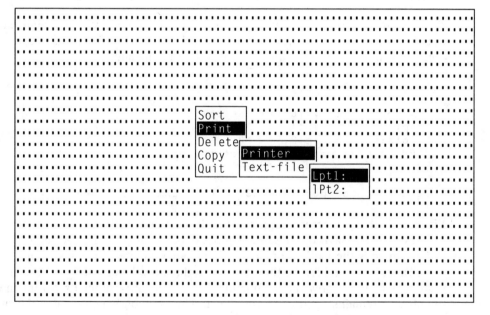

Figure 3–7   Pop-up menu with three levels active

1. Create and initialize the menu data structure for menu 3.
2. Pass the menu structure to **pop_up( )**, to create menu 3.
3. Examine the return code from **pop_up( )** and decide what value to return to menu 2. If a 0 is returned to menu number 2 it will stay open; if a non-0 is returned it will close. As the programmer writing this function, you must decide which of these two actions you want the parent menu to take.

Let's take a specific example from our sample menu system in Figure 3–7. Suppose that, after selecting the option "Lpt1:" (and hypothetically configuring the printer port), we wish menus 2 and 3 to close down, leaving only the initial menu.
If we represent the intervening call to **pop_up( )** by ">p_u>", the calling sequence to the function **1pt1( )** would look like this:

```
start() >p_u> prtdemo() >p_u> printer >p_u> 1pt1()
```

The function **1pt1( )** can close down its parent menu by returning a non-0 number of **pop_up( )**. After **pop_up( )** closes the menu, it passes the non-0 back to its calling function, **printer( )**, which in turn passes that back to its parent menu. At this step in the return trip, **prtdemo( )** returns a 0 to the first menu, which allows it to stay open.
Putting it all together, the calling/return sequence looks like this:

```
Calling:
    start() >p_u> prtdemo() >p_u> printer() >p_u> 1pt1() >⌐
                                                            |
    start() <p_u< prtdemo() <p_u< printer() <p_u< 1pt1() ←⌐
Return value:    0                 1                1
```

At this point the menu created by **start( )**, via **pop_up( )**, is still active, awaiting user input.
The take-home message is this: *plan each step of your menu*. Each function called by a menu may close down the menu or may keep it open, depending on the return code. These return codes may be passed back up the line to parent functions, which can take appropriate actions. In our example, the return codes were all 0s and 1s. In actual applications you could use other non-0 return codes to communicate with parent functions.

Full versus Partial Menus

One technique that you often see in commercial applications is the use of two interchangeable menus which perform the same task within the application. The program may initially have a simplified menu that gives only the most essential options. This simplified menu is less intimidating to the novice user. Later, as

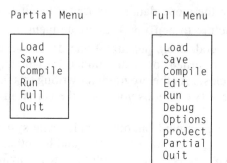

Figure 3–8 Partial and full menus

confidence is gained, the user may select a menu option which activates the full menu system. The program two-way.c (in the Source Code section) uses the full and partial menus shown in Figure 3–8. Notice that the partial menu has an option "Full" which activates the full menu, and the full menu has the option "Partial" which activates the partial menu.

This type of menu system is quite easy to build, based on the modular techniques that were described in the preceding pop-up section. Let's examine the code we would need to build a full-and-partial menu system. Two menu structures are needed, one for each menu.

The return codes are defined as follows:

```
#define FULL     1

#define PARTIAL  2
```

The data structures **partial** and **full** are created:

```
struct pop_struc partial[7]={          /* partial menu */
/*  *name   (*fun)()  select_id  */
   " Load    " ,fake,    0,
   " Save    " ,fake,    0,
   " Compile " ,fake,    0,
   " Run     " ,fake,    0,
   " Full    " ,NULL,    FULL,      /* return "FULL" */
   " Quit    " ,NULL,    0,
   "\0"        /* mark the end of the options list */
};

struct pop_struc full[11]={                /* full menu */
/*  *name   (*fun)()  select_id  */
   " Load    " ,fake,    0,
   " Save    " ,fake,    0,
   " Compile " ,fake,    0,
   " Edit    " ,fake,    0,
   " Run     " ,fake,    0,
   " Debug   " ,fake,    0,
```

```
        " Options " ,fake,    0,
        " proJect " ,fake,    0,
        " Partial " ,NULL,    PARTIAL,         /* return "PARTIAL" */
        " Quit    " ,NULL,    0,
        "\0"        /* mark the end of the options list */
    };
```

Before creating the menu itself, we set a special structure pointer to the partial menu, which therefore becomes the default:

```
struct pop_struc *menu;

menu= partial;  /* set *menu to point to the partial menu */
```

Next, a loop is entered which passes **pop_up( )** the pointer **menu.** If the user selects the full menu, FULL is returned and **menu** is set to the full structure. If PARTIAL is returned, **menu** is set to the partial structure.

```
for(;;){

/* call pop_up() giving it the partial menu */
 return_code= (pop_up(menu,33,10,scr.normal,scr.inverse));

    switch (return_code){
      case FULL:    menu=full;break;      /* select full menu */
      case PARTIAL: menu=partial;break;   /* select partial menu */
    }
   if (return_code==0) return(0);         /* Quit or Escape */
}
```

You could also create a new menu to temporarily disable, or remove from view, specific options. This same technique may be used for all the types of menus in this book.

TECHNIQUES

One of the useful features of this menu system is automatic window sizing that is performed by the function **pop_up( )**. Let's examine what goes on behind the scenes.

    The function **pop_up( )** is passed the menu structure, the coordinates of the upper left corner of the window, and the text attributes to use in the window. The first task for **pop_up( )** is to ascertain the width and height of the window that will contain the options. The menu array, which is passed to the function, is scanned until the terminator ('\0') is located. The number of actual options found yields the height of the window. Next, the option names are scanned to find the maximum width. This becomes the window width. A window of the proper size is created at the location specified, and the cursor is turned off (the highlighter acts as a cursor).

A for(;;) loop is entered, which will loop continuously until a break command is issued. This loop constitutes the main body of the function. Within this for(;;) loop, the keyboard is read for user input, the input is evaluated, and the appropriate action is taken.

There are three variables of particular interest: **cur_opt, found,** and **return_code.**

The variable **cur_opt** keeps track of the currently selected option. Initially set to 0, this value is incremented or decremented, depending on the user selection. If the user presses the up cursor key, **cur_opt** is decreased by 1, and if the down cursor key is pressed, **cur_opt** is increased by 1. Adjustments to **cur_opt** are made to "wrap" the cursor around the window. In other words, if the user presses a down cursor key when the highlighter is on the last option, the highlighter moves to the first option.

At the very beginning of the for(;;) loop, the options are printed, one per line, within the options window. The option indicated by **cur_opt** is printed with the character attribute **inverse.** All the other options are printed using the attribute **normal** (these variables were passed to the function **pop_up()**). The **scr.bold_caps** variable is set to TRUE, which causes the capital letter found within each option to be shown with the intensity set high.

The variable **found** is set TRUE when the user touches a key that matches one of the quick keys, or when the Enter key is pressed to select a highlighted option. When **found** is TRUE, the function pointer is examined, and if it is found to be NULL the variable **return_code** is set to the return code specified by **select_id** and the break command is issued. If a function pointer is given for the selected option, the function is called and the return value is examined. If the return value is non-0, **return_code** is set to the return value and a break is issued. If the user presses the Escape key, the menu terminates.

When an option is selected, either by point-and-shoot or by quick keys, the menu is redrawn and the quick keys are printed without the intense attribute. This is done so that the user is not confused by parent quick keys which may still be visible on the screen. In other words, quick keys are printed with intense characters *only within the active menu.* This convention is also used by all the other menu systems.

The get_key Function

One problem we encounter for the first time in this program is recognizing the cursor keys. As you may recall, the normal ASCII character set is represented by integer values 0 through 127; ASCII values 128 and above represent the extended character set. The extended character set consists of foreign language characters, math symbols, and other symbols such as "smiley faces."

Some of the lower 128 characters represent nonletter keys such as Enter,

Back Space and Escape, but nowhere do you find ASCII characters for Home, PgUp, PgDn, the function keys, or the cursor keys. This is not surprising, since these keys are not standard on all computer systems.

The IBM PC uses an interesting technique to represent these special keys. When a special key is pressed, an ASCII code beginning with 0 means that one of the special keys (such as Home) has been touched. The 0 is followed immediately by another number, an extension, which represents the special key that has been pressed. The most common of these keys are defined in mydef.h. For example, here are the definitions for the up and down cursor keys:

```
#define UP      0x48

#define DOWN    0x50
```

The function prototype for **get_key( )** is defined in mydef.h as

```
void get_key(char *ch, char *ext);
```

The function **get_key( )** is found in the library file L_getkey.c. This function uses the C function **getch( )** to read a character, and if it is 0, to read the extension.

```
void get_key(char *ch, char *ext)

{
  *ch=getch();       /* get the character */

   if(!*ch){   /* if the character is zero (a special key) */
     *ext=getch(); /* get the extension */
   }
}
```

From this point on, we will read all keystrokes via **get_key( )**. By doing so, we have the opportunity to enhance our programs with special features that are accessible by pressing hot keys. We define a *hot key* as a special key which, when pressed, will perform a particular task. In Chapter 7, we will create a modified version of **get_key( )** which will open a help window any time the function key F1 is pressed.

SOURCE CODE

POPDEMO.C

```
/********************  POPDEMO.C  *************************/

/* demonstrates the use of pop-up menus */
```

```
#include "mydef.h"
#include <stdio.h>

/* function prototypes */

int fake(void);
int prtdemo(void);
int printer(void);
int lpt1(void);
int lpt2(void);
int text(void);

int start()
{
extern struct screen_structure scr;
extern struct window_structure w[];

int i;
char string[MAX_STRING];

 /* set up menu structure */

 struct pop_struc pop_menu [6]={
/*   *name    (*fun)()  select_id  */
    " Sort   " ,fake,    0,
    " Print  " ,prtdemo,0,
    " Delete " ,fake,    0,
    " Copy   " ,fake,    0,
    " Quit   " ,NULL,    1,  /* returns a 1 when selected */
    "\0"         /* mark the end of the options list */
 };

cls();

/* fill the screen with dots '.'*/
/* make up a string of '.' wide enough to fill each row */

  for(i=0;i<scr.columns;i++) string[i]='.';  /* build the string */
  string[i]= '\0';                            /* terminate it */

/* now fill each row of the screen with the string of '.' */

  for (i=1;i<=scr.rows;i++) print(1,i,string);

/* create the pop-up menu */
return (pop_up (pop_menu,33,10,scr.normal,scr.inverse));
        /* pop-up appears at column,row 33,10 */

}  /* end of start(); */

int prtdemo()
{
```

```
extern struct screen_structure scr;
extern struct window_structure w[];

int return_code;

 /* set up menu structure */

 struct pop_struc pop_menu [3]={

/*  *name           (*fun)()  select_id  */
 " Printer    "  ,printer,  0,
 " Text-file "  ,text,     0,
 "\0"       /* mark the end of the options list */
 };

/* call routine to handle menu */
return_code= (pop_up (pop_menu,41,13,scr.normal,scr.inverse));
             /* pop-up appears at column-row */
             /* 41,13 */

/* we could examine return_code here if necessary */

return(0); /* return to zero so the parent menu does not close */
}

int printer()
{
extern struct screen_structure scr;
extern struct window_structure w[];

 /* set up menu structure */

 struct pop_struc pop_menu [3]={

/*  *name           (*fun)()  select_id  */
 " Lpt1:  ",   lpt1,     0,
 " lpt2:  ",   lpt2,     0,
 "\0"       /* mark the end of the options list */
 };

/* call routine to handle menu */
return (pop_up (pop_menu,53,15,scr.normal,scr.inverse));
        /* pop-up appears at column-row 53,15 */
}

int lpt1(void)
{
return(1);  /* return a non-zero number to close menu */
}

int lpt2(void)
{
```

```
return(1);  /* return a non-zero number to close menu */
}

int text(void)
{
return(1);  /* return a non-zero number to close menu */
}

int fake(void)
{
return(0);  /* return a zero so the menu does not close */
}
```

L_GETKEY.C

```
/********************* L_GETKEY.C *************************/

#include "mydef.h"

/***************************************************************

 Usage: void get_key(char *ch, char *ext);

   char *ch=  character to read from keyboard.

   char *ext= extended character (if any).

   Reads character and extended character from keyboard.

 ***************************************************************/
void get_key(char *ch, char *ext)
{
  *ch=getch();       /* get the character */

    if(!*ch){        /* if the character is zero (a special key) */
      *ext=getch(); /* get the extension */
    }
}
```

L_POPUP.C

```
/********************* L_POPUP.C *************************/
#include "mydef.h"
#include <stdio.>

/***************************************************************
```

```
Usage: int pop_up(struct pop_struc pop_menu[],int x,int y,
                  char normal, char inverse)

   struct pop_struc pop_menu= data structure containing menu
                              options.

   int x,y= upper left corner of pop_up window.

   char normal,inverse= text attributes used for regular and
                        high-lighted options.

   Creates and manages a pop-up menu at the location specified.

******************************************************************/


int pop_up(struct pop_struc pop_menu[],int x,int y, char normal,
           char inverse)
{
extern struct  screen_structure scr;
extern struct window_structure w[];

int col;              /* screen column */
int i=0,j;            /* general purpose index variables */
int width;            /* width of window */
int nu_opt;           /* number of options */
int cur_opt;          /* current option (highlighted */
char ch,ext;          /* character and extension */
int found = FALSE;    /* flag to indicate option found(selected) */
int return_code;      /* return code */
int pop_window;
int old_caps=scr.bold_caps; /*the original value of bold caps*/
/* set on bold caps to highlight menu quick keys */
scr.bold_caps=ON;

/* figure how many options there are */

nu_opt=0;

/* loop until empty string found */
while (pop_menu[i++].name[0]!='\0');

nu_opt=i-1;   /* set nu_opt to the number of options found */

/* figure size of box */

  width=0;      /* figure max length of window */

  for (i=0;i< nu_opt;i++){                    /* for each option */
```

```
        /* find largest option length */
        if (strlen(pop_menu[i].name) > width){
         width= strlen(pop_menu[i].name);
        }
      }

/* make a window based on x,y parameters
   and calculated width and height */

pop_window= win_make(x,y,width,nu_opt,STD_FRAME,
            "",normal,normal);

cursor(NO_CURSOR):      /* hide cursor */

scr.current = scr.normal;

cur_opt = 0;    /* first option */

   /* infinite loop */
   for(;;){

   scr.bold_caps=!found; /* turn off scr.bold_caps if true */

       /* print menu options, highlight current option */
          col=1; /* start at first column */
          for(i=0;i< nu_opt;i++){     /* print each option */
           /* highlight current option */
            if(i == cur_opt) scr.current= inverse;
            else scr.current=normal; /* else normal */
            print(1,col++,pop_menu[i].name);
          };

           if(found ) {              /* selection found */

            /* return specified code if NULL */
            if(*pop_menu[cur_opt].fun==NULL){
            return_code=pop_menu[cur_opt].select_id;
            break;
            }
            else
               /* a function was specified by pointer,
                  call the function and get code */

               return_code=(*pop_menu[cur_opt].fun)();

               win_pop_top(pop_window);
               /* a non-zero value is signal to exit */
               if(return_code!=0) break;
               found = FALSE;
               /* make sure keyboard buffer is clear */
               if (kbhit()) getch();
```

```
                    } /* end if(found) */

                    else{   /* not found */
                     /* read keys until selection is made */
                     get_key(&ch,&ext); /* get a character */
                     ch=toupper(ch);      /* make it upper case */
                    }
                     if (ext == DOWN)  cur_opt++;  /* move down */
                     if (ext == UP)    cur_opt--;  /* move up */
                     /* wrap if boundaries exceeded */
                     if (cur_opt >= nu_opt) cur_opt =0;
                     if (cur_opt < 0) cur_opt = nu_opt-1;

                    if (ch== 13) found = TRUE;

                    if(ch!='\0'){   /* do we have a letter? */
                      for(i=0;i<nu_opt;i++){    /* scan each option? */
                       j=0;

                        /* check each letter within option */
                        while(pop_menu[i].name[j]!=0){
                          /* ignore spaces in string */
                          if (pop_menu[i].name[j++]==ch && ch != ' '){
                          cur_opt = i;
                          found = TRUE;
                          }
                        } /* end while */
                      }
                    } /* end ch!='\0' */

                    if (ch==ESCAPE){  /* EXIT IF ESCAPE KEY */
                    return_code=0;
                    break;
                    }
                    ext=' ';ch=' ';
             } /* end for(;;)*/

        scr.bold_caps=old_caps;     /* restore bold caps */
        win_delete_top();           /* remove top window */

        return (return_code);
        }
```

TWO_WAY.C

```
/******************** TWO-WAY.C ************************/
/* demonstrates partial/full menus */

#include "mydef.h"
#include <stdio.h>
```

```
/* defines */

#define FULL     1
#define PARTIAL  2

/* function prototypes */

int fake(void);

int start()
{
extern struct screen_structure scr;
extern struct window_structure w[];

struct pop_struc *menu;
int return_code;
int i;
char string[MAX_STRING];

 /* set up menu structure */

 struct pop_struc partial[7]={        /* partial menu */
 /* * name    (*fun)()  select_id */
    " Load    " ,fake,    0,
    " Save    " ,fake,    0,
    " Compile " ,fake,    0,
    " Run     " ,fake,    0,
    " Full    " ,NULL,    FULL,        /* return "FULL" */
    " Quit    " ,NULL,    0,
    "\0"       /* mark the end of the options list */
 };


 struct pop_struc full[11]={          /* full menu */
 /* *name    (*fun)()  select_id */
    " Load    " ,fake,    0,
    " Save    " ,fake,    0,
    " Compile " ,fake,    0,
    " Edit    " ,fake,    0,
    " Run     " ,fake,    0,
    " Debug   " ,fake,    0,
    " Options " ,fake,    0,
    " proJect " ,fake,    0,
    " Partial " ,NULL,    PARTIAL,          /* return "PARTIAL" */
    " Quit    " ,NULL,    0,
    "\0"       /* mark the end of the options list */
 };

menu= partial;        /* set *menu to point to the partial menu */

    /* loop until user presses "Escape" or selects "Quit" */

    for(;;){
```

```
    /* call pop_up() giving it the partial menu */
    return_code= (pop_up(menu,33,10,scr.normal,scr.inverse));

      switch (return_code){
        case FULL:     menu=full;break;      /* select full menu */
        case PARTIAL: menu=partial;break;   /* select partial menu */
      }
      if (return_code==0) return(0);         /* Quit or Escape */
  }
}

int fake(void)
{
return(0);  /* return a zero so the menu does not close */
}
```

INTRODUCTION TO THE MOVING LIGHT BAR MENU

The moving light bar menu is most often thought of in connection with Lotus 1-2-3. It is very similar to the pop-up menu in that options may be selected by the point-and-shoot technique or by the use of quick keys. The pop-up menu is sometimes referred to as a *vertical light bar menu* and the Lotus 1-2-3 menu as a *horizontal light bar menu*.

GOALS

The moving light bar menu is presented in a horizontal format with all the parent options presented on one line. A second line, usually directly under the menu line, gives information about the highlighted option. This information line is optional. When present, it may explain the current option in detail or list suboptions. In some cases it is omitted entirely.

The sample menu shown in Figure 3–9 has the same options that appeared in the pop-up menu shown in Figure 3–7. The program bardemo.c in the Source Code section will produce this menu. Note that the selected option "Quit" has no suboptions. Therefore, the information line is used to explain what the selected option will do.

Now let's see what happens when we choose an option that possesses suboptions. The second option, "Print", is highlighted (shown in Figure 3–10 as an

```
┌─────────────────────────────────────────────────────┐
│ Sort   Print Delete   Copy Quit                       │
│ Exit   the program and   return to DOS                │
└─────────────────────────────────────────────────────┘
```

Figure 3–9 Moving light bar menu

```
Sort  Print  Delete  Copy  Quit
Printer, Text-file
```

Figure 3–10 Suboptions of moving light bar menu

underline). On the second line we see the two options which would be presented
if we chose "Print". Because this information line provides a preview of suboptions, the user need not select an option just to see what is available.

One very interesting variation of the horizontal light bar menu is the ability
to stack menus. Suppose the user has highlighted and selected the second option,
"Print". The conventional procedure is to replace the parent menu window with
the new options. For example, the window that would appear after selecting
"Print" would look like Figure 3–11. An alternative technique is to leave the
original option line on the screen, and show the new options beneath, as in Figure
3–12. From this stacked menu we can see that the option "Print" has been selected
from the first menu, and the user must now choose the destination "Printer" or
"Text file". The quick keys on the first menu are no longer highlighted, so that
there is no conflict with the quick keys on the new menu. The "Printer" option
is highlighted, and the user sees that printer output can go to 1pt1: or 1pt2:.

```
Printer  Text-file
Lpt1:    1Pt2:
```

Figure 3–11 Child menu

Assume that the user now selects "Printer", the currently highlighted option. The actual screen output of the stacked display looks like Figure 3–13. On
the third level menu, the information line does not list suboptions (there are none),
it merely describes the highlighted option. The program bardemo2.c, found in the
Source Code section, demonstrates the use of multilevel menus. It is very similar
to the regular bar menu, bardemo.c, the major difference being that a new window
is created for each menu level in bardemo2.c.

The option levels shown so far have been in framed windows, which is
somewhat wasteful of space. The windows could be unframed and would look
like this:

```
Sort Print Delete Copy Quit
Printer Text-file
Lpt1:    1Pt2:
Send output to the printer on port Lpt1:
```

```
Sort  Print  Delete  Copy  Quit

Printer  Text-file
Lptl:    1Pt2:
```

Figure 3–12   Stacked menu

The multilevel menu provides an excellent sense of navigation through the menu system. The user can see one level ahead, and can look backwards to the beginning of the menu.

In summary, the moving light bar menu has the following advantages:

- The light bar menu uses less space than the pop-up menu. If presented in an unframed window with no information line, the light bar only takes up one line of the screen.

- The information line provides more information to the user; an option need not be selected in order to discover the suboptions available.

- When the light bar menu is presented in a multilevel fashion, the user is provided with a sense of navigation through the options.

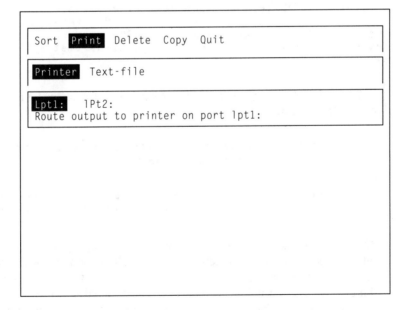

Figure 3–13   Screen output of stacked menu

APPLICATION

Although the outward appearance of light bar menus differs markedly from pop-ups, you will see that the programming is remarkably similar and employs portions of code that function in similar ways.

The function **bar_menu( )** found in the library module Lbar.c creates the moving light bar menu. The structure for the bar menu is defined in mydef.h as:

```
struct bar_struc{
  char *name;            /* the name of the function */
  char *info;            /* the info line appearing under options */
  int  (*fun)();         /* the pointer to function */
  int select_id;         /* the list-select return code */
};
```

With the exception of the **info** pointer, this is identical to the pop-up structure. In the program bardemo.c, the first menu is initialized as follows:

```
struct bar_struc main_menu [6]={

/* *name        *info                          (*fun)()  select_id */

  "Sort",      "Sort the data file",         fake,      0,
  "Print",     "Printer, Text-file" ,        prtdemo,   0,
  "Delete",    "Delete current data file",   fake,      0,
  "Copy",      "Copy data file to backup",   fake,      0,
  "Quit",      "Quit and return to DOS",     NULL,      1,
  "\0"         /* mark the end of the options list */
};
```

After initializing the structure, the function **bar_menu( )** is called. The prototype for **bar_menu( )** is:

```
    int bar_menu(struct bar_struc menu[], char normal,
              char inverse);

    normal = Normal text attribute to use in menu.
    inverse= Inverse text attribute to use in menu.
```

The bar menu uses the same convention as the pop-up menu when dealing with return codes. Anytime a function automatically called by **bar_menu( )** returns a 0, the menu remains open. If a non-0 number is returned, the menu closes and the number is returned to the function which called **bar_menu( ).**

The program bardemo.c sets up a menu similar to that shown for the pop-up menu. Once again, only the "Print" and "Quit" menu options operate in this example. When selected, the "Print" submenu uses the same window as the parent menu. In other words, this is an unstacked menu.

The menu window must be created before calling **bar_menu( )**. If a menu window is not created, the currently active window is used. The **bar_menu( )** function creates the menu line on the first line of the active window; the information line occupies the second line. If there is an information line you must have an active window with a height of at least two lines; if you don't, the menu will scroll out of view.

If you don't wish an information line in your menu, simply put a " " (empty string) where the text would usually go in your structure. If there is no information line, the menu window need only be one line high.

When creating unstacked light bar menus, the same window is used for all menus. The new menu replaces the old menu within the window. Functions which need to create a new menu create a new data structure and make a call to **bar_menu( )**. As you examine bardemo.c you will see that the calling sequence and return codes are almost identical to popdemo.c.

The program bardemo2.c illustrates the creation of a multilevel menu. The only difference between the two programs is that a new window is created for each menu. The menu is created two rows down from the previous window, thus creating a slight overlap.

The multilevel menu gives the user a better feel for navigation within the menu, but each level obscures more of the screen underneath. There is also a limit to how many levels can be shown on the screen. Use of unframed menu windows can save some space.

TECHNIQUES

The internal workings of **bar_menu( )** are very similar to **pop_up( )**. All the **name** elements are scanned until the empty string terminator is located and **nu_opt** is set to the number of menu options. The variable **cur_opt** is initially set to 0, and represents the currently highlighted option.

A for(;;) loop is entered, which continues until the menu is terminated. The first step within this loop is to print all the menu options horizontally across the menu window. The option indicated by **cur_opt** is highlighted and the options are separated with three spaces. As with all our menus, the quick key for each option is displayed with intensity set ON.

Once the menu options have been printed the **info** pointer (**menu[cur_opt].info**) is checked to see if there is a valid information line to print. If there is, **ceol( )** is called to erase any existing text on the menu's second line. The new information line is then printed.

Other than these slight differences in printing the menu, the user input and processing are identical to **pop_up( )**. See the commented Source Code for details.

SOURCE CODE

BARDEMO.C

```
/********************    BARDEMO.C    *************************/

/* Demonstration of un-stacked horizontal moving light bar menu.*/

#include "mydef.h"
#include "stdio.h"

/* function prototypes */

int fake(void);
int prtdemo(void);
int printer(void);
int lpt1(void);
int lpt2(void);
int text(void);

int start(void)
{
extern struct screen_structure scr;
extern struct window_structure w[];

int win1;
int return_code;

  struct bar_struc main_menu [6]={

  /* *name         *info                         (*fun)()  select_id */

    "Sort",      "Sort the data file",         fake,     0,
    "Print",     "Printer, Text-file" ,        prtdemo,  0,
    "Delete",    "Delete current data file",   fake,     0,
    "Copy",      "Copy data file to backup",   fake,     0,
    "Quit",      "Quit and return to DOS",     NULL,     1,
    "\0"         /* mark the end of the options list */
  };

cls();

/* make a window for the bar menu */
win1=win_make(2,2,scr.columns-2,2,STD_FRAME,"",
            scr.current,scr.current);

/* call the bar menu*/

return_code= bar_menu(main_menu,scr.normal,scr.inverse);

win_delete(win1);  /* delete window */
return(return_code):  /* pass along the return code */
}
```

```
int prtdemo(void)
{
extern struct screen_structure scr;
extern struct window_structure w[];

int win1;
int return_code;
 /* set up new menu */
 struct bar_struc main_menu [3]={

  /*
  *name          *info                          (*fun)() select_id */
  "Printer",    "Lpt1:, Lpt2:",                  printer, 0,
  "Text-file", "Send output to a text file", text,    0,
  "\0"        /* mark the end of the options list */
 };

 cls();  /* clear the existing menu window */
 return_code= bar_menu(main_menu,scr.normal,scr.inverse);

 return(0); /* return a zero instead of "return_code"
           so previous menu remains open
           so we don't close the main menu */
}

int printer(void)
{
extern struct  screen_structure scr;
extern struct window_structure w[];

int win1;
int return_code;

 struct bar_struc main_menu [3]={

 /*
  *name       *info                               (*fun)() id */

  "Lpt1:", "Route output to printer on port lpt1:", lpt1,    0,
  "lPt2:", "Route output to printer on port lpt2:", lpt2,    0,
  "\0"       /* mark the end of the options list */
 };

cls();  /* clear the existing menu window */

return(bar_menu(main_menu,scr.normal,scr.inverse));

 }

int lpt1(void)
{
return(1);  /* return a non-zero number so that menu closes down */
 }
```

```
int lpt2(void)
{
return(1);  /* send back a non-zero number to close the menu */
}

int text(void)
{
return(1);  /* send back a non-zero number to close the menu */
}

int fake(void)
{
return(0);  /* send back a zero and keep the menu open */
}
```

BARDEMO2.C

```
/********************** BARDEMO2.C **************************/

/* Demonstration of a stacked (multi-level) horizontal
   moving light bar menu. */

#include "mydef.h"
#include <stdio.h>

/* function prototypes */

int fake(void);
int prtdemo(void);
int printer(void);
int lpt1(void);
int lpt2(void);
int text(void);

int start(void)
{
extern struct screen_structure scr;
extern struct window_structure w[];

int win1;
int return_code;

  /* prepare menu */
  struct bar_struc main_menu [6]={
          "Sort",       "Sort the data file",           fake,     0,
          "Print",      "Printer, Text-file",           prtdemo,  0,
          "Delete",     "Delete current data file",     fake,     0,
          "Copy",       "Copy data file to backup",     fake,     0,
          "Quit",       "Quit and return to DOS",       NULL,     1,
          "\0"          /* mark the end of the options list */
  };
```

```
    cls();
    /* make a window for the menu */
    win1=win_make(2,2,scr.columns-2,2,STD_FRAME,"",
                scr.current,scr.current);

    /* create the first menu */
    return_code= bar_menu(main_menu,scr.normal,scr.inverse);

    win_delete(win1);        /* remove window */
    return(return_code);  /* pass along the return code */
}

int prtdemo(void)
{
extern struct screen_structure scr;
extern struct window_structure w[];

int win2;
int return_code;

struct bar_struc main_menu [3]={
            "Printer",   "Lpt1:, Lpt2:",                        printer, 0,
            "Text-file", "Send output to a text file", text,    0,
            "\0"         /* mark the end of the options list */
};

    win2=win_make(2,4,scr.columns-2,2,STD_FRAME,"",
                scr. current,scr.current);

  return_code= bar_menu(main_menu,scr.normal,scr.inverse);

    win_delete(win2);

    return(0); /* we don't want to close the parent menu
                so we return a zero value instead of
                "return_code" */
}


int printer(void)
{
extern struct screen_structure scr;
extern struct window_structure w[];

int win3;
int return_code;

 struct bar_struc main_menu [3]={
  "Lpt1:",   "Route output to printer on port lpt1:", lpt1, 0,
  "1Pt2:",   "Rout output to printer on port lpt2:",  lpt2, 0,
  "\0"        /* mark the end of the options list */
};
```

```
        win3=win_make(2,6,scr.columns-2,2,STD_FRAME,"",
                      scr.current,scr.current);

    return_code= bar_menu(main_menu,scr.normal,scr.inverse);

     win_delete(win3);
     return(return_code);
    }

    int lpt1(void)
    {
    return(1);   /* return a non-zero number to close menu */
    }

    int lpt2(void)
    {
    return(1);   /* return a non-zero number to close menu */
    }

    int text(void)
    {
    return(1);   /* return a non-zero number to close menu */
    }

    int fake(void)
    {
    return(0);   /* return a zero to close menu */
    }
```

L_BAR.C

```
/********************     L_BAR.C     *************************/

#include "mydef.h"
#include "stdio.h"

/*****************************************************************


  Usage: int bar_menu(struct bar_struc bar_menu[], char normal,
                      char inverse)

   struct bar_struc bar_menu=data structure containing menu options.

   char normal,inverse= text attributes used for regular and
                        highlighted options.

   Creates and manages a moving light bar menu at the first line of
   the topmost (active) window.

*****************************************************************/
```

```
int bar_menu(struct bar_struc menu[], char normal, char inverse)
{

extern struct  screen_structure scr;
extern struct window_structure w[];

int x=1;        /* x screen location */
int y=1;        /* y screen location */
int i,j;        /* index variables */
int nu_opt;     /* number of options in menu */
int old_caps=scr.bold_caps;  /* original value of bold_caps */

int cur_opt;    /* current menu (highlighted option) */

char ch;        /* char and extension variables */
char ext;

int found = FALSE;    /* selection made (found) flag */
int return_code=0;
int my_win=scr.active;

cls();
cursor(NO_CURSOR); /* turn off cursor */
 /* set number of options to max */

/* figure how many options there are */

for(i=0;i<MAX_BAR;i++){
   if (menu[i].name[0] == '\0'){
    nu_opt = i;
    break;
   }
 }


 cur_opt = 0;

    for(;;){        /* loop infinite */
          x=1;

        scr.bold_caps=!found;  /* turn off caps when found */

       for(i=0;i< nu_opt;i++){     /* print all options */
          if(i == cur_opt) scr.current= inverse;
          else scr.current= normal;
          print(x,y,menu[i].name);
          x=x+strlen(menu[i].name)+3; /* move option location */

       };  /* end of menu printing loop */

         if(menu[cur_opt].info[0]!='\0'){ /* is there info? */
          scr.current=normal;      /* then print it on next line */
          scr.bold_caps=FALSE; /* don't highlight bold caps */
```

```
            ceol(1,y+1);      /* clear to end of line
                               to clear old info */
            /* print new information */
            print(1,y+1,menu[cur_opt].info);
          }

if(found ){           /* selection made.
                         return correct return code if function
                         pointer NULL */
 if(menu[cur_opt].fun==NULL) return(menu[cur_opt].select_id);
    else{  /* else run option to get code */
      return_code= (*menu[cur_opt].fun)();
      win_pop_top(my_win);
      ceol(1,1);
    }
      found = FALSE;    /* reset flag, ready for new selection */

    if (kbhit()) getch(); /* make sure keyboard buffer is clear */

}
  else{        /* selection not made
                  read keys until selection is made */

      get_key(&ch,&ext); ch=toupper(ch);  /* get a character */
      if (ext == RIGHT)  cur_opt = cur_opt +1;  /* move right */
      if (ext == LEFT)  cur_opt = cur_opt -1;   /* move left */
      if (cur_opt >= nu_opt) cur_opt =0;        /* wrap if out of
                                                   bounds */
      if (cur_opt < 0) cur_opt = nu_opt-1;

      if (ch== RETURN) found = TRUE;

    /* if we have a valid character then it may be a quick key */
    if(ch!='\0'){
        for(i=0;i<nu_opt;i++){     /* does it match an option?  */
        j=0;                       /* scan each menu option name */

      /* check each letter within option */
      while(menu[i].name[j]!= '\0'){
          /* if match and not space */
          if ( ch==menu[i].name[j++] && ch != ' '){
          cur_opt = i;             /* mark found flag and break */
          found = TRUE;
          break;
          }
      }
      if(found==TRUE) break;   /* break if found */
    }
  }
          if (ch==ESCAPE)}        /* EXIT IF ESCAPE KEY */
            return_code = 0;      /* exit but don't close down */
            break;               /* parent menu */
            }
            ext=ch=' ';
```

```
           }   /* end else */
           /* a non-zero return code means exit menu */
           if (return_code!=0) break;

       } /* end for(;;)*/
      scr.bold_caps=old_caps; /* restore old value */
      return (return_code);
    }
```

GOALS FOR PULL-DOWN MENUS

Pull-down menus are certainly one of the more popular types of menu systems available. They have found a home in both text- and graphics-based displays.

In many ways pull-down menus are a hybrid between horizontal light bar menus and pop-up menus. Initially, a horizontal bar parent menu appears at the top of the screen. When an option is selected from this menu, a vertical pop-up child menu appears beneath the selected option. The user may select from this menu, escape back to the top menu, or pull down adjacent menus by using the cursor keys.

Pull-down menu systems also provide an excellent navigation sense, as the menu path is visible on the screen.

Our menu can work in either an expert or novice mode. The *expert* mode is ideal for users who use the quick keys (pressing a single key to select an option). In this mode the pull-down menus are made visible only when the user selects an option with a quick key. The pull-down menu disappears when the final selection is made.

In the *novice* mode, the pull-down child menus for each highlighted main menu option stay visible while the user browses from option to option on the main menu.

To illustrate the differences between these two modes, let's look at each menu in actual use.

Expert

Take, for example, the sample menu (it should look familiar by now) in Figure 3–14. Note that the pull-down menus corresponding to the highlighted options *do not appear initially*. This is an important distinction from horizontal light bar menus that have an information line corresponding to each option.

```
┌─────────────────────────────────────┐          ┌──────────────────────────────────────┐
│ Sort   Print   Delete   Copy   Quit  │          │ Sort   Print   Delete   Copy   Quit  │
└─────────────────────────────────────┘          └──────────────┬───────────┬───────────┘
                                                                 │ Printer   │
                                                                 │ Text-file │
                                                                 └───────────┘
```

Figure 3–14   First level of pull-down menu   **Figure 3–15**   Menu with one pull-down

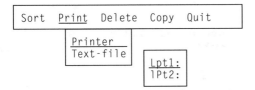

Figure 3–16   Second pull-down

Figure 3–17   Main menu after child menus close

For example, when the expert user touches a ''p'' in the menu in Figure 3–14, the ''Print'' option is highlighted and the pull-down appears, as in Figure 3–15. The quick key highlighting on the main menu is turned off. Let us assume the expert user now selects the ''Printer'' option by again pressing ''p''. A new menu appears, as in Figure 3–16. By convention, this is usually a pop-up menu, and the user can now choose between the final two options ''Lpt1:'' and ''1Pt2:''. Once again, the quick key highlighting of the parent menu is turned off, so that quick key highlighting appears only in the current menu. The purpose of this is to eliminate confusion for the user about which quick keys are active.

The user now selects the final option from this menu by pressing an ''l'' or ''p'', the task is carried out, and all the child menus close down. Note that the last option selected from the main menu (Print) is still highlighted, as shown in Figure 3–17.

Novice

We can assume that the novice is less confident than the expert user. Novice behavior is characterized by use of the cursor keys to position the highlighter, or pressing Enter to pull down the menu.

Once a menu is pulled down in the novice mode, the user may use the Right and Left cursor keys to move to adjacent pull-down menus. When the Right cursor key is pressed, the current pull-down is removed and the parent (horizontal menu) highlighter is moved to the right. The pull-down for this new option is automatically activated. The novice user may also move the highlighter up and down with the cursor keys to highlight options within the pull-down. The novice selects an option by pressing Enter when the desired option is highlighted, or may select by means of the quick keys.

Figure 3–18 contains a sample of the screen as it appears to the novice user. The initial screen starts in the expert mode: The user presses the Right cursor key to move the highlighter to ''Print''. This action activates the novice mode and the pull-down appears, as in Figure 3–19. The user now selects ''Printer'' by

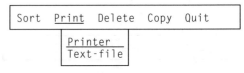

Figure 3–18   Initial screen: expert mode

Figure 3–19   Novice mode: pull-down active

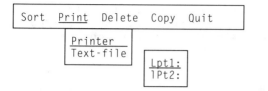

Figure 3–20 Novice mode: pop-up active   **Figure 3–21** Novice mode: return to pull-down

pressing Enter or "p", which activates the pop-up menu as in Figure 3–20. The final selection is made from the pop-up menu; the pop-up disappears, *but the pull-down remains active*, as in Figure 3–21. The user may now move the Right or Left cursor keys to preview or select other options. The novice mode remains in effect until the user exits the pull-down by pressing Escape.

When using an application for the first time, most users will prefer to pull down the menus and work in the novice mode. Later, as confidence grows, they are more likely to operate as experts.

APPLICATION

The program pd.c creates and manages the pull-down menu. There are several define statements in mydef.h which are used to control the pull-down menu. They are defined as follows:

```
#define MAIN_OPT    5    /* the actual number of options
                            appearing in the main menu */
#define PD_SUB      3    /* the maximum number of sub-
                            options in the pull-down
                            menus */
#define PD_SUB_ROW 4     /* the row that the pull-down
                            window appears */
#define PD_MAIN_FRAME STD_FRAME /* frame used for the
                                    main menu window */
#define PD_SUB_FRAME PD_FRAME   /* frame used for the
                                    pull-down menu
                                    window */
```

These numerical values (5,3,4) or frame definitions (STD_FRAME, PD_FRAME; see definitions in the header file mydef.h) may be altered according to your menu requirements. A series of menus which have been modified by changing these values or definitions appears near the end of this Application section.

The data structure for the pull-down menu is somewhat different from that used in the previous menus. The structure is as follows:

```
struct pd_str{
  char *main;              /* option to appear in main menu */
```

```
char *sub[PD_SUB];     /* array of options to appear in Pull-down*/
int (*fun[PD_SUB])();  /* array of function pointers for pull-down*/
int select_id[PD_SUB]; /* array of list-select return code */
};
```

This structure is initialized as an array with five (MAIN_OPT) elements, each of which defines one of the five main-menu options and its respective pull-down.

Take a look at this excerpt from the source code for pd-demo.c. Pay particular attention to the initialization of the pull-down menu. Note that each main menu option is listed, followed by an array of pull-down options, the matching array of function pointers, and the **select_id** return codes. The data elements have been positioned so that they may be viewed in columns. There are numerous fake options added to the pd-demo.c demonstration menu so that it will appear more realistic when run.

```
struct pd_str m_menu   [MAIN_OPT]={

/* main menu    sub-menu            *function   list select values */

"   Sort   ",
                " Ascending  ",
                " Descending ",
                "\0",
                                    demo,
                                    demo,
                                    NULL,
                                                0,
                                                0,
                                                0,
" Print ",
                " Printer    ",
                " Test-file ",
                "\0",
                                    printer,
                                    demo,
                                    NULL,
                                                0,
                                                0,
                                                0,
" Delete ",
                " Data-file    ",
                " program-File ",
                " Programmer    ",
                                    demo,
                                    demo,
                                    NULL,
                                                0,
                                                0,
                                                0,
```

```
" Copy ",
                " Block ",
                " Line    ",
                "\0",
                                        demo,
                                        demo,
                                        NULL,
                                                        0,
                                                        0,
                                                        0,
" Quit ",
                " Exit program        ",
                "\0",
                "\0",
                                        NULL,
                                        NULL,
                                        NULL,
                                                        1,
                                                        0,
                                                        0,
};
```

This data array is auto-initialized. This means that the specified values are placed sequentially in the data array. Therefore, unused options must still be assigned a value. PD_SUB is set to three, which means that each submenu can contain up to three "real" options. However, the option "Print" has only two menu options which appear in the pull-down submenu; therefore its last option is padded to fill out the third option. You can see from the listing that the submenu items which are not used are filled with an empty string (" "). The unused submenu options must have the function pointer filled with NULL and the list-select values padded with 0s.

The pull-down data structure is slightly more difficult to design and initialize than previous menus; however, putting many of the menu definitions in one structure allows us to simplify the call to **pull_down( )**.

One important difference between the pull-down menu and previous menus is that two menu levels are created and controlled by one function call to **pull_down( )**. With the pop-up menu, for example, selection of the option "Print" from the first menu resulted in a function call to **prtdemo( )**, which then defined the second menu level, and called **pop_up( )** to actually create the menu. In the case of the pull-down menu, both the main menu and the pull-down sub-menu are controlled by **pull_down( )**. Therefore, the options in the main menu represent only logical groups of options, and not actual function calls as they would in previous menus.

Only selection of an option within the pull-down submenu causes the associated function to be called. Look at the example in Figure 3–22. The option "Print" has been selected from the main menu and the pull-down submenu ap-

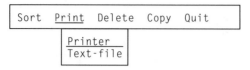

Figure 3–22 Pull-down submenu example

pears. At this point, selection of the option "Printer" causes the specified function, **printer( )**, to be called.

The pull-down menu no longer has control at this point, and will have no control until **printer( )** terminates. The function **printer( )** now assumes the task of creating the pop-up menu which will appear next to the pull-down submenu. In the following section of code the function **printer( )** defines the pop-up and calls **pop_menu( ):**

```
struct pop_struc pop_menu [3]={
            "Lpt1:    " ,NULL,    0,
            "lPt2:    " ,NULL,    0,
            "\0"        /* mark the end of the options list */
};
return (pop_up (pop_menu,29,5,scr.normal,scr.inverse));
```

*The function **printer( )** could have created any type of menu-pop-up, light bar, or another pull-down.* As many additional menus may be created as needed.

When the functions called by **pull_down( )** terminate, they are expected to return an integer value. Depending on the value returned, **pull_down( )** takes the action indicated in Table 3-1. Our pull-down menu has one fixed window which contains the main options as well as one relocatable pull-down window which contains the suboptions. The frame style is defined in mydef.h and can be any of our predefined frame types, including unframed.

In previous pop-up and light bar menus we could control the placement of the menu window on the screen. The main window of a pull-down menu, by

TABLE 3–1   CODES RETURNED TO **PULL-DOWN( )**

Return value	Action
>0	Pull-down menu closes down completely. This value is returned to the function which originally called **pull_down( )**.
0	The pull-down menu continues normal operation. If the expert mode is active, the pull-down submenu closes and only the main menu is visible. If the novice mode is in effect, the submenu remains active.
<0	The pull-down submenu remains active regardless of the expert/novice setting. This may be used to keep a pull-down menu open so that several options may be selected. This may help avoid annoying returns to the main menu in cases where the user may need to make several selections within a submenu. Returning a negative value may also be used to override the expert mode, keeping the menus always in novice mode.

convention, appears on the first line of the display. The pull-down menu function, **pull_down( )**, automatically places the main window for you. If the window is framed (see frame types in Windows, Chapter 2), the top left interior is placed at 2,2. If the window is unframed, the interior begins at 1,1. The window is automatically created as wide as the screen width permits.

The pull-down menu always appears beneath the main menu option which called it. You can control the vertical placement of the window by altering PD_SUB_ROW, which sets the row at which the upper left corner of the pull-down window appears. *If you change the values defined in mydef.h, don't forget to recompile the module pd.c.*

Perhaps you noticed that the pd.c module does not have the l_ prefix, and therefore is not a library module. The reason for this is that, unlike previous menus, the pull-down menu has several aspects controlled by #define statements in mydef.h. These values are very likely to change, and would entail recompilation and replacement of the module in the library file. However, if you are content with the default values, you may rename the file l_pd.c and place it in the library.

The following are examples of menus you can produce by changing the #define statements. These are the default values:

```
#define PD_SUB_ROW 4
#define PD_MAIN_FRAME STD_FRAME
#define PD_SUB_FRAME PD_FRAME
```

The frame types are indicated in Figure 3–23.

Figure 3–23   Frame types used in pull-down menus

When the pull-down window is drawn with the upper left corner at row 4, the top of the pull-down frame merges with the bottom of the main menu frame providing a smooth blending of the frames. Had we used the STD_FRAME definition for both frames, there would be a tiny gap where the frames joined, as in Figure 3–24. In Figure 3–25 is the actual screen output from pd-demo.c, using the parameters just shown. The pop-up menu is also displayed. This is typical of pull-down

Figure 3–24   Frame gap

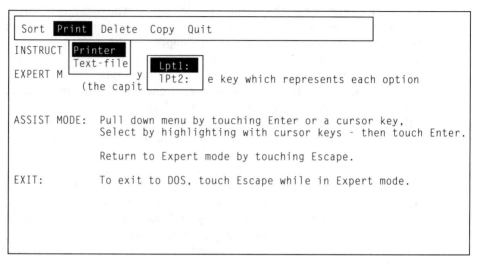

Figure 3–25   Pull-down with framed main menu

menus you see in commercial applications. However, as we discussed in Chapter 2, the window frames waste precious screen space.

Now let's look at a screen layout which uses slightly less space. Here we use an unframed main menu window and standard frame (STD_FRAME) for the pull-down. Since there is no frame around the main menu, the interior colors are set to inverse so that the main menu will stand out from any other text which may be on the screen. The location of the pull-down window is moved up so that it is closer to the main menu.

```
#define PD_SUB_ROW 3

#define PD_MAIN_FRAME NO_FRAME
#define PD_SUB_FRAME  STD_FRAME
```

Figure 3–26 shows the actual screen output

This approach produces a somewhat cleaner appearance. We could have used an unframed window for the pull-down window, setting it off from the rest of the screen with inverse text. If the pull-down window is displayed as inverse text, then the highlighter would need to be normal text so it would stand out from the inverse background. Unfortunately, if we have a pull-down window with only two options, the user might be confused as to which option is highlighted, since by convention the highlighter is usually displayed in inverse text. For this reason, it is probably best to keep the pull-down window framed, use normal attributes for the window, and reserve inverse attributes for the highlighter.

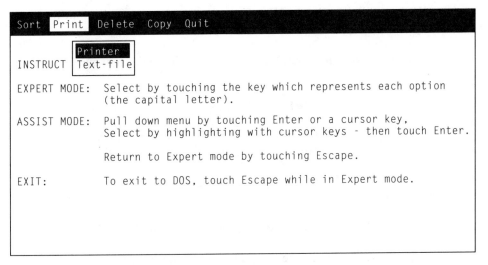

Figure 3–26   Pull-down with unframed main menu

So, how do we specify the attributes for the windows? There are so many attributes that need to be specified (i.e., the window frame, and the interior, normal, and highlight attributes for each window created), that it is more appropriate to place them in a data structure which can be passed *en masse* to **pull_down( )**.

The data structure **window_colors** is defined in mydef.h as:

```
struct window_colors{
  char main_frame;        /* attribute used for main menu frame */
  char main_interior;     /* " " " " menu interior */
  char main_inverse;      /* " " " " menu highlighter */

  char pd_frame;          /* " " " pull-down frame */
  char pd_interior;       /* " " " pull-down interior */
  char pd_inverse;        /* " " " pull-down highlighter */
};
```

The program pd-demo.c applies this structure to the external data structure **color** which is then initialized prior to calling the function **pull_down( )**. The text attributes specified will automatically be used when the menu is created.

Once the structures **pd_str** and **window_colors** have been applied and initialized, the actual pull-down menu is created with a call to **pd_menu( )**. The prototype for **pull_down( )** is:

```
int pull_down (struct pd_str m_menu[], struct window_
colors color);
```

We have discussed several steps necessary to create the pull-down menu. Let us review the steps again. To create a pull-down menu:

1. Alter the following define statements in mydef.h as needed:

```
#define MAIN_OPT   5
#define PD_SUB   3
#define PD_SUB_ROW   4
#define PD_MAIN_FRAME STD_FRAME
#define PD_SUB_FRAME PULL_DOWN
```

2. Create and initialize the external data structure:

```
struct window_colors color;
Fill in the text attributes you desire for your menu.
```

3. Create and initialize the pull-down menu structure:

```
struct pd_str m_menu [MAIN_OPT]={
    /* put initializing code here */
};
```

4. Pass the menu and color structure to the function **pull_down( )**:

```
return_code=pull_down(m_menu,color);
```

The function **pull_down( )** handles all the details of menu operation. The function exits when any called function returns a value greater than 0, when a list selection is made, or Escape is pressed at the main menu level (the same as in previous menus).

Please examine the sample program pd-demo.c at the end of this section for details.

TECHNIQUES

As we mentioned in the Goals section, the main portion of a pull-down menu is very similar to a horizontal light bar menu, while the pull-down submenu is basically a pop-up-style menu. Most of the concepts used to read keyboard input, print the options, and make function calls are almost identical to those used in the previous menus. Rather than spend a great deal of time on those issues, let's look at the unique aspects of the pull-down menu programming. Specifically, we will examine:

- The two-way communication between the main menu and the pull-down submenu.

- Calculating the location of the pull-down window.
- The effect of the expert/novice status on the program flow.

The pull-down menu system is controlled by two functions: **pull_down( )**, which creates the main menu, and **pull_down_sub( )**, which creates and manages the pull-down sub-menu. Both of these functions are found in the module pd.c. The function **pull-down_sub( )** is of type *static*, and cannot be called from outside the module pd.c.

The most important aspect of the menu operation deals with the communication between **pull_down( )** and **pull_down_sub( )**. The function **pull_down_sub( )** must "know" which main menu option has been selected from the main menu so it can create the correct pull-down submenu. The expert/novice status of the user must also be known, so that the menu operation is appropriate. In addition, the menu structure and color structure must be made available to the function **pull_down_sub( )**.

One important role for the function **pull_down_sub( )** is to inform **pull_down( )** of any changes in the expert/novice status as well as the exit status (did the user press Escape or a Right or Left cursor key?). Also, **pull_down_sub( )** must relay to **pull_down( )** any return code from called menu functions. The prototype for **pull_down_sub( )** is:

```
static int pull_down_sub(struct pd_str m_menu[],struct
    window_colors color,int option, char *ext,
    int *expert);
```

m_menu	=	Pull-down data structure.
color	=	Color data structure.
option	=	The number of the selected option.
*ext	=	Extension to show exit status (Escape, cursor, etc.).
*expert	=	Expert/novice status.

The actual function call made from **pd_menu( )** is:

```
return_code =(pull_down_sub(m_menu,color,cur_opt,&ext,
&expert));
```

Note that **pull_down( )** passes to **pull_down_sub( )** the actual address of **ext** (the extended keyboard return code) and the address of **expert**. Since **pull_down_sub( )** then has the address of the actual variable instead of a copy, any changes to these variables made within **pull_down_sub( )** are therefore visible to **pull_down( )**.

The function **pull_down( )** calls **pull_down_sub( )** when the user selects an option by pressing a quick key (expert mode), or by browsing via the Enter or cursor keys (novice mode).

The function **pull_down_sub( )** calculates the width and height of the pull-

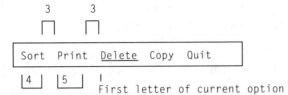

Figure 3–27   Calculating the position of
the pull-down

down submenu window using techniques described in the chapter on pop-up
menus. One special problem is figuring where to draw the submenu window. The
row is set equal to PD_SUB_ROW, which is defined in mydef.h as 4. The column
at which the upper left corner of the window appears is calculated by summing
the widths of the main menu options, up to the current option. The three-column
separation between options must be added in. For example, suppose we are drawing the pull-down submenu for the third main menu option, as shown in Figure
3–27. The first two menu options are ''Sort'' and ''Print''. Adding up the string
lengths plus column separation gives us $4 + 5 + 3 * 2 = 15$. After creating the
pull-down submenu window in the proper position, the user input is evaluated.
Any options selected from the submenu are called and the return code is examined.

Remember, the return codes from called functions have the following mean-
ings:

     0   Proceed as usual.
   >1 Close down all menus.
   <1 Keep the submenu active regardless of expert/novice status.

Any of the following events cause the function **pull_down_sub( )** to terminate.

- The return code from a called function is >0. This code is returned to
  pull_down( ).
- The return code from a function is 0 and **expert** equals TRUE. The 0 return
  code tells **pull_down_sub( )** to proceed as usual. If **expert** equals TRUE, this
  means to close down the submenu.
- The user presses the Right or Left cursor keys. This action indicates that
  the user is finished with the current submenu, and wishes to go to an adjacent
  menu.
- The user may press Escape, at which time **pull_down_sub( )** terminates, and
  ext is set to ESCAPE. Escaping from a submenu restores **expert** status.

When **pull_down_sub( )** terminates, **pull_down( )** examines **return_code**. If re-
turn_code is found to be any value other than 0, **pull_down( )** exits, returning the
value to the calling function.

If the variable **ext** equals LEFT or RIGHT then the highlighter is moved in the appropriate direction and **pull_down_sub( )** is called to display the new submenu. If **ext** equals ESCAPE then **expert** is set to TRUE.

CONCLUSION

In spite of the appearance of complexity, the pull-down menu is, when split into component parts, fairly simple. The following commented code should help answer any remaining questions.

SOURCE CODE

PD-DEMO.C

```
/********************  PD-DEMO.C  *************************/

/* Link with pd.c and library */

#include "mydef.h"
#include <stdio.h>
#include <ctype.h>
#include <dos.h>
#include <stdlib.h>

/* the number of main options is defined in mydef.h as MAIN_OPT */

/* the maximum number of suboptions is defined in
   "menu.h" as PD_SUB */

/* function prototypes */

int demo();
void howto(void);
int printer(void);

int start(void)
{
extern struct screen_structure scr;
extern struct window_structure w[];

char ch,ext;
int return_code;
int i;
int menu_win;

struct pd_str m_menu [MAIN_OPT]={
```

```
/* main menu    sub-menu            *function        list select values */

"Sort",
                " Ascending   ",
                " Descending  ",
                "",
                                    demo,
                                    demo,
                                    NULL,
                                                     0,
                                                     0,
                                                     0,
"Print",
                " Printer    ",
                " Text-file ",
                "",
                                    printer,
                                    demo,
                                    NULL,
                                                     0,
                                                     0,
                                                     0,
"Delete",
                " Data-file     ",
                " program-File ",
                " Programmer    ",
                                    demo,
                                    demo,
                                    demo,
                                                     0,
                                                     0,
                                                     0,
"Copy",
                " Block ",
                " Line   ",
                "",
                                    demo,
                                    demo,
                                    NULL,
                                                     0,
                                                     0,
                                                     0,
"Quit",
                " Exit program ",
                "",
                "",
                                    NULL,
                                    NULL,
                                    NULL,
                                                     1,
                                                     0,
                                                     0,
    };
```

```
/* colors for main and pull-down windows */
struct window_colors color;

/*initialize window colors*/

if (scr.mode==COLOR_80){
 color.main_frame=set_color(YELLOW,BLACK);
 color.main_interior=set_color(WHITE,BLUE);
 color.main_inverse=set_color(BLUE,WHITE);

 color.pd_frame=set_color(YELLOW,BLACK);
 color.pd_interior=set_color(WHITE,BLUE);
 color.pd_inverse=set_color(BLUE,WHITE);
 }
 else{

 color.main_frame=scr.normal;
 color.main_interior=scr.normal;
 color.main_inverse=scr.inverse;

 color.pd_frame=scr.normal;
 color.pd_interior=scr.normal;
 color.pd_inverse=scr.inverse;
 }

howto();          /* SHOW INSTRUCTIONS */

   return_code=pull_down(m_menu,color);

cursor(NORMAL_CURSOR);  /* restore normal cursor */

cls();

return(return_code);
}

void howto()
{
  if (scr.mode==COLOR_80)
   scr.current=  set_color(GREEN,BLACK);
    else
     scr.current = NORMAL;

 cls();
 print (1,4,"INSTRUCTIONS:");
 print(1,6,"EXPERT MODE: Select by touching the\
 key which represents each option");
 print (14,7,"(the capital letter).");

 print (1,10, "ASSIST MODE: Pull down menu by touching\
 Enter or a cursor key.");
 print (14,11,"Select by highlighting with cursor keys -\
 then touch Enter.");
```

```
    print (14,13,"Return to Expert mode by touching Escape.");

    print (1,15,"EXIT:          To exit to DOS, touch\
    Escape while in Expert mode.");

}

int demo(void)
{
int demo win;
char ch,ext;

  demo_win=win_make(24,10,30,5,STD_FRAME," Demo window ",
                    scr.normal,scr.normal);

   print(1,1,"Make believe window");

    scr.bold_caps=TRUE;
      print(1,3,"TOUCH ANY KEY TO EXIT");
    scr.bold_caps=FALSE;
       get_key(&ch,&ext);
    win_delete(demo_win);
  return(0);
}

int printer(void)
{
extern struct screen_structure scr;
extern struct window_structure w[];

  /* set up menu structure */

  struct pop_struc pop_menu [3]={
            " Lpt1:    " ,NULL,   0,
            " 1Pt2:    " ,NULL,   0,
            "\0"        /* mark the end of the options list */
  };

  /* call routine to handle menu */
  return (pop_up (pop_menu,25,5,scr.normal,scr.inverse));
  }
```

PD.C

```
/******************     PD.C     **************************/

#include "mydef.h"
#include <stdio.h>

int pull_down (struct pd_str m_menu[], struct window_colors color)
{
```

```
extern struct screen_structure scr;
extern struct window_structure w[];

int i,j;                /* general index variables */
int cur_x,cur_y;        /* screen coordinates */
int cur_opt=0;          /* the current option (highlighted) */
int found=FALSE;        /* flag to indicate if option found */
int expert=TRUE;        /* flag to indicate expert/novice mode */
char ch=' ', ext=' ';   /* character and extension from keyboard */
int return_code;        /* return code */
int main_win;           /* integer handle for main options window */

/* find out if a frame is requested and make window */

if (PD_MAIN_FRAME[0]=='\0')  /* no frame requested */
   main_win=win_make(1,1,scr.columns,1,PD_MAIN_FRAME,""\
   ,color.main_frame,color.main_interior);
  else       /* frame requested */
    main_win=win_make(2,2,scr.columns-2,1,PD_MAIN_FRAME,"",\
    color.main_frame,color.main_interior);

  cursor(NO_CURSOR);   /* turn off cursor */

  for(;;){
      /* if a true letter is pressed */
      if(ch!= ' '&& ch!=RETURN){
        for(i=0;i<MAIN_OPT;i++){   /* for each main option */
         j=0;
        while(m_menu[i].main[j]!= '\0'){   /* scan each letter */
         /* if quick key found */
          if (m_menu[i].main[j++] ==ch && ch != ' '){
           found= TRUE;         /* mark found true */
           cur_opt = i;         /* mark it as current option */
           break;
          }
        }
       }
     }
          if (ch==RETURN){        /* if Enter (return) is pressed */
           found = TRUE;          /* accept current option */
           expert = FALSE;        /* action indicates non-expert */
          }

        /* reset variables */
        ch=' ';
        cur_x=1;cur_y=1;

      /* turn on bold caps if necessary */
         if (found !! !expert )scr.bold_caps=FALSE;
           else scr.bold_caps=TRUE;

         for(i=0;i< MAIN_OPT;i++){   /* print options */
             if(i == cur_opt) scr.current= color.main_inverse;
```

```
          else scr.current= color.main_interior;
           print(cur_x,cur_y,m_menu[i].main);
      /* move to next screen location*/
      cur_x= cur_x+strlen(m_menu[i].main)+3;
    }

    if (!expert) found = TRUE; /* if not expert then    */
                               /* force found=TRUE so    */
                               /* sub-menu always called */

    if (found){                    /* enter here if found==TRUE */

      /* redraw main menu with bold_caps off */
      scr.bold_caps=FALSE;

      /* call function to create pull-down */
      return_code =(pull_down_sub(m_menu,color,cur_opt,
                   &ext, &expert));
      win_pop_top(main_win);
      if(return_code!=0) break;

      /* reactivate expert mode */
      if (ext == ESCAPE) expert = TRUE;

      /* if cursor keys used then not expert */
      if (ext == RIGHT || ext == LEFT) expert = FALSE;

      /* if cursor keys then adjust counter */
      if (ext==RIGHT) cur_opt++;
      if (ext ==LEFT) cur_opt--;
      ch= ' ';
      ext= ' ';

    } /* end if found */
     else
    {    /* if selection not made then get key */
     ch=' ';
     get_key(&ch,&ext);
     ch=toupper(ch);
    } /* end not found */

    if (ch==ESCAPE) break;    /* exit if "Escape" pressed */

    /* if cursor keys then not expert */
    if (ext ==RIGHT || ext == LEFT) expert = FALSE;
    /* adjust counter if cursor key used */
    if (ext == RIGHT)  cur_opt++;
    if (ext == LEFT)  cur_opt--;
    if (cur_opt >= MAIN_OPT) cur_opt =0;
    if (cur_opt < 0) cur_opt = MAIN_OPT-1;
    ext=' ';
    found=0;
```

```
  } /* end for(;;) */
  /* close window and return return-code */
  win_delete(main_win);
  return(return-code);
}

static int pull_down_sub(struct pd_str m_menu[],
                         struct window_colors color,int option,
                         char *ext, int *expert)
{

char ch=' ';

int i,j;                /* general index variables */
int y;                  /* y screen coordinate (row) */
int start,width;        /* info for pull-down window */
int nu_opt;             /* the number of options in pull-down */
int cur_opt=0;          /* the current (highlighted) option */
int found= FALSE;       /* flag to indicate selection made (found)*/
int pd_win;             /* handle of pull-down window */
int return_code=0;      /* return code */

nu_opt=PD_SUB;     /* set nu_opt to maximum value */

scr.bold_caps=TRUE;     /* turn on bold_caps */

/* find out how many options are in pull-down menu */

for(i=0;i<nu_opt;i++){
  /* scan until empty string found */
  if (m_menu[option].sub[i][0] == '\0'){
   nu_opt = i;
   break;
  }
}

start=3;   /* Figure where to draw pull-down box.
              The column must begin at least on the 3rd column.
              We can calculate the column at which to place
              the pull-down window by adding up the lengths
              of the main menu options appearing before
              the current option. */

  for(i=0; i< option; i++) start= start+strlen(m_menu[i].main)+3;

  width=0;        /* figure max length of window, assume 0 to start */
  for (i=0;i< nu_opt;i++){
   if (strlen(m_menu[option].sub[i]) > width){
    /* set width to largest strlen */
    width= strlen(m_menu[option].sub[i]);
   }
  }
```

```
/* move box to left if it will spill off right side */
if(start+width+1>scr.columns) start = scr.columns-width-2;

/* create pull-down window based on calculated values */
pd_win= win_make(start++,PD_SUB_ROW,width,nu_opt,PD_SUB_FRAME,"",\
        color.pd_frame,color.pd_interior); /*make a window */
cursor(NO_CURSOR); /* turn off cursor for this window */

y=1;   /* reposition in pull-down window for writing */

  for(;;){       /* begin endless loop while we process input */
        y=1;
        /* if a selection is made, turn off bold_caps */
        if (found )scr.bold_caps=FALSE;
        else scr.bold_caps=TRUE;

    /* print options in pull-down menu highlighting current option */
        for(i=0;i< nu_opt;i++){
          if(i == cur_opt) scr.current= color.pd_inverse;

            else scr.current= color.pd_interior;
            print(1,y++,m_menu[option].sub[i]);
        };

      if(found ) {  /* an option is selected */

        scr.bold_caps=FALSE;  /* turn off bold caps */
         /* if function pointer =NULL return specified code */
         /* else call function */
         if (m_menu[option].fun[cur_opt]==NULL)
          return_code=m_menu[option].select_id[cur_opt];
          else
          return_code=(*m_menu[option].fun[cur_opt])();
          win_pop_top(pd_win);

        /* exit pull-down if expert and return_code >0 */
        if(*expert==TRUE && return_code >=0)break;

        if(return_code>0) break;
        /* reset for next pass */
        if(return_code <0) return_code=0;
        found = FALSE;
        scr.bold_caps=TRUE;
        /* make sure keyboard buffer is clear */
        if (kbhit()) getch();
      } /* end found */
        else {          /* begin not found */

        /* get a character */
        get_key(&ch,ext); ch=toupper(ch);

        /* adjust cur_opt if up or down cursor key pressed */
```

```
            if (*ext == DOWN )  cur_opt = cur_opt +1;
            if (*ext == UP)  cur_opt = cur_opt -1;


            /* test for boundary and wrap if necessary */
            if (cur_opt >= nu_opt) cur_opt =0;
            if (cur_opt < 0) cur_opt = nu_opt-1;

          /* has a regular letter key been pressed? */
          if(ch='\0') *expert=FALSE;

          if (ch== RETURN){   /* user pressed "Enter" */
            found = TRUE;
            *expert=FALSE;
          }

          if(ch!='\0'){      /* check for quick keys */
           for(i=0;i<nu_opt;i++){    /* do for each option */
            j=0;

           /* check each letter in option to
              see if it matches character */

             while( m_menu[option].sub[i][j]!='\0'){
              if ( m_menu[option].sub[i][j++]==ch && ch != ' '){
               cur_opt = i;
               found = TRUE;
               break;
              }
             }
           } /* end for(); */
          }   /* end if(ch) */
         }    /* end else */

          /* check for options which would exit pull-down */
          if (*ext==LEFT || *ext==RIGHT) break;
          if (ch==ESCAPE){               /* EXIT IF ESCAPE KEY */
           *ext = ch;
           break;
          }
          *ext=' ';ch=' ';
   } /* end for(;;)*/

   /* exit pull-down */
   win_delete(pd_win);
   return (return_code);
}
```

Chapter 4

The Data Input Screen

In this chapter we will:

- Discuss standard field editing features.
- Create a field editor with full support for editing keys.
- Create a multifield data input screen with data verification.

INTRODUCTION

C language programmers are often faced with the task of obtaining one or more lines of text from the user via the console. Although the function **gets( )** may be used for this task, its lack of editing features often makes it unsuitable for use in a modern, user-friendly application.

Field input functions, or field editors, do not require complex features found in full-featured word processors. For example, search and replace options and blockmoves are unnecessary when the user is inputting only a single line of text.

A few simple editing features, such as an insert/overtype mode, are not only useful, but many of them have become standard in many applications. We will, of course, implement these standard features in our field editor, along with a few enhancements.

In the remainder of this chapter, we will discuss the field editor and the data input screen manager. The latter is simply a function that manages the task of entering multiple fields of text.

GOALS

The Field Editor

The field editor, as the name implies, allows input and editing of a field of text. A typical application would be to prompt the user to enter a file name, then read the user input. Fields may be longer than one line, but never take up more than one screen. Editors that process more than one screen of continuous information are generally referred to as text editors or word processors.

Field editors are generally used whenever more than one letter of input is required from the user. In many cases the field in which the user types information is highlighted or demarcated in some manner. There is often a prompt before the field, to indicate what the user should enter.

In the following example, the brackets indicate cursor position, and the underline represents the highlighted screen display which marks the field limits:

PLEASE ENTER PATH/FILENAME: [_] _____

In some cases the field may be partially filled with default values. The purpose of this is to reduce the amount of repetitious typing required of the user. For example:

PLEASE ENTER PATH/FILENAME: a:\my.doc[_] _____

In this situation the user may accept the current field by pressing Enter or may edit the field.

Editing features vary among different field editors but a few features come close to being universal. Because adherence to these standard features makes transition from application to application easier for the user, we will incorporate in our field editor the following features:

- The length of the input field can be set for each field.
- The editor can input new text, or edit existing text.
- The cursor can be positioned anywhere within the field prior to editing existing text.
- Left and Right cursor keys move the cursor within the field for editing.
- Home and End keys move the cursor to the beginning and end of the text within the input field.

- The Delete key deletes the text under the cursor.
- The Back Space key deletes the text to the left of the cursor.
- The field editor operates in two modes, insert and overtype. *Insert* mode allows text to be entered at the current cursor location, pushing text to the right of the cursor. *Overtype* mode replaces text underneath the cursor with new text. The Insert key acts as a toggle, flipping between insert and overtype modes.
- The cursor changes size to reflect the state of the insert/overtype toggle. A small cursor indicates overtype mode, while a large cursor indicates insert mode. In contrast to applications that have a status line containing the word "Overtype" or "Insert", the cursor change allows the user to know the status while looking directly at the text (this saves screen space too!). The precedent for this feature came from the IBM Basic language interpreter, which means it should be recognized by a great many people.

The Data Input Screen Editor

In addition to the basic field editor, we will construct a data input screen editor. We can use this function to input an entire screen of data, containing as many fields as will fit on the display. Our data input screen will have the following features:

- The cursor automatically jumps to the next field when the user presses Enter.
- The user may use the up and down cursor keys to move between fields (pressing the up cursor key moves to the previous field, pressing the down key moves to the following field).
- Data entry terminates when the user presses Enter on the last field, or the user presses PgUp, PgDn or Escape.
- A special field verification routine allows the fields to be examined after each field is entered.

A special data structure will be created for the input screen. Within this structure we can specify for each field:

- The screen location (column, row).
- Prompt for each field.
- String to receive input, or to be edited.
- Maximum length of string.
- Text attribute for prompt and field highlighting.

The screen input routine will automatically create the screen and handle all editing functions.

APPLICATION

The library files L_getfld.c and L_input, contain the functions which handle field and screen input, respectively.

The basic function that we use to input text is **getfield( )**. The prototype for **getfield( )** is:

```
char getfield(char *string, int inlength, int start,
char attribute);
```

The values passed to **getfield( )** are:

char *string	= A pointer to the string which receives text.
int inlength	= The maximum allowed input length.
int start	= The location within the string to start editing. (first location is 0)
char attribute	= The text attribute used to highlight the input field.

The function **getfield( )** will print the string at the current cursor location, and edit the string until the user touches one of the following keys, at which time the editing will terminate. The return value will be one of those shown in Table 4–1. The return codes ENTER, UP, DOWN, PGUP, PGDN, and ESCAPE are macros which represent the keys, and they are defined in mydef.h.

TABLE 4–1   RETURN CODES FOR **GETFIELD( )**

User presses	Return code
Enter	ENTER
down cursor	DOWN
up cursor	UP
PgUp	PGUP
PgDn	PGDN
Escape	ESCAPE

The pointer **string** should point to a '\0'-terminated string which is empty "" or has existing text such as "This is a test". The memory set aside for the string should be wide enough to hold the number of characters indicated by **inlength** plus one (for the '\0' terminator).

The variable **start** specifies the location within the string at which editing will begin. For example:

```
char string[30];
char ext;
```

```
strcpy(string,"hello");
print (1,1,"EDIT THIS STRING: ");
getfield(string,20,3,scr.current);
```

This code would allow **string** to be edited starting at position three. The screen display would look like this:

EDIT THIS STRING: hel<u>l</u>o

In the example just shown, the current screen attribute **scr.current** is specified in the function call, and the field is not visibly highlighted. You may use **scr.inverse** to highlight the input field with the predefined inverse text.

Data Input Screens (Multiple Fields)

The purpose of a data input screen is to allow multiple fields of text to be entered or edited on the same screen. The function responsible for managing a data input screen must prepare the screen for input by placing the prompts and highlighted fields on the screen, and then make repeated calls to **getfield( )** to input each field at the correct location. The function **input( )**, found in the library module l_input.c, performs this task.

The data structure **in_struc** (defined in mydef.h) is designed to contain all the information necessary to construct the data input screen. This is its structure:

```
struct in_struc {
   int x;       /* x position for data input field (start of label)*/
   int y;       /* y position for data input field (start of label)*/

   char *prompt;/* the prompt for the field */
   char *ptr;   /* pointer to string to edit */
   int  length; /* the maximum length of the field */

   unsigned int label_f,label_b; /* label foreground,background color */
   unsigned int input_f,input_b; /* input field foreground,background
                                     color */
   };
```

This data structure is applied to the data array **in_scrn** and is initialized with the information describing the input screen. Once the data structure is created and initialized, it is passed to **input( )** and the screen is created.

Let's take a look at the sample program in-demo.c (found at the end of this chapter) and see the process at work. The data structure **in_scrn** is created and initialized with descriptions for each field. Note that the last field has only a 0 for the X screen coordinate. Since our screen coordinate system starts numbering with 1, the illegal value 0 serves as a terminator to mark the end of the field list. The macro MAX_FIELD is defined in this example as 12.

```
struct in_struc in_scrn[NUMBER_FIELDS+1]= {
/*
X    Y    Label name         Ptr    Length   Label-color     Field color */

1,   1,   "First Name:"      ,NULL  ,10,     YELLOW,BLACK,   BLACK,WHITE,
1,   2,   "Last Name :"      ,NULL  ,15,     YELLOW,BLACK,   BLACK,WHITE,
40,  2,   "Middle init:"     ,NULL  ,1,      YELLOW,BLACK,   BLACK,WHITE,
1,   4,   "Age:"             ,NULL  ,3,      CYAN,BLACK,     BLACK,CYAN,
12,  4,   "Sex:"             ,NULL  ,1,      CYAN,BLACK,     BLACK,CYAN,
25,  4,   "Date of Birth:"   ,NULL  ,10,     CYAN,BLACK,     BLACK,WHITE,
1,   7,   "Street address:"  ,NULL  ,30,     GREEN,BLACK,    BLACK,GREEN,
1,   8,   "City :"           ,NULL  ,20,     GREEN,BLACK,    BLACK,GREEN,
1,   9,   "State:"           ,NULL  ,2,      GREEN,BLACK,    BLACK,GREEN,
12,  9,   "Zip:"             ,NULL  ,11,     GREEN,BLACK,    BLACK,GREEN,
1,   11,  "Current Title:"   ,NULL  ,40,     WHITE,BLACK,    WHITE,RED,
1,   13,  "Comments:"        ,NULL  ,160,    WHITE,BLACK,    WHITE,RED,
0    /* terminator */
};
```

The X-Y screen coordinate specifies the location at which each field's label is printed. The input field is placed one space beyond the end of the label.

The screen output from in-demo.c uses this structure to generate the upper part of the display shown in Figure 4-1. Notice that the structure string pointers **ptr** are initially set to NULL, to indicate that no memory has been allocated. These pointers must be set to point to a suitable string storage location. The

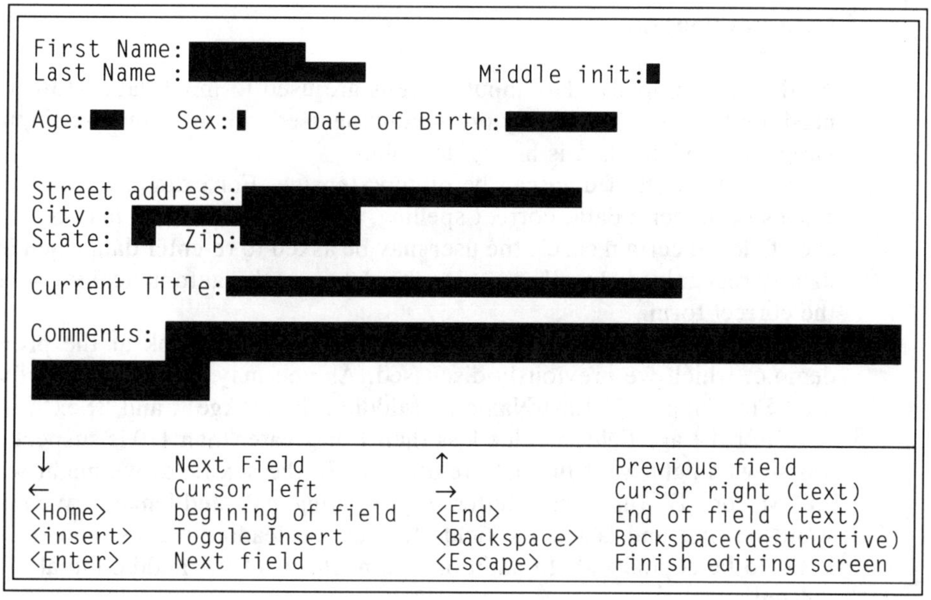

Figure 4-1 Data input screen created by in-demo.c

TABLE 4–2   RETURN CODES FOR **INPUT( )**

Key	Return value
Enter	ENTER (This works on the last field only)
PgUp	PGUP
PgDn	PGDN
Escape	ESCAPE

memory locations to which you direct each pointer must be large enough to store the corresponding string.

Once memory is allocated, it could be filled with text prior to calling **input( )**. If **ptr** points to existing strings, then **input( )** would allow the text in these strings to be edited.

After the structure has been initialized and the memory allocated, the following call is made to create the input screen.

```
input(in_scrn);
```

All the editing features are handled by **input( )**, which terminates when the user finishes editing by pressing one of the keys listed in Table 4–2. All information entered by the user is treated as text, even numerical information such as "Age". The text may be converted to numerical values using functions such as **atoi( )** (ASCII to integer).

Data Verification

As the name implies, data input screens are used to input data. However, they need not be limited to merely prompting the user and obtaining user input. Some verification of the data is highly desirable.

Verification of data can be quite extensive. For example, we could check ranges of numeric data, correct spelling, or specify what text may be allowed in each field. In certain cases, the user may be asked to re-enter data when incorrect data is recognized. In other cases, the data may be automatically converted to the correct form.

As an example of data verification, let's take a look at the program in-demo.c, which we previously discussed. As you may recall, the first five fields are "First Name", "Last Name', "Middle Init", "Age", and "Sex".

For the age field, a value less than 1 or greater than 110 is suspect. In such a case we might want the data re-entered. In the sex field, we might want only an "M" or "F" (uppercase letters representing male and female). We might also want the first and last name fields to have no leading blanks, and for the first letter to be capitalized. In addition, we might want the middle initial to be capitalized.

All these tasks can be accomplished with the field verification routine **val_field( )**. The function **val_field( )** is called by **input( )** immediately after each field is entered. The prototype for **val_field( )** is:

```
int val_field( char *string,int length,int field_number)
```

    string   = The text string just edited.

    length   = The maximum allowed string length.

    field_number = The number of the field in the data input screen.

The function **val_field( )** can evaluate or modify the text string in any manner it chooses. The only restriction is that the string, after modification, must not be larger than the maximum allowed length.

    The function returns one of the values that are defined in mydef.h and shown in Table 4–3.

TABLE 4–3 RETURN CODES FOR **VAL_FIELD( )**

Macro name	Value	Meaning
OK	0	Field OK - go to next field
REDO	1	Field not correct; re-edit this field
REDRAW	2	The field was altered by **val_field( )**; redraw and go to the next field.

Within **val_field( )** you can do almost anything with the field just entered. Data values can be tested to assure they fall within specified ranges, and alterations may be made to the data just entered. Here is the function **val_field( )** from the program in-demo.c. Note that the parameter **length** is not used in this example, since nothing is done which could make the string longer than the allowed value.

```
/* This function evaluates the data input and does the following
   for each field

   Field:        Action

" First Name" Trims leading spaces,capitalizes first letter.
" Last Name"  "      "        "       "  "          "     "
" Middle Init" Capitalizes
" Age"        If age is <1 or >110 a re-edit is requested
" Sex"        If sex equals 'm' or 'f' then it is capitalized
              if it is any other letter, then re-edit.  */

int val_field( char *string,int length,int field_number)
```

```
{
  /* Note: In this demo "length" is not used. */
  int age;

  switch (field_number){
    /* trim leading spaces off field zero */
    case 0: trim_left(string);
            /* make first letter uppercase */
            string[0]=toupper(string[0]);
            return(REDRAW);
            /* trim leading spaces off field one */
    case 1: trim_left(string);
            /* make first letter uppercase */
            string[0]=toupper(string[0]);
            return (REDRAW);
    case 2: string[0]=toupper(string[0]);
            return(REDRAW);

    case 3: age=atoi(string);    /* convert string to integer */
            if (age<0 || age>110) return(REDO);
            break;
    case 4: if (string[0]=='m'){string[0]='M'return(REDRAW);}
            if (string[0]=='f'){ string[0]='F'; return(REDRAW);}
            if(string[0]!='M' && string[0]!='F')return (REDO);
            break;
  }
  return (OK);
}
```

Note: The *trim* functions, which remove leading and trailing blanks from strings, are found in the library module 1_trim.c.

When developing the **val_field( )** function, it is important to try to foresee the types of errors that the user might make during data input, and to customize error checking to the data requirements of each field. Data input is typically a boring, error-prone task. Automating the task of capitalizing letters for example, can save the user time and avoid errors in the long run. Remember, you can do any manipulation to the string that you desire, as long as you do not exceed the maximum length of the string. If you do alter the string, return REDRAW, so that the screen is updated.

If you do not wish to do any verification, alter **val_field( )** so it does nothing but return an OK (0).

TECHNIQUES

Creating a field editor can be quite a programming task. The editor is actually doing two tasks: managing the on-screen editing, and manipulating text strings stored in memory. It is reasonable to assume that there is a correspondence between the action on the screen and the string manipulation.

On-screen, the user moves a cursor to edit the text. Text is always inserted at the current cursor location. It is therefore reasonable to assume that within memory there are two text strings: the string to the left of the cursor, and the string under and to the right of the cursor.

Suppose, for example, we start with an empty data field ready for user input. Both strings are empty at this point and can be represented with brackets.

                              [ ]   [ ]

In Table 4–4 is an example of the string contents as a user types in "The quick fox", backs up three columns using the cursor key, and inserts the word "brown" (insert is ON). At the time the user touched Enter, the right string was merged with the left string and the editing terminated.

TABLE 4–4 EXAMPLES OF STRING CONTENTS

User input	On-screen	String contents
"The quick fox"	The quick fox	[The quick fox] [ ]
three left cursor moves	The quick fox	[The quick] [fox]
"brown"	The quick brown fox	[The quick brown] [fox]
presses Enter		[The quick brown fox] [ ]

As you can see, such a function spends a lot of time taking the ends off one string and moving them to the other. To make the programming task somewhat easier, we create a set of "chip" functions. These functions literally take a "chip off the old block." Here is the prototype for **chip_right( )** which is found in the file L_chip.c:

```
void chip_right(char *chip,char *block,int number);
```

    chip   = Pointer to string that receives text.
    block   = Pointer to string that loses text.
    number = Amount of text to move.

Assume that **block** points to the string "The quick fox", and the **chip** points to an empty string. We make this call:

```
                    chip_right(chip,block,3);
```

We therefore end up with:

    block = "The quick "
    chip   = "fox"

The function **chip_left( )** works the same way, only on the left side of the block. The functions **chip_left( )** and **chip_right( )** make use of the function **copy( )**, as in this example.

```
void copy (char *from,char *to,int first,int length);
```

The parameters are defined as follows:

from   = String to copy from.
to   = String to copy to.
first   = Position within "from" string to start copying.
length = Number of characters to copy.

For example, if the variable **str1** equals " " and **str2** equals "this is a test", then the command "copy (str2,str1,0,4);" would yield:

str1 = "this"
str2 = "this is a test"

The Screen Display

Although we now have a method of manipulating the user input, we must try to represent these strings on the display.

Displaying user input is a very easy task at first. We simply read the character typed by the user, place it on the screen and move the cursor forward. If the user moves the cursor forward or backward with the cursor keys, the program simply moves the cursor to reflect the action. Of course, a lot of string manipulation is going on behind the scenes.

At all times the program checks to see if the cursor is being moved beyond the window boundaries and wraps the text if needed. The input string length is monitored, and the user is not allowed to exceed the specified value.

Let's look again at the example we cited earlier, in which the user typed "the quick fox", moved left three columns via the cursor keys, and typed "brown". This time we will focus on the screen update.

As the user types the first phrase, the program gets the characters and echoes them to the screen. When the user moves the cursor left (with cursor keys), the cursor is moved to the left, and no other screen update is performed.

When the user types "brown", we have a more complicated situation. The program must echo the new characters to the screen as well as push the text, which is under and to the right of the cursor, to the right. This is handled by printing the new character at the current cursor position, storing the current cursor position, and then printing the string **right**. The string **right** contains the text under and to the right of the cursor.

Each character of input that is echoed to the screen overwrites the first character of the existing text. Printing the string **right** therefore totally overwrites the old text which is to the right of the cursor (it overlaps by one character). After overwriting the old text and making it appear to be pushed over, the cursor is moved back to its old position.

Let's take a look at how some of the other editing commands are performed.

Back space

STRING = The Back Space key is destructive; it deletes the text to the left of the cursor. In terms of string manipulation, the rightmost character of the string **left** is removed. No change is made to the **right** string.

SCREEN = On the screen it appears that the text to the left of the cursor is erased as the cursor moves over it. The text to the right of the cursor is dragged along with the cursor. The screen update is done by moving the cursor to the left. Then the cursor position is stored, and the **right** string is printed. An extra blank space must be printed in order to cover up all the old string. The cursor is then moved back to the original position.

Delete

STRING = The leftmost character of the **right** string is the character which appears under the cursor; therefore it must be removed.

SCREEN = The character under the cursor appears to disappear, with the text to the right being pulled over. This is accomplished by saving the cursor position and printing the **right** string (which has had the leftmost character removed). The **right** string is not long enough to totally overwrite the screen text, so one extra space must be printed at the end of **right** to overwrite all the previous text. The cursor is restored.

Home

STRING = The **right** and **left** strings are combined, and their contents are stored in **right**; **left** is set to empty " ".

SCREEN = The cursor is moved to the beginning of the input field. This is easily accomplished as the initial cursor position is saved in **orig-x** and **orig-y** when editing begins.

End

STRING = The **left** and **right** strings are combined and stored in **left**; **right** is set to empty.

SCREEN = The cursor is moved to the end of the **right** string. This is accomplished by printing the **right** string. The cursor is left at the end of the string.

Text entry is completed when the user touches the Enter, Escape, PgUp, PgDn, or the Up or Down cursor keys. The return code for the function represents the key used to terminate editing. See the tables in the Application section for the return codes.

Allowing the field editor to terminate when the user presses the Up or Down cursor key is necessary to allow the field editor to be used in a multiple field input screen format.

The data screen function **input( )** does the following:

- For each data field, the prompt is printed and the field highlighted to show the limits of data input. This is done prior to any data input. The prompts, field size, and text attributes are contained in the data structure **in__scrn**, which is passed to the function **input( ).**
- The variable **i** is set to 0, and is used to keep track of the field being edited.
- The cursor is moved to the home position at the beginning of the first input field, and the function **getfield( )** is called to edit the field.
- The variable **ext** is set to the value returned by **getfield( )**. Depending on the value returned (ENTER, UP, DOWN, or ESCAPE), the variable **i** is adjusted so that the proper field is edited. The function **val__field( )** is called immediately after each field is edited. Redrawing or re-editing is performed if requested by **val__field( ).**

The complete listing of **getfield( )** may be found in the Source Code section in the module l_getfld.c.

SOURCE CODE

IN-DEMO.C

```
/ * * * * * * * * * * * * * * * * * * * * *     IN-DEMO.C      * * * * * * * * * * * * * * * * * * * * * * * * * * * /
#include "mydef.h"
#include <stdio.h>
#include <ctype.h>

#define NUMBER_FIELDS 12 /* the maximum number of fields */

/* for memory allocation */
#if defined QUICKC
```

```
#include <malloc.h>
#include <memory.h>

#endif

#if defined TURBOC

#include <alloc.h>
#include <mem.h>
#include <string.h>
#include <stdlib.h>
#include <dir.h>

#endif

/* function prototypes */

void help();
int val_field( char *string,int length,int field_number);

int start(void)
{
extern struct screen_structure scr;
extern struct window_structure w[];

int i;
int helpwin, mainwin; /*window handles*/

/* make a help screen */

helpwin= win_make(1,20,78,5,STD_FRAME,"",scr.normal,scr.normal);

help(); /* display help */

/*make the main window*/
mainwin=win_make (1,1,78,17,TOP_FRAME,"",scr.normal,scr.normal);

demo(); /*do input demo*/

/*remove windows */

win_delete(helpwin);
win_delete(mainwin);

return(0);
}

demo()
{
extern struct screen_structure scr;
extern struct window_structure w[];
```

```
int field_attr;
int ret_code;
char ch,ext;
      /* make in_scrn large enough to include zero terminator */
struct in_struc in_scrn[NUMBER_FIELDS+1] = {
/*
X    Y    Label name          Ptr    Length    Label-color     Field color */

1,   1,   "First Name:"       ,NULL   ,10,   YELLOW,BLACK,  BLACK,WHITE,
1,   2,   "Last Name :"       ,NULL   ,15,   YELLOW,BLACK,  BLACK,WHITE,
40,  2,   "Middle init:"      ,NULL   ,1,    YELLOW,BLACK,  BLACK,WHITE,
1,   4,   "Age:"              ,NULL   ,3,    CYAN,BLACK,    BLACK,CYAN,
12,  4,   "Sex:"              ,NULL   ,1,    CYAN,BLACK,    BLACK,CYAN,
25,  4,   "Date of Birth:"    ,NULL   ,10,   CYAN,BLACK,    BLACK,WHITE,
1,   7,   "Street address:"   ,NULL   ,30,   GREEN,BLACK,   BLACK,GREEN,
1,   8,   "City:"             ,NULL   ,20,   GREEN,BLACK,   BLACK,GREEN,
1,   9,   "State:"            ,NULL   ,2,    GREEN,BLACK,   BLACK,GREEN,
12,  9,   "Zip:"              ,NULL   ,11,   GREEN,BLACK,   BLACK,GREEN,
1,   11,  "Current Title:"    ,NULL   ,40,   WHITE,BLACK,   WHITE,RED,
1,   13,  "Comments:"         ,NULL   ,160,  WHITE,BLACK,   WHITE,RED,
0    /*terminator */
};
int i;

/* We must allocate enough memory for each field, allowing for the
   '\0' terminator. */

   for (i= 0 ;i<NUMBER_FIELDS;i++){
   in_scrn[i].ptr= malloc((in_scrn[i].length+1)*sizeof(char));
   if(in_scrn[i].ptr==NULL) exit(1);
   in_scrn[i].ptr[0]='\0';
   }


/* call input function, pass it the input structure */

ret_code=input(in_scrn);

cls();

/* show that we really got data */
if (ret_code==ESCAPE) print(1,1,"Escape pressed, no data entered");
 else {
  print (1,1, "The following data were returned from input():");
  gotoxy(1,3);
    for(i=0;i<NUMBER_FIELDS;i++) {
      print(1,i+2,in_scrn[i].prompt);
      print_here(in_scrn[i].ptr);
    }
   print (1,i+4, "Touch any key to quit");
 }

    for(i=0;i<NUMBER_FIELDS;i++)
     /* free memory if it has been allocated*/
```

```
        if (in_scrn[i].ptr!=NULL)
            free(in_scrn[i].ptr);

get_key(&ch,&ext);
return(0);

}
void help()
{
int x=1, y=1;

print(x,y++,"\x19            Next Field            \x18\
            Previous field");
print(x,y++,"\x1b            Cursor left            \x1a\
            Cursor right (text)");
print(x,y++,"<Home>        beginning of field  <End>\
        End of field (text)");
print(x,y++,"<insert>      Toggle Insert          <Backspace>\
    Backspace(destructive)");
print(x,y++,"<Enter>       Next field             <Escape>   \
    Exit (Abandon record)");

}

/* This function evaluates the data input and does the following
   for each field.

   Field:          Action

   "First Name"  Trims leading spaces, capitalizes first letter.
   "Last Name"   "       "       "       "   "               "      "
   "Middle init" Capitalizes
   "Age"         If age is <1 or >110 a re-edit is requested
   "Sex"         If sex equals 'm' or 'f' then it is capitalized
if it is any other letter, then re-edit.    */

int val_field( char *string,int length,int field_number)

{
 /* Note: In this demo "length" is not used. */
 int age;

 switch (field_number){
  /* trim leading spaces off field zero */
  case 0: trim_left(string);
          /* make first letter uppercase */
          string[0]=toupper(string[0]);
          return(REDRAW);
          /* trim leading spaces off field one */
  case 1: trim_left(string);
          /* make first letter uppercase */
          string[0]=toupper(string[0]);
          return (REDRAW);
```

```
      case 2: string[0]=toupper(string[0]);
              return(REDRAW);

      case 3: age=atoi(string);      /* convert string to integer */
              if (age<0 || age>110) return(REDO);
              break;
      case 4: if (string[0]=='m'){ string[0]='M';return(REDRAW;}
              if (string[0]=='f'){ string[0]='F'; return(REDRAW);}
              if(string[0]!='M' && string[0]!='F')return (REDO);
              break;

   }
   return (OK);
   }
```

L_GETFLD.C

```
/********************      L_GETFLD.C      *************************/

#include "mydef.h"
#include "stdio.h"

/******************************************************************

Usage: char getfield( char *string, int inlength, int start,
                      char attribute);

  char *string=   string to edit (if empty "" then accepts new text.
  int inlength=   maximum string length allowed.
  int start=      position within string to start editing.
  char attribute= text attribute to use to highlight field.

  Allows input of text.  If *string contains text, then *string
  may be edited.

  Editing keys (home, end etc) allowed.

********************************************************************/

char getfield(char *string,int inlength,int start, char attribute)
{
extern struct  screen_structure scr;
extern struct window_structure w[];

int width;
char left[255], right[255], chip[255];
char ch=' ',ext2=' ';
int i,x,y,orig_x,orig_y,temp_x,temp_y;
int insert=FALSE;
int letter=0,len_left=0, len_right=0;
int return_code;
int old_attribute=scr.current;
```

```
scr.current=attribute:        /* use specified attribute */
wherexy(&orig_x,&orig_y);   /* save original cursor position */
x=orig_x;y=orig_y;            /* set x,y to current cursor location */

hilight_field(x,y,inlength,attribute);   /* highlight input area */

width=scr.right-scr.left +1;  /* get the width of the window */

chip[0]= '\0'; left[0]= '\0';right[0]= '\0';

  strcpy(right,string);
  i=strlen(right);
  if(start>i)        /* break up string into left and right
                        components, depending on the requested
                        start position */
    chip_left(left,right,i);
  else
    chip_left(left,right,start);

print(x,y,left);        /* print left string*/
wherexy(&x,&y);         /* store cursor edit position */
print_here(right);      /* print right string */
gotoxy(x,,y);           /* move cursor back to edit location */

for (;;){     /* begin input cycle */
  ext2= 0; ch= 0;letter=0;

  len_left=strlen(left);      /* get string lengths */
  len_right = strlen(right);

  get_key(&ch,&ext2);

  if (ch >=32) letter =TRUE;

  if (ext2 == INSERT){       /* toggle inset/overtype mode */
    insert = !insert;
    if(insert) cursor(2);  /* make big cursor to show insert */
    else cursor(1);
 }

  if(len_right>0) trim_right(right); /* Trim trailing blanks
                                        so we avoid problems
                                        with the insert
                                        feature. */
len_left=strlen(left); len_right = strlen(right);

  if (!letter){            /* not regular letter */

  if (ext2 == LEFT && len_left >0){  /* if it is a left arrow */

    chip_right(chip,left,1);  /* remove end of left and */
    strcat(chip,right);        /* add to right           */
    strcpy(right,chip);
    x--; len_left--;
  }
```

```
if (ext2 == HOME && len_left >0){ /* home */
 strcat(left,right);       /* concat stings */
 strcpy(right,left);       /* copy combined strings to right */
 len_left = 0;             /* set left length variable to zero */
 len_right = len_left+len_right;  /* set new right length */
 left[0] ='\0';                     /* set left string to "" */
 x=orig_x; y=orig_y;  /* move cursor to beginning of field */
}

if (ext2 == END){            /* end */
 print (x,y,right);          /* print right part of string */
 wherexy(&x,&y);             /* get cursor location */
 strcat(left,right);         /* combine left and right in left */
  len_right = 0;             /* new length to be zero */
  len_left = len_left+len_right;   /* new right length */
 right[0] ='\0';                   /* right ="" */
}

if (ext2 == RIGHT && len_right> 0){  /* if it is right arrow */
 chip_left(chip,right,1);       /* chip left end off right string */
 strcat (left,chip);           /* add it to left string */
 x++;                 /* update cursor location */
 len_right++;         /* adjust length */
 gotoxy(x,y);         /* move cursor */
}
if (ext2 == DELETE && len_right >0){  /* delete */
 chip_left(chip,right,1); /* chip left end of right string */
 len_right--;            /* update length */
}

} /* end if not letter */
 if (ch == BACKSPACE && len_left >0) {    /* if it is backspace */
  chip_right(chip,left,1);     /* chip right end of left string */
  x--;                         /* up-date cursor */
  len_left--;                  /* up-date length */
}

  /* enter here if it is letter  */
   if (letter){

    /* insert mode on and no room for char */
    if ((insert && (len_left +len_right >= inlength))){
    putchar(BELL);  letter = 0;  /* no room for char */
    }
    else{
     if(insert){            /* insert mode on */
      x++;                  /* update cursor location */
      /* add char to string */
      left[len_left++] = ch; left[len_left]= '\0';
     }
     if(!insert){        /* in overtype mode */
        if( len_left ==inlength){    /* no room for character */
        putchar(BELL);                 /* "beep" the user */
```

```
      letter =0;
    }
    else
    {
    /* add new character, overtype old character */
    chip_left(chip,right,1);    /* chip off left end of
                                       right string */
    left[len_left++] = ch ;/* add new character */
    left[len_left]= '\0';
    len_right--;        /* record new right length */
    x++;
    }
  } /* not insert */

  }
}             /* end if (letter) */

    /* check for boundary conditions */

  if (x<1 && y == orig_y) x=1; else

  if (x<1){ y--; x=width;}
  if (x>width){    /* have we reached the end of the window ? */
    y++;x=1;
  }

  if (ext2 == LEFT !! ext2 = = RIGHT!! ext2 == HOME) gotoxy(x,y);

  /* if backspace or delete then redraw the line */
  if( ch == BACKSPACE !! ext2 == DELETE){
      gotoxy(x,y);
      temp_x=x; temp_y=y;
      /* print right string (don't move cursor) */
      dma_print(&temp_x,&temp_y,right);
      /* print  blanks to cover old trailing text */
      dma_print(&temp_x,&temp_y," ");
  }
      if (letter ){
        chip[0]=ch;chip[1]='\0'; /* turn character into string */
        print_here(chip);  /* print string at current location */
        wherexy(&x,&y);    /* get new location */
          if (insert){
            temp_x=x; temp_y=y;
            dma_print(&temp_x,&temp_y,right);
          }
        }

  if (ch==ESCAPE !! ext2 == UP !! ext2 == DOWN) break;
  if (ext2 == PGUP !! ext 2 == PGDN) break;
  if (ch==RETURN) break;

} /* end of for loop */
```

```
    switch(ext2){
     case UP  :return_code=UP;break;
     case DOWN:return_code=DOWN;break;
     case PGUP:return_code=PGUP;break;
     case PGDN:return_code=PGDN;break;
    }

   if (ch==RETURN) return_code = RETURN;
   if (ch==ESCAPE) return_code = ESCAPE;
    strcat(left,right);
    strcpy(string,left);
   cursor(NORMAL_CURSOR); /* set normal cursor */
   scr.current=old_attribute;
   return(return_code);

    }


/***************************************************************************

  Usage: static hilight_field (int x, int y, int length,
                               char attribute);

   int x,y =         column,row to place highlighted field.
   int length=       length of highlighted area.
   char *attribute= text attribute to use for highlighted area.

   Creates a highlighted area on the screen.

 ***************************************************************************/
void hilight_field (int x, int y, int length, char attribute)
{
extern struct  screen_structure scr;
extern struct window_structure w[];

char hilight [MAX_STRING];
int i;
char old_attribute=scr.current;  /* save current attribute */
scr.current=attribute;  /* set current attribute */

    for(i=0;i<length;i++){  /* build a string of blanks */
      hilight[i]=' ';
    }
    hilight[i]='\0'; /* terminate string */

    dma_print(&x,&y,hilight); /* use dma_print which does
                                   not move the cursor */

    scr.current=old_attribute; /* restore current attribute */

}
```

L_INPUT.C

```
/********************       L_INPUT.C       *************************/

#include "mydef.h"
#include "stdio.h"

/*******************************************************************

  Usage: int  input(struct in_struc in_scrn[]);

   in_scrn[] = a array of struct in_struc.

   Creates a data input screen based on the data structure in_scrn[].
   Allows full editing of input screen until the user presses "Enter"
   on the last field, or presses "PgUp", "PgDn" or "Esc".

 ********************************************************************/
int  input(struct in_struc in_scrn[])
{
extern struct  screen_structure scr;
extern struct window_structure w[];

int number=0;
int i,x,y,done=FALSE;
char old_current=scr.current; /* save current attribute */
char temp_attr;
char ext;
int val_code;

/* search for terminating zero in data structure */
for (;;){
 if (in_scrn[number++].x==0) break;
 if (number==1000) return(1);  /* count too high, must not
                                  have terminator */
}
number--;  /* reset to correct value */

  /* write field prompts and highlight input area */
  for(i=0;i<number;i++){
    x= in_scrn[i].x; y= in_scrn[i].y;   /* calc. x-y coordinates */

    if (scr.mode==COLOR_80) /*if color then set label x_attribute */
        scr.current= set_color(in_scrn[i].label_f,
                                in_scrn[i].label_b);

      else
       scr.current=scr.normal;

    print(x,y,in_scrn[i].prompt);    /* print input label */
```

```
   if (scr.mode==COLOR_80)
     scr.current = set_color(in_scrn[i].input_f,in_scrn[i].input_b);
   else
       scr.current = scr.inverse;

   x=x+strlen(in_scrn[i].prompt)+1; /* move past input label */
       hilight_field(x,y,in_scrn[i].length,scr.current);

   }
   print(x,y,in_scrn[i].ptr); /* show contents */
   /* At this point we have set up the screen,
      we now input the data. */

   }
   print(x,y,in_scrn[i].ptr); /* show contents */
   /* At this point we have set up the screen,
      we now input the data. */

   i=0;   /* use first field */

   /* this is the main loop in which editing occurs */
   while(!done){
     x= in_scrn[i].x; y=in_scrn[i].y;        /* get x,y coordinates */
     x=x+strlen(in_scrn[i].prompt )+1;       /* move past label */
/* set up field attribute */
       if (scr.mode==COLOR_80)
         scr.current = set_color(in_scrn[i].input_f,in_scrn[i].input_b);
         else
         scr.current=scr.inverse;

   for (;;){   /* loop until a valid field is read */
      gotoxy(x,y);
      /* get the string */
      ext=getfield(in_scrn[i].ptr,in_scrn[i].length,0,scr.current);

      if (ext==ESCAPE) break; /* don't validate if Escape pressed */

      /* validate the field */

      temp_attr=scr.current;   /* save our attribute */

      /* validate data entered */
      val_code=val_field(in_scrn[i].ptr,in_scrn[i].length,i);
      scr.current=temp_attr;

          if (val_code==REDO) putchar(BELL);
          if (val_code==OK) break;

      if (val_code==REDRAW) {          /* redraw field is requested */
         /* highlight input field to erase current contents */
         hilight_field(x,y,in_scrn[i].length,scr.current);
         print (x,y,in_scrn[i].ptr); /* print new contents */
         break;
      }
   }   /* end for(;;) */

      if (ext== UP) i--;
      if(ext== DOWN!! ext==RETURN) i++;
```

```
        if(ext== ESCAPE || ext== PGUP || ext==PGDN) break;

        if (i==number && ext==RETURN ){        /* last field? */
          ext=RETURN;
          break;
        }
        if (i<0) i=(number-1);    /* check boundary conditions */
        if (i> (number-1)) i=0;

        }    /*end while (!done)*/

    scr.current=old_current;
    return(ext);
}
```

L_CHIP.C

```
/********************        L_CHIP.C        ************************/

#include "mydef.h"

/******************************************************************

Usage: void chip_left(char *chip,char *block,int number);

  char *chip  = string to receive characters.
  char *block = string to lose characters.
  int  number = number of characters to move.

 Takes a "chip off the old block", removing characters from the
 left side of "block" and placing them in "chip".

  Example: block= "this is a test"
           chip= ""
           chip_left(&chip,&block,4);

           results: chip= "this"
           block= " is a test"
********************************************************************/

void chip_left(char *chip,char *block,int number)
{
char temp[MAX_STRING];

strcpy(chip,"\0");
 if (number <1 ) return;    /* nothing to chip */
 /* are we trying to chip too much off block? */
 if (number > strlen(block)) number=strlen(block);
 strcpy (temp,block);
 copy (block,chip,0,number);
 copy(block,temp,number,strlen(block)-number);
 strcpy (block,temp);
 return;
}
```

```
/ ********************************************************************
  Usage: void chip_right(char *chip,char *block,int number);

    char *chip  = string to receive characters.
    char *block = string to lose characters.
    int  number = number of characters to move.

    Works just like chip_left() but moves characters from the
    right side.

 ********************************************************************/
void chip_right(char *chip,char *block, int number)
{
char temp[MAX_STRING];
strcpy(chip,"\n");
if (number <1 || number >strlen(block))return;
copy(block,chip,strlen(block)-number,number);
copy (block,block,0,strlen(block)-number);
return;
}
```

L_COPY.C

```
/ *********************            L_COPY.C           *********************/

#include "mydef.h"

/ ********************************************************************
  Usage: void copy (char *from,char *to,int first,int length);

    char *from  = string to copy from.
    char *to    = string to copy to.
    int  first  = position within string to start copying.
    int  length = number of character to copy.

    Copies a section of text, beginning at position "first" in
    string "from" and copies "length" number to string "to".
    (zero based counting, begins at zero not one)

    Example: copy ("test",&to 1,2);
             results: to = "es"

 ********************************************************************/
void copy (char *from,char *to,int first,int length)
{
int i;
 if ( (first <0) ) return; /*  invalid number */
```

```
/* if attempt made to copy beyond end of string then adjust*/
if((first+length+1 ) > strlen(from))length=strlen(from)-first ;

 for(i=0;i<length;i++)
  to[i]= from[(first)+i];
 to[i]='\0';
}
```

L_TRIM.C

```
/********************     L_TRIM.C      **************************/

#include "mydef.h"

/**********************************************************************

 Usage: void make_string(char *string,char letter,int count);

  char *string = pointer to string to build.
  char letter  = letter to replicate.
  int count    = length of string.

  Builds a string consisting only of the character specified
  by "ch". The string is the length specified by "count".

  Example: make_string (string,'x',10);
          results: string = "xxxxxx"

**********************************************************************/
void make_string(char *string,char letter,int count)
{
int j;
for (j=0;j<count;j++) string[j]=letter;
string[j]='\0';
}

/**********************************************************************

 Usage: void trim_left(char *string)

  char *string = string to strip of left spaces.

  Removes all the leftmost spaces from the string specified by
  "string".

**********************************************************************/

void trim_left(char *string)
{
```

```
int i=0;
int j=0;

if (!strlen(string)) return;

while(string[i]== ' ' && string[i] != '\0') i++;

while (string[i] != '\0')
 string[j++]= string[i++];

string[j]='\0';
}
```

```
/******************************************************************

 Usage: void trim_right(char *string);

  char *string = string to strip of right spaces.

  Removes all the rightmost spaces from the string specified by
  "string".

 ******************************************************************/
void trim_right(char *string)
{
int pos;
pos = strlen(string)-1;
  while(string[pos]==' '){
   string[pos--]= '\0';
   if (pos < 0) break;
  }
}
```

```
/******************************************************************

Usage: void trim(char *string)

 char *string = string to strip of left and right spaces.

 Removes all the leftmost and rightmost spaces from the string
 specified by "string".

 ******************************************************************/
void trim(char *string)
{
trim_left(string);
trim_right(string);
}
```

Chapter 5

List Selection

In this chapter we will:

- Create a list selection function with both point-and-shoot and speed search features.

INTRODUCTION

In Chapter 3 we saw how the menus that we created could be used for simple list selection if they were used to return a number, as opposed to automatically calling functions. There were two important limitations with this technique:

- The items had to be hard-wired into the application, and could not be changed at run-time.
- The items offered for selection had to fit within the menu window. It was not possible to page through a list of options that was longer than the window.

With these limitations in mind, we will create an improved system which allows far more flexibility and which will permit us to build a directory function in Chapter 6.

GOALS

We want our menu options to be displayed vertically within a window, with the first option highlighted. The user may point to any option by moving the highlighter with the cursor keys. When the highlighter reaches the bottom of the window, the window scrolls up one line and a new option appears at the bottom of the window. The user may also use the PgUp and PgDn keys to rapidly move through the list of options a page (or window) at a time.

Alternately, the user may *speed search* by starting to type the name of the option, and the highlighter will automatically jump to the option which most closely matches the user input. When the desired option is highlighted, the user presses Enter to make the selection, and an integer representing the item is returned to the calling function. Speed searching is very useful when the name of the option is known and there are many options to choose from. Without speed search, the user would be forced to page to the desired option.

The user may press Escape to exit the list select window without making a selection.

On the surface, this sounds very much like a pop-up menu. There are several important differences to keep in mind.

- The list-select function cannot directly call functions; it only returns the number of the option selected.
- The number of possible options is limited only by the available memory. An unlimited number of options may be displayed via paging.
- The options list may be created at any time, unlike menus whose options must be known at the time of compilation. Lists may be constructed from information provided by the user, or from data read from attached devices, such as file names read from a disk drive.
- Quick keys (single key selection based on the capitalized letter within an option) are not used. If a list contained hundreds of options, there would not be enough letters to go around. Instead, the speed search feature allows the user to start typing out the name of an option, and the most closely matching option is highlighted.

APPLICATION

The list selection function is **list_select( )** and is found in the library module L_list.c. The function prototype for **list_select( )** is:

```
int list_select (char *ptr[]);
char *ptr[]= Array of pointers.
```

The function returns the number of the option selected. A return value of -1 indicates that no selection was made (i.e., the user pressed Escape). The steps required to utilize the list selection function **list_select( )** are:

- Create an array of pointers, each element of which points to a string representing the option. The last pointer in the array should be set to NULL to mark the end of the list.
- Create the window in which the list is to appear. If no window is specifically created, the active top window is used by **list_select( )**.
- Call **list_select( )** and give it the address of the array as in the following statement.

```
selection=list_select(ptr);
```

To demonstrate how the function **list_select( )** can be integrated into an application, let's look at the sample program listdemo.c, found in the Source Code section. The following array of pointers is created by the demo program list-demo.c:

```
char *ptr[11]= {
              "Apple   ", "Boat      ", "Berry      ",
              "Car     ", "Computer ", "Denver     ",
              "Donut   ", "Dog       ", "Elephant   ",
              "Egg     ", NULL
              };
```

A window is made in which the list will appear, and then the function **list_select( )** is called:

```
select_win= win_make(1,2,10,5,STD_FRAME,"",scr.normal,scr.normal);
selection=list_select(ptr);
```

In this demo, options are displayed in a window with ten columns and five rows. Of course, by adjusting the appropriate parameters in **win_make( )**, the width and length of the window can be customized to occupy a greater or lesser portion of the screen.

TECHNIQUES

In this section we will concentrate on two portions of code for the function **list_select( )**. One portion deals with the point-and-shoot process, and the other deals with the speed search feature.

The first task for **list_select( )** is to scan the array of pointers, and set the variable **last** to the number of the last valid option. There are three important variables used to create and manipulate this display. The variable **top_opt** represents the first option in the window, **current_opt** represents the highlighted option, and **offset** represents the distance between the two. The initial values are **top_opt** = 0, **current_opt** = 0, and **offset** = 0.

A conditional loop within **list_select( )** prints the options whenever the variable **redraw** is set to TRUE. Since **redraw** is initially set to TRUE, the drawing of the window occurs immediately.

The actual screen image produced by the program listdemo.c is shown in Figure 5–1 and has been magnified to show the window. The function now evaluates user input and mode of selection, and moves the highlighter or pages the display in response. Since **list_select( )** operates in two distinct modes, point-and-shoot and speed search, we will examine each mode separately.

Point-and-Shoot

In this mode, the user may move the highlighter through the options list by pressing the cursor keys, or may press the PgUp or PgDn key to view a new windowfull of options.

Given the window shown in Figure 5–1, let's assume the user presses the Down cursor key. The variable **current_opt** is increased by 1 and the window is updated to reflect the movement of the highlighter.

Figure 5–1   Screen image produced by listdemo.c

The easiest way to update the window would be to set the variable **redraw** to TRUE and have all the options reprinted. However, why waste time reprinting all the options when only two changes are required? Instead, the previously highlighted option is rewritten with the highlighting turned off, and the new current option is printed with highlighting turned on. In this case we print two options, as illustrated in Figure 5–2, as opposed to the five options required to redraw the entire window. If the options were displayed in a larger window, say with 23 options, even more time would be saved.

```
Apple          ← redraw this line without highlighting
Boat           ← redraw with highlighting
Berry
Car
Computer
```

Figure 5–2   Redrawing the highlighter

Much more screen manipulation is necessary when the highlighter is at the bottom of the options window and the Down cursor key is pressed. The screen must be scrolled up and a new option added to the bottom of the window. Before scrolling the window up, the currently highlighted option must be unhighlighted. Now, in Figure 5–3, **top_opt** = 1 and **current_opt** = 5.

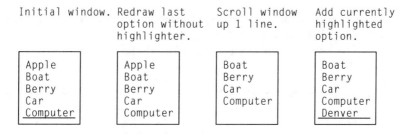

Figure 5–3 Redrawing and scrolling

The same technique (with downward scrolling of window contents) is used when the cursor is at the top of the window and the Up cursor is pressed. The window is not scrolled if there are no more options to display; such would be the case at the beginning or end of the options list.

If the user presses the PgDn key, an entire windowfull of new options is displayed in the window. Assume that we have the options window shown in Figure 5–4. In order to display the next page, we add the height of the window to **top_opt** (top_opt + = height;). We want the highlighter to remain in the same relative position, so we set **current_opt** to **top_opt** plus **offset**, thus: current_opt = top_opt + offset;.

```
┌──────────┐   top_opt      = 0
│ Apple    │   current_opt  = 1
│ Boat     │   offset       = 1
│ Berry    │
│ Car      │
│ Computer │
└──────────┘                   Figure 5–4  Display before paging
```

The variable **redraw** is set to TRUE and the window shown in Figure 5–5 is produced. A similar technique is used when PgUp is pressed.

```
┌──────────┐   top_opt      = 5
│ Denver   │   current_opt  = 6
│ Donut    │   offset       = 1
│ Dog      │
│ Elephant │
│ Egg      │
└──────────┘                   Figure 5–5  Display after paging
```

The techniques used for point-and-shoot are quite simple, which probably explains why point-and-shoot selection is standard on so many applications. The programming is considerably more complex when dealing with speed searching, but the user will appreciate the time-saving results of your efforts.

Speed Search

The concept of programming a speed search is to take text input from the keyboard and to highlight options that match the text.

The key variables that we use for this task are:

```
char ch;                    /*  character read from keyboard */
char search[MAX_STRING]; /* a string built out of characters
                                read from keyboard */
int sub_search=0;           /* index to character within "search"
                                string */
int sub_option=0;           /* index to character within
                                highighted option */
```

The string **search** is filled in with the text entered by the user. The variable **sub_search** is an index to the current position within **search** and the variable **sub_option** is an index to a letter within the currently highlighted option.

Initially, both **sub_search** and **sub_option** are set to 0. The speed search feature is activated when the user presses a character key (as opposed to a cursor key or page key). At this point, we assume the user is typing the name of an option. Let's look at a specific example using the demo program listdemo.c.

Assume that we have the screen and variables that appear in Figure 5–6. The user touches the "b" key and the character is stored in the variable **ch.** The list of options is scanned, comparing the letter in **ch** to the first letter in each option. Letters are compared in uppercase form and leading spaces are ignored.

In this example, the first letter of the option "Boat" matches the letter in the variable **ch** so the highlighter is moved to the option "Boat". The window is paged to the matching option if that option is not currently displayed.

The letter stored in **ch** is added to the **search** string. The index variables **sub_search** and **sub_option** are both increased by one, since we have matched the first letter and are now ready to examine the second letter. Although in this example, **sub_search** and **sub_option** have identical values, this would not be true if the highlighted option had leading spaces. When leading spaces are present,

```
 Apple
 Boat        sub_search = 0
 Berry       sub_option = 0
 Car         search     = ""
 Computer    ch         = 'b'
```

Figure 5–6 Speed search: initial screen and variables

sub_option is adjusted to indicate the position of the first *real* characters (not blanks).

After these changes, the screen display and variables now appear as in Figure 5–7. If "Boat" were the option the user wanted, the Enter key could be pressed to make the selection.

```
┌─────────┐      sub_search  = 1
│ Apple   │      sub_option  = 1
│ Boat    │      search      = "b"
│ Berry   │      ch          = 'b'
│ Car     │
│ Computer│
└─────────┘
```

Figure 5–7 Speed search: screen and variables after update

Let's assume the user does not want the option "Boat", and so now presses the letter "e". We are not dealing with the first letter of a search operation and the logic flow is somewhat different. Since we already matched the first letter ("b"), we must see if the new letter ("e") matches the second letter of the currently highlighted option. When we examine the second real character of the option "Boat" (indicated by **sub_option**), we see that the match fails.

When the match fails on the current option, we must scan the entire list of options, starting at the beginning, to see if the text entered by the user matches any other options. Before doing this, we must finish building the string **search** by adding the new letter and the '\0' terminator. We now have what is shown in Figure 5–8.

```
┌─────────┐      sub_search  = 1
│ Apple   │      sub_option  = 1
│ Boat    │      search      = "be"
│ Berry   │      ch          = 'e'
│ Car     │
│ Computer│
└─────────┘
```

Figure 5–8 Speed search: search fails at current option

We will perform the search for "be" using the function **pos( )** which is found in the library module Lstring.c. The prototype for **pos( )** is:

```
int pos(char *string,char *pattern);
```

*string   = String to search.

*pattern   = Substring to find.

return value = The offset within string of pattern. The integer −1 is returned if no match is found. (Case is ignored when comparing text.)

For example, after the call "x = pos("this is a test", "TEST");", the variable **x** would equal 10.

In our example, we now utilize **pos( )** to scan the options list to discover if any other options begin with "be". The option "Berry" begins with "be", and the screen is adjusted to highlight that option, as shown in Figure 5–9. Had the option "Berry" not existed, all our searches would have failed and the variables would be reset, ready to begin the next search. The search would also reset if a noncharacter key, such as PgUp or Back Space, were pressed.

```
Apple       sub_search  = 2
Boat        sub_option  = 2
Berry       search      = "be"
Car         ch          = 'e'
Computer
```

Figure 5–9 Speed search: screen adjusted for current best match

The speed search feature is not particularly useful for such a small list of options as we used in our example. However, speed search really proves its worth when searching a large list, such as a list of clients, students, products, or a DOS directory listing.

In the next chapter, we will use **list_select( )** to build a DOS file selection (directory) function.

SOURCE CODE

LISTDEMO.C

```
/*********************** LISTDEMO.C ****************************/

#include "mydef.h"
#include <stddef.h>

int start(void)          /* start is the entry point */
{
extern struct screen_structure scr;
extern struct window_structure w[];

char string[30];
int select_win;
int selection;
char *ptr[11]= {
                    "Apple     ", "Boat       ", "Berry     ",
                    "Car       ", "Computer   ", "Denver    ",
                    "Donut     ", "Dog        ", "Elephant  ",
                    "Egg       ", NULL
                    };

cls();

select_win= win_make(1,2,10,5,STD_FRAME,"",scr.normal,scr.normal);
```

```
selection=list_select(ptr);

win_delete(select_win);

  if (selection==-1) print(1,1,"No selection made");
   else {
     sprintf(string,"Item number %i was selected",selection);
     print(1,1,string);
   }

return(0);
 }
```

L_LIST.C

```
/************************* L_LIST.C *************************/
#include "mydef.h"    /* always include this */
#include "stddef.h"   /* we need the definition of NULL from here */
#include "dos.h"      /* directory related header files */

#include "stdio.h"
#include "string.h"

/* load memory allocation header files for specific compiler */

#if defined QUICKC

#include "malloc.h"
#include "memory.h"

#endif

#if defined TURBOC

#include "alloc.h"
#include "mem.h"
#include "stdlib.h"
#include "dir.h"

#endif

/********************************************************************

 Usage: int list_select (char *ptr[]);

        char *ptr[]= Array of pointers, each of which points to
                     an option. The pointer following the last
                     option must be NULL.
```

This function allows selection from a list of options. The user
may point to the option using the Up/Down cursor keys, and select
by pressing Enter. Pressing Escape exits without making a selection.

The user may also Speed Search by typing in the option. As the
user types in the text, the option most closely matching the typed
text is highlighted. Actual selection must still be made by
pressing Enter.

The number corresponding to the selection is return. A -1
indicates the user pressed Escape without making a selection.


```
*****************************************************************/

int list_select (char *ptr[])
{
extern struct  screen_structure scr;
extern struct window_structure w[];

int current_opt=0;      /* highlighted current option */
int top_opt=0;          /* first option in window */
int offset=0;           /* distance between top_opt and current_opt */
int last_opt;           /* the last option which was highlighted */
int height;             /* height of the window */
int last=0;             /* last element in pointer array */
int i=0,y,j=0;          /* general purpose */
char ch,ext;            /* character and extension*/
int sub_search=0;       /* index for location within search string */
int sub_option=0 ;      /* index for location within list options */
char search[MAX_STRING]; /* holds the speedsearch characters */
int redraw=TRUE;             /* flag which forces a redraw of selection
                                  window */
int start,end;             /* pre-existing start end scan lines */
height = scr.bottom-scr.top +1;   /* height of selection window */

/* find out how many options are in the NULL terminated
   array of pointers */

for(last=0;ptr[last++]!NULL;);
last-=2;     /* decrease by one so "last"
                 now indicates the last option */

scr.current=scr.normal;
what_cursor(&start,&end);

/* draw initial window */

cursor(NO_CURSOR); /* turn off cursor */
y=1;

/* begin loop to process use selection */
```

```
for(;;){

  if(redraw){        /* redraw the window contents */
  alt_screen(ON); /* turn on alternate screen so that
                      redraw appears to be instantaneous */
  cls();
  y=1;      /* y location (row) to print option */
  scr.current=scr.normal;        /* start with normal attribute */

    for(i=top_opt;i<top_opt+height;i++){
    if (ptr[i]==NULL) break;        /* stop if we go too far */
     if (i==current_opt)scr.current=scr.inverse;

      /* highlight current option */
      print (1,y++,ptr[i]);
      scr.current=scr.normal;     /* reset to normal */
    }
  alt_screen(OFF);
  redraw=FALSE;
  } /* end if (redraw) */

ch='\0';ext='\0';        /* reset character and extension */
get_key( &ch, &ext);     /* get character and extension */

/* scan list of options match search key */

/* make sure we have a valid letter, number or punctuation */
if (ch>=32 && ch <=126 ) {

/* here we search to find match for speed search letters */
last_opt=current_opt;        /* save the highlight position */

if(sub_search==0){        /* are we looking for the first letter
                             of the word? */
  for(i=0;i<=last;i++){  /* scan each list option */
    sub_option=0;     /* look for the first letter within option */
    while(ptr[i][sub_option]==' ') sub_option++; /* skip spaces */

      if(toupper(ptr[i][sub_option])==toupper(ch)){ /* match*/
          search[sub_search]=ch;  /* add it to the speed search
                                      string */
          offset=current_opt-top_opt;  /* difference between window
                                          top and highlighter */
          current_opt=i;        /* set current_opt to option found */
          sub_search++;         /* reposition indexes within search*/
          sub_option++;         /* string and option */

          break;
      }
  } /* end scan each list option */
} /* end first letter */
else{    /* No longer the first letter. */
```

```
                         The next loop examines further letters within the
                         current highlighted option to see if they still
                         match ch.*/

      if(toupper(ptr[current_opt][sub_option]) != toupper(ch)){
            /* Match with current highlighted option fails.
               Scan list to see if we can match string elsewhere. */

         search[sub_search]=ch;   /* finish building string */
         search[sub_search+1]='\0';
         sub_search=0;      /* reset to begin search at first letter */

          /* see us a match exists anywhere else */

          for(i=0;i<=last;i++){     /* examine each option */
            sub_option=0;            /* start at beginning of
                                          each option */
            while(ptr[i][sub_option]==' ') /* skip space */
               sub_option++;

               j=pos(&ptr[i][sub_option],search); /* is search string
                                                         in option? */
               if (j==0){                     /* search string found */
                 offset=current_opt-top_opt;  /* calculate distance
                                                    (top to current)*/
                 current_opt=i;
                 sub_search=strlen(search);
                 sub_option=j+strlen(search);
                 break;
               }
          } /* end (examine each option) */
      } /* end failed to match within current option */
        else
         {   /* current option still matches search key */
           search[sub_search]=ch;
           sub_search++;
         }
      } /* end of (not first letter) */

   /*the following code moves the highlighter or
     requests a redraw as needed */

         /* is new selection beyond window? */

         if(current_opt >top_opt+ height-1 || current_opt < top_opt){
            top_opt=current_opt-offset;   /* keep the offset the same */
            if (top_opt <0) top_opt=0;    /* correct if off top of window */
            redraw=TRUE;                  /* redraw window */
         } else{
```

```
                    /* new option is within displayed page */
                    /* un-highlight old position and redraw highlight */
        scr.current=scr.normal;   /* over-write highlighter with
                                        normal attribute */
        print(1,last_opt-top_opt+1,ptr[last_opt]);

        scr.current=scr.inverse;   /* print new highlighter */
        print(1,current_opt-top_opt+1,ptr[current_opt]);
      }


}  /* end valid letter */

else  /* not valid letter */
{
  sub_search=0;   /* reset sub_search to look for first letter */

    if(ch==RETURN !! ch==ESCAPE){  /* selection made or Escape key */
        scr.current= scr.normal;
        set_cursor(start,end);
      if (ch==RETURN) return(current_opt); /* item selected */
        else
          return(-1);              /* no selection */
    }
      y=current_opt-top_opt+1;     /* y = distance from top of window
                                        to highlighter */

  /* down arrow and not at bottom of window */
  if (ext==DOWN && y<height && current_opt<last ){
    /* overwrite highlighter with normal attribute */
    scr.current=scr.normal;
    print(1,y,ptr[current_opt]);

    scr.current=scr.inverse;
    current_opt++;                          /* increment list pointer */
    print(1,y+1,ptr[current_opt]);   /* print new highlighter */
  }
    else   /* down arrow and bottom of window */

  if (ext==DOWN && y==height && current_opt<last){

    /* rewrite current line with normal attribute */
    scr.current=scr.normal;
    print(1,y,ptr[current_opt]);
    scroll_up (1);                         /* scroll window up */
    current_opt++;                         /* increment positions */
    top_opt++;
    scr.current=scr.inverse;               /* print a new highlighter */
    print(1,y,ptr[current_opt]);
  }
```

```
    if (ext==UP && y>1){    /* up arrow and not at top of window */
      /* rewrite current line with normal attribute */
      scr.current=scr.normal;
      print(1,y,ptr[current_opt]);

      scr.current=scr.inverse;
      current_opt--;                    /* increment list pointer */
      print(1,y-1,ptr[current_opt]); /* print new highlighter */
    } else
    if (ext==UP && y==1 && current_opt>0){  /* up arrow and top
                                                of window */
    /* rewrite current line with normal attribute */
     scr.current=scr.normal;
     print(1,y,ptr[current_opt]);
     scroll_down (1);                        /* scroll window down */
     current_opt--;                          /* move current_opt back */
     top_opt--;

       scr.current=scr.inverse;          /* print new highlighter */
      print(1,y-1,ptr[current_opt]);
    }

  /* page down and not at end of selection list */
  if(ext==PGDN && top_opt!= last) {
  offset=current_opt-top_opt; /* how far is the highlighter
                                 from the top of window? */
  top_opt+=height;              /* increase top_opt by the height
                                 of screen */
  current_opt=top_opt+offset; /* increase current_opt for
                                 new location */
   /* check for boundary errors */
  if(top_opt>last) top_opt=last;
  if(current_opt>last) current_opt=last;
  redraw=TRUE;  /* force a redraw of list options */

  }
  if(ext==PGUP && top_opt !=0){  /* PgUp pressed and not at top
                                    of window */
    offset=current_opt-top_opt;  /* move all positions up */
    top_opt-=height;
    current_opt=top_opt+offset;

    if(top_opt<0){      /* out of bounds ?*/
     top_opt=0;         /* reset */
     current_opt=offset;
    }
    redraw=TRUE;

  } /* end ext==PGUP */
  } /* end of not valid letter */

 } /* end of for(;;) loop which reads user selection*/
 }
```

L_STRING.C

```
/************************** L_STRING.C **************************/

#include "mydef.h"

/***************************************************************

  Usage: int pos(char *string, char *pattern)

   char *string= string to search.

   char *pattern= text to search for.

   Returns an integer value representing the location of
   pattern within string.

   Example:   string= "this is a test"
              i=  pos(&string,'test');

              results: i=10

 ***************************************************************/

int pos(char *string,char *pattern)

{
   int i,j,found=0;

    for(i=0;i<= strlen(string)-strlen(pattern);i++){

     /* find first location */
     if (toupper(string[i]) == toupper(pattern[0])){
      found=1;

        for (j=1;j<=strlen(pattern)-1;j++){
           if (toupper(string[i+j]) != toupper(pattern[j])) {
           found=0;
           break;
           }
        }
     }
     if(found) return (i);
    }
return (-1);
}


/***************************************************************

  Usage: int caps(char *string);
```

```
char *string= string to make upper case

Converts all letters in string to uppercase.

******************************************************************/
/***CAPS***/
void caps(char *string)
{
 int i;

 for (i=0;string[i] != '\0';i++) string[i]= toupper(string[i]);
}
```

Chapter 6

Directories

In this chapter we will:

- Discuss the techniques used to read directory information.
- Create a function for selecting files from a given directory.

INTRODUCTION

Displaying and selecting files from a directory is a task familiar to most programmers. Some programmers provide absolutely no directory access or information within their applications, which forces the user to guess at file names or exit to DOS to view the directory. Other programmers make use of the *system* command, such as "system ("dir *.*");" to print the directory on the screen. The system command loads a copy of command.com which processes the command. Once the directory is displayed, the user types in the desired file name.

Many of today's commercial applications use a point-and-shoot technique to allow users to select options from a directory window. This is a versatile, attractive, and efficient technique which we will emulate.

GOALS

We will create a file select function which allows the user to make selections from a list of files, using one of two methods. Please refer to Chapter 5 for a detailed discussion of how these two methods work. Here, we will focus on techniques for retrieval and selection of information from DOS directories.

Point-and-shoot.   The user moves the highlighter to the desired option and presses Enter.

Speed Search.   The user begins to type the name of the desired file and the highlighter automatically moves to the file which matches the text. When the proper file is highlighted, the user presses Enter.

APPLICATION

The directory function is **dir( )** and is found in the library module L_dir.c The prototype for **dir( )** is:

```
int dir(char *filespec, char *selection);
```

char *filespec   = Wildcard specification for the path and files (e.g., *.*, *.c, and so on).

char *selection = Pointer to a location suitable for storage of a 13-character array. The name of the selected file is copied to this location. If the user presses Escape, no selection is made and **selection** = " ".

Before calling **dir( )**, create a directory window with a width of at least 12 columns. The 12 columns will accommodate the maximum width of a DOS file name; that is, an 8-character file name plus the period ('.') that separates the file name from the 3-character extension. If no window is created, the active window is used.

The following lines from dir_demo.c create the directory window and call **dir( )**.

```
dir_win= win_make(35,2,12,20,STD_FRAME,"",scr.normal,scr.normal);
dir("*.*",selection);
```

As you can see, this is a very easy function to use. Shown in Figure 6–1 is an actual screen capture of the dir_demo.c display. The program dir-demo.c, found in the Source Code section demonstrates the use of **dir( )**.

Another function found in the L_dir.c module is **file_count( )**.

```
int file_count(char *filespec);
```

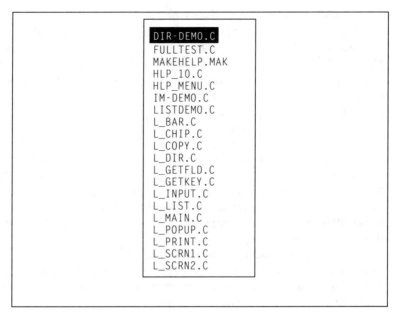

```
DIR-DEMO.C
FULLTEST.C
MAKEHELP.MAK
HLP_10.C
HLP_MENU.C
IM-DEMO.C
LISTDEMO.C
L_BAR.C
L_CHIP.C
L_COPY.C
L_DIR.C
L_GETFLD.C
L_GETKEY.C
L_INPUT.C
L_LIST.C
L_MAIN.C
L_POPUP.C
L_PRINT.C
L_SCRN1.C
L_SCRN2.C
```

Figure 6–1 Screen capture of dir__demo.c

The function **file_count( )** returns the number of directory entries which match the file specification. This function is used by **dir( )**, but may be accessed by other functions.

TECHNIQUES

The **dir( )** function gives us an excellent opportunity to use the function **list_select( )** to display the directory and process user input. Before calling **list_select( )**, we must create the array of pointers to each file name.

The quickest way to create an array of pointers is to define an array of pointers to characters:

```
char *list[600];
```

Once the array is created, memory can be allocated for each file name in the directory:

```
list[i]= (char *) malloc(DIR_NAME_LENGTH*sizeof(char));
```

DIR_NAME_LENGTH is the maximum length of a directory entry (equals 13, including the 12 characters possible in a DOS file name plus the '\0' string terminator).

A problem sometimes arises when a large array is created within a function. By default, such allocations have a "volatile" storage class; that is, their memory is allocated upon entry to the function and de-allocated when the function terminates. Some compilers store these variables in the *stack*. Stack space is usually limited—typically only about 4000 bytes for Turbo C and QuickC. Creation of large arrays could cause unexpected stack errors, especially with highly recursive programs.

A relatively undesirable way to remedy this problem would be to set the stack to a larger size or to make the pointer array of *external* or *static* storage class (which would not be stored in the stack). Using either of these options would be wasteful of memory since we don't need this extra memory except when we are reading the directory. A better approach is to allocate the memory when we need it, and release it when done. The only slight problem is that we must allocate the array of pointers in a contiguous unit (in other words, it must be large enough to hold a pointer to each directory entry).

A fast, albeit memory-inefficient approach, would be to allocate a section of memory large enough to hold all the pointers we anticipate. If we assume that MAX_DIR is defined as the maximum number of directory entries we might expect, we could use the following technique:

```
char **list;      /* a pointer to a character pointer */
/* allocate memory */

list =(char **)malloc (MAX_DIR*sizeof(char *));
```

We could then allocate space for individual file names as needed.

```
/* allocate memory */
list[i]= malloc (DIR_NAME_LENGTH*sizeof(char));
```

There are several disadvantages to this technique. If we underestimate the number of directory entries, the directory function will not operate correctly. If we make the pointer array excessively large, we waste memory.

Another approach, which solves these problems and which we will use, is to:

1. Scan the directory and count the number of files.
2. Allocate the memory for the array of pointers.
3. Allocate memory for each file name (which the array of pointers points to).
4. Then scan the directory again, copying the file names to their allocated memory.

As you see, this technique requires scanning the directories twice via DOS. This slows down the process only very slightly, and it is much more memory-efficient than the other technique mentioned earlier.

Both Turbo C and QuickC have library functions which can obtain file names from a given directory. These functions fall into the category of MS-DOS Extensions and are not part of ANSI C. Their names and calling conventions differ in Turbo C and QuickC. We must resort to conditional compilation statements (of the form #if defined TURBOC or #if defined QUICKC) to handle the differences.

Under both compilers, obtaining file names is a two-step process. One must find the first directory entry, and then find subsequent entries, as shown in Table 6–1. The functions **findfirst( )** and **_dos_findfirst( )** each take three parameters:

File specification   = Such as *.c or myfile.dat.

File attribute   = Hidden, read-only, archive, and system.

Disk Transfer Area = A location at which the function will store the directory information.

TABLE 6–1. FUNCTIONS FOR FINDING FIRST DIRECTORY ENTRY

Objective	Turbo C	QuickC
Find the first entry	findfirst()	_dos_findfirst()
Find subsequent entries	findsecond()	_dos_findnext()

The Disk Transfer Area or DTA has a very specific structure which is defined as in Table 6–2. We assign these structures in L_dir.c as follows:

```
#if defined TURBOC
 struct ffblk DTA;
#endif

#if defined QUICKC
 struct find_t DTA;
#endif
```

TABLE 6–2. THE DISK TRANSFER AREA STRUCTURE

Turbo C	QuickC
`struct ffblk {`	`struct find_t {`
`    char      ff_reserved[21];`	`    char reserved[21];`
`    char      ff_attrib;`	`    char attrib;`
`    unsigned ff_ftime;`	`    unsigned wr_time;`
`    unsigned ff_fdate;`	`    unsigned wr_date;`
`    long      ff_fsize;`	`    long size;`
`    char      ff_name[13];`	`    char name[13];`
`};`	`};`

We then call the appropriate compiler-specific function to obtain the first directory name:

```
#if defined TURBOC
  done=findfirst(filespec,&DTA,0);
#endif

#if defined QUICKC
  done=_dos_findfirst(filespec,_A_NORMAL,&DTA);
#endif
```

Not only do the names differ between the two compiler functions, but they also use different parameter sequences. In the Turbo C **findfirst( )** the DTA is the second parameter; in the QuickC **_dos_findfirst( )** the DTA is the last parameter. A *normal* file attribute is specified in both cases. For **findfirst( )** it is 0; for **_dos_findfirst( )** it is defined as **_A_NORMAL**. See your compiler manual for lists of all the attributes.

Both functions return a 0 if an entry is found; otherwise they return an error code. If an entry is found, the file name, date, and other file-related information are stored in the DTA. We can extract the file name from the DTA and store it in our list of files.

```
#if defined TURBOC
    sprintf(list[i],"%-12s",DTA.ff_name);
#endif

#if defined QUICKC
    sprintf(list[i],"%-12s",DTA.name);
#endif
```

If we succeed in finding one file name matching the file specification, we can look for others:

```
#if defined TURBOC
  done=findnext(&DTA);
#endif

#if defined QUICKC
  done=_dos_findnext(&DTA);
#endif
```

Once the last file name is found, the array of pointers is sent to **list_select( )**. The function **list_select( )** returns the number of the option selected by the user, and the name of the file is copied to **selection.** After freeing up the allocated memory, **dir( )** exits.

Although **dir( )** only displays file names, other information such as the file attribute, size, and date are stored in DTA. The **sprintf** statement could easily be modified so that this information is displayed as well. If you make such changes, don't forget to increase the size of DIR_NAME_LENGTH so that enough memory is allocated for the string, and increase the size of the window accordingly.

The function **file_count( )** is internally very similar to **dir( )**. The main difference is that it does not process the DTA information, but instead counts the number of files matching the file specification.

CONCLUSION

A point-and-shoot directory function gives a more professional look to any application. Note how the modular design of our functions made it especially easy for us to integrate the list select function into the design of our directory function.

SOURCE CODE

DIR-DEMO.C

```
/*************************  DIR-DEMO.C  **************************/
#include "mydef.h"
#include <stddef.h>

int start(void)
{
extern struct screen_structure scr;
extern struct window_structure w[];

int dir_win;         /* handle for directory window */
char selection[13]; /* string to receive the name of file selected */

cls();

dir_win= win_make(35,2,12,20,STD_FRAME,"",scr.normal,scr.normal);

dir("*.*",selection);
win_delete(dir_win);

if (strlen(selection)==0) print (1,1, "No file selected.");
 else
   print(1,1,"The selected file was "); print_here(selection);

return(0);
}
```

L_DIR.C

```
/************************** L_DIR.C **************************/

#include "mydef.h"
#include "stddef.h"
#include "dos.h"
#include "stdio.h"

#define DIR_NAME_LENGTH 13  /* length of directory entry
                                (includes '\0') */
#if defined QUICKC

#include "malloc.h"
#include "memory.h"

#endif

#if defined TURBOC

#include "alloc.h"
#include "mem.h"
#include "string.h"
#include "stdlib.h"
#include "dir.h"

#endif

/**********************************************************************

  Usage:    int dir(char *filespec,char *selection);

    char *filespec=  Wildcard specification for directory
                     ("*.*" ,"*.c") etc.

    char *selection= Pointer to a location suitable for storage of
                     a DIR_NAME_LENGTH character array. The name of
                     the selected file is copied to this location. If
                     the user presses Escape, no selection is made
                     and *selection = "".

    Returns a 1 if memory is unavailable, otherwise returns a 0.

    Allows list selection of directory files specified by filespec.
    Makes use of the list_select() function. Allows point-and-shoot
    or Speed key selection.   The list is displayed in the currently
    active (top) window.

**********************************************************************/

int dir(char *filespec, char *selection)
{
```

```
extern struct screen_structure scr;
extern struct window_structure w[];

int done;                    /* flag */
int filecount=file_count(filespec);

#if defined TURBOC
   struct ffblk DTA;
#endif

#if defined QUICKC
   struct find_t DTA;
#endif

char **list;     /* a pointer to a character pointer */

int i,j,number;

/* allocate array */

/* note: we allocate an extra list pointer for the null terminator */
   list =(char **)malloc ((filecount+1)*sizeof(char *));

 if (list==NULL)return(1);

 /* null the list of pointers */
 for(i=0;i<=filecount;i++) list[i]=NULL;

  /* get the first directory listing */
  /* different techniques used by Turbo C and QuickC */

#if defined TURBOC
   done=findfirst(filespec,&DTA,0);
#endif

#if defined QUICKC
   done= _dos_findfirst(filespec,_A_NORMAL,&DTA);
#endif

/* the first step is to set pointer array to memory allocated
   for each directory entry */

i=0;
 while(!done){  /* loop to get any additional entries */

  if(i==filecount) break;     /* stop if we exceed our pointers */
  /* allocate memory */
  list[i]=  malloc (DIR_NAME_LENGTH*sizeof(char));

  if(list[i] !=NULL){ /* if we have memory for directory entry */

/* copy the directory listing to the allocated space */
```

```
#if defined TURBOC
        sprintf(list[i],"%-12s",DTA.ff_name);
#endif

#if defined QUICKC
        sprintf(list[i],"%-12s",DTA.name);
#endif


        /* get the next directory listing */
#if defined TURBOC
        done=findnext(&DTA);
#endif

#if defined QUICKC
        done=_dos_findnext(&DTA);
#endif


    }  /* end if != NULL */
     else return (1);    /* error allocating memory */
    i++;                      /* inc index */

} /* end while(!done) */

/* now we call on list_select() to process directory list */

   if(i>0){   /* if any entries were found */

    number=list_select(list);   /* Call list_select so user can
                                   make selection. Upon return,
                                   "number" equals the file selected
                                   or -1 if user "Escaped". */
    if(number==-1) strcpy(selection,"");
     else
       strcpy(selection, list[number]);

    for(j=0;j<=filecount-1;j++){    /* free up allocated memory */
     if (list[j]!= NULL){
      free(list[j]);
      list[j]=NULL;
     }
      else
       break;
 }
  if (list!=NULL){
    free (list);
    list=NULL;
  }
}
  return(0);
}


int file_count(char *filespec)
{
```

```
extern struct screen_structure scr;
extern struct window_structure w[];

int done;                    /* flag */
int count=0;

#if defined TURBOC
   struct ffblk DTA;
#endif

#if defined QUICKC
   struct find_t DTA;
#endif

#if defined TURBOC
   done=findfirst(filespec,&DTA,0);
#endif

#if defined QUICKC
   done= _dos_findfirst(filespec,_A_NORMAL,&DTA);
#endif
   if(!done)count++;

/* first step is set pointer array to memory allocated
   for each directory entry */

 while(!done){          /* if we have at least one entry,
                           loop to get the rest */

/* get the next directory listing */

#if defined TURBOC
        done=findnext(&DTA);
#endif

#if defined QUICKC
        done=_dos_findnext(&DTA);
#endif

  if(!done) count++;

 } /* end while(!done) */

 return (count);
}
```

Chapter 7

Help Screens

In this chapter we will build:

- A function to view help screens from your applications.
- An editor for creating disk-based help screens.

INTRODUCTION

Help screens are certainly one of the more useful features that can be added to an application. The help screen feature gives an application a very polished and professional appearance. Most users feel more confident using an application which provides on-line help features.

Some software developers reduce the size of their user's manual, or eliminate the manual entirely, and put most of the instructions in the program's help screens. This, of course, saves on production costs.

Several approaches are used to create help screens. The simplest method is to have a menu-based help system. In such a system, help is only available when the "Help" option is selected from a menu. A more versatile approach is the context-specific help system. The user can, at any point, press a hot key (such as F1) and have a help screen appear to explain the current task. For example, the user could press F1 while editing text to find out more about the text editing features.

Sometimes the help system is "hard-wired" into the application. In that case, the help screens are created by means of print statements contained within the program. The obvious disadvantage of the hard-wired approach is that the program must be recompiled every time a help screen is changed. The program may become excessively large if all the help screens are stored within the program.

A better approach is to have the help screens stored on disk. The program then reads the help as needed.

GOALS

In the following pages, we will build:

- A help function which can be linked with each application and is capable of reading help files from the disk and displaying them on-screen.
- A help screen generator which can be used to create and edit the help screen file.

Each help file consists of a series of pages, each page representing a windowfull of text. All the pages within a help file are the same size. The width and height of the help page is specified when the file is created. Multiple help files can be used by an application.

The help screen generator is intended to streamline and greatly facilitate the task of producing help screen displays. In the process of building the help screen generator we will have an opportunity to use many of the functions we created earlier in this book. We will utilize several windows, moving light bar menus, directory functions and data input screens. We will see how the modules can easily be combined into one application.

APPLICATION

Adding help screens to an application is a two-step process. The first step is to create a help screen and save it to disk. Second, we must have a way to read the help file from within an application, and display it on the screen. We will discuss the latter step first, to illustrate the ease with which help screens may be incorporated into any application.

Let's assume that we have already created the help file, and now wish to use the file from within an application.

Adding Help Screens to Your Application

The help system is contained in the module readhlp.c, and linking this module to any application gives it the capability of reading help files. This module contains the function **read_help( )** which creates and manages the help system. Also included in readhlp.c is a modified version of the function **get_key( )** which will recognize the F1 key. These functions will be discussed more fully in the Techniques section.

The only requirement, other than linking readhlp.c, is that the application must specify which help file and page are currently active. This information is represented by the data structure **help_structure** which is defined in mydef.h as:

```
struct help_structure{
    char filename[80];   /* the current help file */
    char message[80];    /* the window title */
    int x;               /* the column for the upper left corner of
                            window */
    int y;               /* the row for the upper left corner of
                            window */
    int page;            /* page within file to use */
    char frame_attr;     /* character attribute for help interior */
    char interior_attr;  /* character attribute for help frame */
    };
```

This structure is applied in L_main.c to the external pointer **hlp:**

```
            struct help_structure hlp;
```

The data elements are initialized by L_main.c with the following default values:

```
hlp.filename[0]='\0';                 /* empty string (no current
                                         help file) */
strcpy(hlp.message,"Esc: to exit");   /* text appearing in window
                                         frame */
hlp.page=0;                           /* page zero */
hlp.x=1;                              /* upper left column of help
                                         window */
hlp.y=1;                              /* upper left row of help
                                         window */
hlp.interior_attr=scr.normal;         /* set window interior to
                                         normal */
hlp.frame_attr=scr.normal;            /* set window frame to normal
*/
```

Since **hlp.filename** is an empty string, no help file is specified. At this point, pressing F1 would have no effect. We need only specify the help file and page to make the help system available. The following function would allow the help system to use page 5 of the file help.hlp.

```
void set_help(){

extern struct help_structure hlp;

 strcpy(hlp.filename,"help.hlp");
 hlp.page=5;
}
```

Now that the help system is configured, pressing F1 would cause page 5 of the file help.hlp to be displayed.

The user could then browse through the entire help file by pressing the PgUp or PgDn keys. Pressing Escape would close the help window and return the user to whatever task was in process when the F1 key was pressed.

It is possible to have the entire help system stored in one disk file. For example, pages 1 through 5 might be devoted to editing features, pages 6 through 10 could cover loading and saving files, and so on. If the help system is all contained in one disk file, it is a good idea to put headers and footers within each help page so that the user knows when a given topic ends. This is a useful feature, since the user may unwittingly (or unintentionally) page past the end of a given subject. Figure 7–1 shows an example. The user knows that the subject is the help system and that the next page should be viewed by pressing PgDn. Note that the window title is ''Esc: to exit'', which is defined by **hlp.message.** This value may be changed to provide additional help.

If you do not want the user paging past the current topic, then create a separate help file for each topic. The page size is specified when the file is created, so you may create different page sizes for each file.

At any point in the application, the help file name and page may be altered to display a different help file and/or page. Should you feel that help is not appropriate for some reason, setting **hlp.page** to 0 will disable the help system.

```
┌Esc:  to exit──────────────────┐
│ SUBJECT:  USING THE HELP SYSTEM.│
│                                 │
│                                 │
│ Help may be activated at any    │
│ time by pressing the F1 key.    │
│ Once the system is active       │
│ you may browse through the      │
│ help screens using the "page"   │
│ keys.                           │
│                                 │
│ Press PgDn for next page.       │
│                                 │
│ PAGE 1 OF 5                     │
└─────────────────────────────────┘
```

Figure 7–1 Help screen with headers and footers

Creating the Help File

Our help files are created by an application called makehelp. To create this help
file generator, link makehelp.c, hlp_menu.c, hlp_io.c, and the library. These files
utilize the header file help.h. When makehelp is run, the text shown in Figure 7–2
appears. The input line contains the current drive and directory. You may finish
typing the name of a help file and press Enter. The extension .hlp will automatically be added to the name.

```
┌──────────────────────────────────────────────────────────┐
│ Please name a file (new or existing), or                 │
│ Press Enter to select from list.                         │
│ C:\DATA\C\_                                               │
└──────────────────────────────────────────────────────────┘
```

Figure 7–2   Choosing a help file

Alternately, if you wish to select from the list of existing files, press Enter.
In order to select from a different drive or directory, alter the data entry line
appropriately. Just make sure you end the line with a ":" or a "\" to indicate a
drive or directory. After pressing Enter the display will look as in Figure 7–3.
The desired file may then be selected from the list.

```
                ┌─Files:─┐
┌───────────────┤        ├──────────────────────────┐
│ Please │HELP.HLP    │ w or existing), or           │
│ Press E│HELP2.HLP   │ from list.                   │
│ C:\DATA│HELP3.HLP   │                              │
└────────┤EDIT.HLP    ├──────────────────────────────┘
         │            │
         │            │
         │            │
         │            │
         └────────────┘
```

Figure 7–3   Directory window

If you had typed the name of a new file instead of selecting from the list,
you would be asked if you wanted to create it. Pressing 'y' would then bring up
the data input screen shown in Figure 7–4. The values you enter will apply to all
the help screen pages used within this help file.

```
┌──────────────────────────────────────────────────────────┐
│ PLEASE ENTER HELP SCREEN SIZE:                           │
│                                                          │
│ Width    (10-78): ___                                    │
│ Height   (5-23):  ___                                    │
└──────────────────────────────────────────────────────────┘
```

Figure 7–4   Defining the help screen size

After creating a new file, or selecting an existing file, the screen shown in Figure 7–5 appears. This screen has an inverse menu line at the top, an inverse status line on the bottom, and an empty help page in the middle. From the status line we see that this is the file c:\data\c\demo.hlp, and there are two pages. The current options are:

Browse   = Examine each page in the file.
Add   = Add a new help page to the file.
New-file = Use a different help file.
Quit   = Return to DOS.

If the option "Add" is selected, the cursor will appear within the help page window, and you may enter text, as shown in Figure 7–6. The editing features provided within the help window are rather rudimentary. You may enter text, and the cursor will advance to the next line when the end of the current line is reached. The cursor keys may be used to position the cursor at any point within the window.

The editor operates in overtype mode only. If mistakes are made, they must be corrected by typing in new text. When you are finished typing, press Escape to exit. You will be given the opportunity to re-edit the window, save the window, or quit. When editing is complete, you are returned to the main menu.

If you select the option "Browse" from the main menu, you are presented with the screen shown in Figure 7–7. You are given the opportunity to view the next or previous page, to edit the current page, or to quit to the main menu. Now let's take an in-depth look at the inner workings of the help functions.

```
 Browse    Add   New-file   Quit
┌Edit:  Then 'Esc'─────────────────┐
│                                   │
│                                   │
│                                   │
│                                   │
│                                   │
│                                   │
│                                   │
└───────────────────────────────────┘



 C:\DATA\C\DEMO.HLP                    Page   0 of 2
```

Figure 7–5 Main menu screen

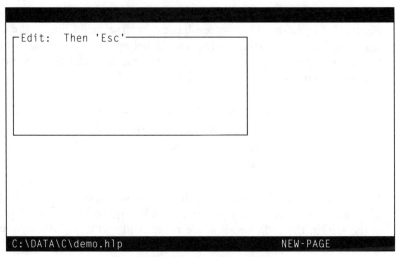

Figure 7–6   Editing the help screen

```
 Next        Previous    Edit    Quit
┌Edit:   Then 'Esc'──────────────────┐
│Demo Help:                          │
│                                    │
│ This is page 1:                    │
│                                    │
│                                    │
│                                    │
└────────────────────────────────────┘



C:\DATA\C\DEMO.HLP                    Page    1 of 2
```

Figure 7–7   Browse menu

TECHNIQUES

The Application makehelp

The makehelp program is quite large and is broken into four parts:

- help.h   = Contains the definitions and prototypes.
- makehelp.c = Contains the function **start()**, and the functions for editing the window and setting up the data input screen.

- hlp_io.c   = Contains all disk input/output functions.
- hlp_menu.c = Contains all the menus.

Our major design considerations for this project are:

- Window placement.
- Help screen editing.
- Saving and retrieving the help pages from the disk.

Window placement.   Since 80 × 25 is a standard screen size supported by all IBM PC compatible computers, we will design our help windows for that size. Our maximum help window size is therefore 78 × 23 (allowing for the frame).

Unfortunately, a full-screen help window causes a few design problems. Take, for example, the process of browsing through the help pages. We would like the current help page to be displayed on the screen so that it may be viewed. In addition, we want a menu showing the current options "Next", "Previous", "Edit", and "Quit". The problem is, where do we display this menu if the help window occupies the entire screen? Most of the menus would obscure the help window contents.

One trick we can use is to create a tiny unframed window, only one row high, on the first line of the display. This tiny window would only obscure the frame of the edit window, not the contents. Within this tiny window we can fit a bar menu with no information line.

Similarly, at the bottom of the screen we can place a one-line unframed window containing the status line. These two windows are placed on top of the help edit window. The only time that the edit window is on top is during the edit process. The help window must be moved to the top during the edit process because only the top window may contain the cursor.

Many of the functions in the program makehelp need to "know" the window handles, as well as the dimensions, of the current help window. The program makehelp.c has the following structure defined in help.h:

```
struct hlp{
        int width;          /* the width of the edit window */
        int height;         /* the height of the edit window */
        char filename[80];  /* name of the help file in use */
        int number_pages;   /* the number of pages in the file */
        int edit;           /* handle for edit window */
        int menu;           /* handle for the menu window */
        int status;         /* handle for the status window */
        };
```

This structure is applied to the external pointer **help** in makehelp.c, and is therefore available to all the functions in the project.

Now that we have decided on a window layout, let's look at the editing process.

Editing.   The function **edit( )** found in makehelp.c allows us to enter text for a new help screen page, or edit the text of an existing page. The internal workings of **edit( )** are quite simple.

The edit window is popped to the top, and the cursor is positioned in the upper lefthand corner. Characters are read from the keyboard and printed to the window at the current cursor location, and the cursor is advanced. When the end of the window is reached, the cursor is moved to the next line. If cursor keys are pressed, the cursor is moved in the appropriate direction. If the Left cursor key is pressed when the cursor is at the left side of the window, the cursor is moved to the right side of the previous line. If the Right cursor key is pressed when the cursor is at the right window border, the cursor is moved to the left side of the next line.

The net result is an extremely simple editor which operates only in the overtype mode. Any corrections must be typed in over existing text. When text entry is complete, the Escape key is pressed. This causes a menu to appear, offering the opportunity to save the help page, edit the page, or quit the edit process without saving. If the "Save" option is chosen, the window contents are copied to the current help file on disk.

Help file structure.   The help file is a random access file consisting of a file header, followed by the help pages. The header consists of two integer numbers: width and height. Our external data structure, **help** has the help screen width and height as the first two elements. Therefore, we can define two variables, **page_size** and **header_size** as follows:

```
page_size=sizeof(char)*(help.width*help.height);
header_size=sizeof(int)*2;
```

After opening a new file, the header may be written with the command:

```
write(handle,(char *)&help,header_size);
```

```
handle=       File handle to write to.
&help=        The buffer to write from.
header_size=  The number of bytes to write.
```

We use the low level **read( )** and **write( )** functions because they allow us to read and write entire buffers at once. Notice how we write only the header of the **help** data structure to the disk file in the example just shown.

We may read the width and height from an existing help file directly into the data structure **help:**

```
read(handle,(char *)&help,header_size);
```

Once the width and height are known, the number of pages in the file may
be calculated by first obtaining the file size. This is done by moving to the end
of the file with **lseek( )**, and examining the return value, which is the number of
bytes in the file. If we subtract header_size, and divide the result by **page_size,**
we obtain the number of pages in the file.

```
read(handle,(char *)&help,header_size);                  /* read the
                                                            header */
page_size=sizeof(char)*(help.width*help.height);         /* calculate page
                                                            size */
offset=lseek(handle,(long)0,SEEK_END);                   /* how many bytes
                                                            in file? */
help.number_pages=(offset-(long)header_size)/(long)page_size;
                                                         /* number of pages */
```

A new page may be added by seeking the end of the file, and writing the help
screen buffer to the file. Of course, the primary problem is that the help screen
window is not contiguous. Each row is contiguous, but the rows are separated
on the screen.

You may remember when we were creating the windowing environment,
that when a new window was created, the contents of the old window were copied
line by line to a contiguous buffer created to hold the window. The window became
virtual at that point, and could later be copied back to the physical screen.

At first glance, it might seem reasonable to use the same routine to copy
the help window to a buffer, then write the entire buffer in one pass to the help
file. Unfortunately there are two problems with this approach. First of all, that
approach would copy the character attributes, along with the actual text, to the
help file. If the user of such a help file had a different video card than the creator
of the help file, unexpected results might occur. Imagine a help screen created
on a color VGA being restored to a monochrome MDA.

A second problem is disk space. We do not really need the attributes, because we can use default attributes on the user's display. Stripping out the character attributes before writing to the disk will cut by half the space required to
store the image.

The function **save_page( )** ignores the attributes as it moves the screen image
to an allocated contiguous section of memory. This buffer is then written to the
disk file as follows:

    handle   = File handle.
    page   = Page to write.
    buffer   = Help page buffer.

```
lseek(file_handle,(long)(header_size+ page_size*page),SEEK_SET);
write(file_handle,buffer,page_size);
```

This page may be read back by the command:

```
lseek(file_handle,(long)(header_size+ page_size*page),SEEK_SET);
read(file_handle,buffer,page_size);
```

This concludes the discussion of the program makehelp. The commented Source Code should answer any specific questions you have. Let us move on to the task of viewing the help pages from other applications.

The Module readhelp.c

As we discussed in the Application section, the module readhlp.c will, when linked with an application, display the help pages when the user presses F1.

The module "readhlp.c" contains two functions, **read_help( )** and **get_key( ).** The task of creating the help window, and the reading of the help page from the disk file, is handled by **read_help( ),** utilizing the same techniques described for the program makehelp.

The function **get_key( )** is the key to the help system's operation. It is this function which recognizes the F1 key and calls **read_help( ).** You may recall that **get_key( )** is one of our library functions and is found in Lgetkey.c. The library version of **get_key( )** is:

```
void get_key(char *ch, char *ext)
{
   *ch=getch();        /* get the character */

    if(!*ch){          /* if the character is zero (a special key) */
      *ext=getch(); /* get the extension */
    }
}
```

At the time I introduced **get_key( ),** I stated that all keyboard input should be routed through this function. In fact, all the line editors and input screen functions use **get_key( )** to read the individual keystrokes entered by the user.

The following modified version of **get_key( )** is found in readhlp.c:

```
void get_key(char *ch, char *ext)
{
   for(;;){
    *ch=' ';*ext=' ';

    *ch=getch();        /* get the character */

     if(!*ch){          /* if the character is zero (a special key) */
       *ext=getch(); /* get the extension */
       if (*ext==F1) read_help():
     }
}
```

```
    if (*ext!=F1) break;   /* if F1 pressed we must read again */
  }
}
```

This version of **get_key**( ) is placed into the final code before the library is linked. Since the linker already has **get_key**( ), it will not attempt to place the library version in the program code. This is a handy trick to use any time you need to use a modified version of a library module. Simply place the name of the modified module in the program list or *make* list, and you lock out the library module.

It would not have been wise to modify the library version of **get_key**( ) because the reference to the function **read_help**( ) would cause the linker to add **read_help**( ) to every application, whether it used the help system or not.

CONCLUSION

The program makehelp.c demonstrates how the elements of screen and menu design can be combined into a functional, although simple application. In this single application we make use of windows, data input screens, moving light bar menus and the directory function.

SOURCE CODE

HELPDEMO.C

```
/********************** HELPDEMO.C **************************/

#include "mydef.h"

/* link with readhelp.c */

start(){
extern struct screen_structure scr;
extern struct window_structure w[];
extern struct help_structure hlp;

char ch;
char ext;
char *ptr;

strcpy(hlp.filename,"helpdemo.hlp");
hlp.page=1;
hlp.interior_attr=scr.inverse;
hlp.frame_attr=scr.inverse;
cls();
print(1,1,"Press F1 to see help page 1, any other key to continue.");
get_key(&ch,&ch);
```

```
hlp.page=2;
print(1,4,"Press F1 to see help page 2, any other key to continue.");
get_key(&ch,&ch);

print (1,6,"bye");
return (0);
}
```

HELP.H

```
/********************     HELP.H     *************************/

/* function prototypes */

/* makehelp.c */

void edit(int x, int y);
int getsize(void);
int val_field( char *string,int length,int field_number);


/* hlp_menu.c */

void main_menu(void);
int browse(void);
int file(void);
int verify_save(void);
int add(void);
void status(int page);


/* hlp_io */

void get_name(char *filename);
int save_page(int page);
int load_page(int page);
int append(char *filename, char *buffer, int page_size);

struct hlp{
        int width;              /* the width of the edit window */
        i'nt height;            /* the height of the edit window */
        char filename[80];      /* name of the help file in use */
        int number_pages;       /* the number of pages in the file */
        int edit;               /* handle for edit window */
        int menu;               /* handle for the menu window */
        int status;             /* handle for the status window */
        };
```

MAKEHELP.C

```
/********************** MAKEHELP.C **************************/

/*
link with :
hlp_menu.c
hlp_io.c
*/

#include "mydef.h"
#include "help.h"
#include <stdio.h>

struct hlp help;

int start(void)        /* start is the entry point */
{
extern struct hlp help;
extern struct screen_structure scr;
extern struct window_structure w[];

cls();
 get_name(help.filename);        /* select a filename */
 if(help.filename[0]=='\0'){    /* if none selected */
  win_delete_top();
  cls();
  print(1,1,"A file must be selected.");
  exit();
 }

  /* make the three windows */
 help.edit= win_make(2,3,help.width,help.height,STD_FRAME,
                  "Edit: Then 'Esc' ",scr.normal,scr.normal);
 help.menu= win_make(1,1,80,1,NO_FRAME,"",scr.inverse);
   cursor(NO_CURSOR);
 help.status= win_make(1,25,80,1,NO_FRAME,"",scr.inverse,
                    scr.inverse);
   cursor(NO_CURSOR);
  main_menu();     /* call the first menu */

/* clean up to exit */
  win_delete (help.edit);
  win_delete (help.menu);
  win_delete (help.status);

return (0);
}

/* this function allows editing of the help window */
```

```
void edit(int x, int y)
{
extern struct screen_structure scr;
extern struct window_structure w[];

char string[2];
char ch,ext;

 scr.current=win_what_attr(help.edit);
 ch= 0;
    while(ch != ESCAPE) {            /* read while key not 'Esc' */
     ch=0;ext=0;
     get_key(&ch,&ext);

      /* break while{} loop if PgUp or PgDn */
      if(ext==PGUP || ext==PGDN) break;

      if(ch  > 31){                     /* if character */
       string[0]=ch;string[1]='\0';/* build a string */
       print_here(string);          /* put on screen */
      x++;                          /* increment cursor location */
      }
      else{
        switch (ext){                 /* if cusor key */
         case UP:y-- ;break;          /* act accordingly*/
         case DOWN:y++ ;break;
         case LEFT:x-- ;break;
         case RIGHT:x++ ;break;
         case HOME:x=1 ;break;
         case END:x=scr.right-scr.left+1;break;
        }
    } /* end else */
      if (ch==BACKSPACE)x--;
      if(ch==RETURN){
       x=1;
       y++;
      }

      /* the following code adjusts the cursor within the window */

      if(scr.left+x-1<scr.left{  /* too far left */
        x=scr.right-scr.left)+1;
        y--;
       }

      if(scr.left)+x-1>scr.right){x=1;y++;};    /* goto next line */
      if(scr.top+y-1<scr.top)y=scr.bottom-scr.top+1;
      if(scr.top+y-1>scr.bottom)y=1;

       if (ch=='\b') print(x,y," ");
       gotoxy(x,y);
```

```
    } /* end while ch!=27 */

    x=1;y=1;
    gotoxy(x,y);
}

/* this function creates an input screen for entry
   of new help screen sizes */

int get_size()
{
char width[3]="";
char height[3]="";

int in_window;
int return_code;

struct in_struc in_scrn[3]= {

/*
X    Y    Label name                Ptr    Length  Label-color  Field color */

1,   3,   "Width (10-78): ", NULL, 2,      WHITE,BLACK, BLACK,WHITE,
1,   4,   "Height (5-23): ", NULL, 2,      WHITE,BLACK, BLACK,WHITE,
0    /* terminator */
};
        in_scrn[0].ptr =width;
        in_scrn[1].ptr =height;

   cls();
   in_window= win_make(1,1,78,5,STD_FRAME,"",scr.normal,scr.normal);

   print(1,1,"PLEASE ENTER HELP SCREEN SIZE:");
   return_code = input(in_scrn);
   if(return_code==ESCAPE)
      return(return_code);
   else{
        help.width=atoi(width);          /* convert to integer */
        help.height=atoi(height);
      }
   win_delete(in_window);
   return(0);
}

/* val_field() is used by input routine to check validity of data */

int val_field( char *string,int length,int field_number)
{
int value;

/* in this demo "length" is not used */

 int age;
```

```
switch (field_number){
  case 0: value=atoi(string);               /* convert string to integer */
      if (value <10 !! value >78) return(REDO);
        break;
  case 1: value=atoi(string);               /* convert string to integer */
        if (value <5 !! value >23) return (REDO);
  }
return (OK);
}
```

HLP_IO.C

```
/********************     HLP_IO.C     *************************/

/*
link with:
makehelp.c
hlp_menu.c
*/

#include "mydef.h"
#include "help.h"

#include <stdio.h>
#include <io.h>
#include <fcntl.h>

#if defined TURBOC

#include <alloc.h>

#endif

#if defined QUICKC

#include <sys\types.h>
#include <malloc.h>
#include <string.h>

#endif

#include <sys\stat.h>

/* get_name allows the user to select a file from a "point and
   shoot" menu containing all the file names matching the wild card
   filename */
```

```
void get_name(char *filename)
{
extern struct screen_structure scr;
extern struct window_structure w[];
extern struct hlp help;

int done=FALSE;
char ch,ext;
int handle;
int i;
int name_win;  /* window handle for name window */
int dir_win;   /* window handle for directory window */
char temp[80];
char dir_name[80];
char orig_dir[80];
int return_code;
long offset;
int page_size;
int header_size;

header_size=sizeof(int)*2;

name_win= win_make(1,1,78,4,STD_FRAME,"",scr.normal,scr.normal);

 while(!done){
  for(;;){  /* loop to get file name */
    cls():
    print(1,1, "Please name a file (new or existing), or");
    print(1,2,"(Press Enter to select from list.");
    gotoxy(1,3);
    getcwd(dir_name,79);  /* get the current directory */
    /* if it doesn't have a backslash then add it */
    if(dir_name[strlen(dir_name)-1]!='\\')
       strcat(dir_name,"\\");                    /* add it */
    scr.current=scr.inverse;
    ext=getfield(dir_name,78,strlen(dir_name),scr.current);
    trim(dir_name);   /* remove spaces from ends of string */
    scr.current=scr.normal;
     if(ext==ESCAPE){  /* escape */
            strcpy(filename,"");
            win_delete(name_win);
            return;
     }

     /* remove any extension from name */
     i=pos(dir_name,".");
     if (i>=0) dir_name[i]='\0';
     /* Did the user enter the name of a path or drive? */
     if(dir_name[strlen(dir_name)-1]=='\\'
        || dir_name[strlen(dir_name)-1]==':'){
     strcpy(orig_dir,dir_name);  /* save the path */
```

```
   strcat(dir_name,"*.hlp");
   strcpy(filename,"");
   dir_win= win_make(10,2,13,10,STD_FRAME," Files: ",
                     scr.normal,scr.normal);
   dir(dir_name,filename);
   win_delete(dir_win);

   if(strlen(filename)>0){ /* was a file selected? (in temp) */
     strcpy(temp,orig_dir);
     strcat(temp,filename);
     strcpy(filename,temp);
     break;    /* we have a name (break for(;;) loop) */
    }
      else  filename[0]='\0'; /* no file selected from list */

   } /* end (is path) */

   else{ /* not path, must be name */
    strcpy(filename,dir_name);
    break;
   }
 }   /* end for(;;) loop to get file name*/

/* entry was not a path or directory, let's try to open it */
/* add the .hlp extension if none was specified */

if(pos(filename,".")==-1)strcat(filename,".hlp");

 /* open for append-create if not exist */

handle= open(filename,O_RDWR!O_BINARY);

if (handle==(-1)) { /* create new file ? */
   cls();
   print(1,1,"The file does not exist:");
   print(1,2,"Create a new file y/n ? ");
    for(;;){    /* find out if user wants a new file */
     get_key(&ch,&ext);
     if (toupper(ch)=='Y'){
         return_code=get_size(): /* prompt user for
                                      size of help screen */
         if (return_code==ESCAPE) break;
         handle= open(filename,O_CREAT!O_BINARY!O_RDWR,
                 S_IREAD!S_IWRITE);

         if(handle==(-1)){
            cls();
            print(1,1,"Error opening file!");
            print(1,2,"Press any key to continue.");
            get_key(&ch,&ext);
            break;
```

```
            }else
            {
             /* write the header */

             write(handle,(char *)&help,header_size);
             close(handle);
             help.number_pages=0; /* new file, no pages yet */
             done=TRUE;
             break;  /* escape the for(;;) loop */
            }

        } /* end of if (toupper(ch)=='Y')*/

         if (toupper(ch)='N'){
          putch(ch);
          strcpy(filename,"");
          break;
         }

       } /* end for(;;) which asks if user wants to create file */

    }  /* end if (handle==(-1))  (create new file?) */

  else{ /* file opened (new or existing), now read header */
     /* read the header */
     read(handle,(char *)&help,header_size);

     /* calculate page size */
     page_size=sizeof(char)*(help.width*help.height);

     /* how many bytes in file? */
     offset=lseek(handle,(long)0,SEEK_END);

     /* calculate the number of pages */
     help.number_pages=(offset-(long)header_size)/(long)page_ size;

     close(handle);
     done=TRUE;
     /*break;*/
  } /* end (read header) */
     print(1,1,"x");
  }  /* end while(!done); */

 win_delete(name_win);
}


int save_page(int page)  /* saves the current help page */
{
extern struct hlp help;
extern struct screen_structure scr;
extern struct window_structure w[];
```

```
int file_handle;
char *buffer=NULL;
char far *temp;
char far *scrn_ptr;
int i,j;
int page_size;
int header_size;

 page_size=sizeof(char)*(help.width*help.height);
 header_size=sizeof(int)*2;

 win_pop_top(help.edit);
 scr.current=win_what_attr(help.edit);
 cursor(NORMAL_CURSOR);

 /* allocate space, allow for \0 terminator */

 buffer=(char *)malloc ((help.width*help.height)*sizeof(char));
 temp=buffer;    /* set temp pointer = pointer */

 for(i=0;i<help.height;i++){  /* get each row */

  scrn_ptr=(char far *)(scr.buffer+(scr.top+i-1)*(scr.columns*2)
          +2*(scr.left-1));
    for(j=0;j<help.width;j++){
      *temp=*scrn_ptr;
      temp++;scrn_ptr+=2; /* adjust pointers, skipping attributes */
    }
 }

 /* save image to file */
 file_handle=open (help.filename,O_RDWR!O_BINARY);
 lseek(file_handle,(long)(header_size+ page_size*page),SEEK_SET);
 write(file_handle,buffer,page_size);
 close(file_handle);

 if(buffer!=NULL)free(buffer);
 win_cls(help.edit); win_redraw_all();win_pop_top(help.menu);
 return(1);
}

int load_page(int page)   /* load a help page from the file */
{
extern struct hlp help;
extern struct screen_structure scr;
extern struct window_structure w[];

int file_handle;
char *buffer;
char *buffer_ptr;
char far *scrn_ptr;
```

```
int page_size;
int header_size;
int i,j;

page_size=sizeof(char)*(help.width*help.height);
header_size=sizeof(int)*2;

buffer=NULL;
buffer=(char*)malloc(page_size);

 /* load help page into buffer */
 file_handle=open (help.filename,O_RDWR!O_BINARY);
 lseek(file_handle,(long)(header_size+ page_size*page),SEEK_SET);
 read(file_handle,buffer,page_size);
 close(file_handle);

 /* copy buffer to active window */

 /* scan the help window for characters */

 buffer_ptr=buffer;      /* set temp pointer = buffer pointer */
 for(i=0;i<help.height;i++){   /* get each row */
   scrn_ptr=(char far *)(scr.buffer+(scr.top+i-1)
              *(scr.columns*2)+2*(scr.left-1);

   for(j=0;j<help.width;j++){
     *scrn_ptr=*buffer_ptr;     /* copy char from buffer to screen */
     buffer_ptr++;scrn_ptr+=2; /* increment both pointers */
   }
}

if(buffer!=NULL) free(buffer);
return(0);
}

/* append a new help page to the file */

int append(char *filename, char *buffer, int page_size)
{
int file_handle;

 /* write record use file_handle int */

 file_handle=open (filename,O_RDWR!O_APPEND!O_BINARY);
 write(file_handle,buffer,page_size);
 close(file_handle);

 return (0);
}
```

HLP_MENU.C

```
/******************** HLP_MENU.C ***************************/

/*
link with:
makehelp.c
hlp_io.c
*/

#include "mydef.h"

#include "help.h"
#include <stdio.h>

#if defined QUICKC

#include <malloc.h>
#include <memory.h>

#endif

#if defined TURBOC

#include <alloc.h>
#include <mem.h>
#include <string.h>
#include <stdlib.h>

#endif

/* these functions create the menus used by makehelp.c */

void main_menu(void)    /* the main menu */
{
extern struct screen_structure scr;
extern struct window_structure w[];

struct bar_struc main_menu [5]={
    "Browse" ,"",browse,0,
    "Add" ,"",add,0,
    "New-file" ,"",file,0,
    "Quit","",NULL,1,
    "\0"
  };

  status(0);

  bar_menu(main_menu,scr.inverse,scr.normal);
  };
```

```
int browse(void)        /* page browsing menu */
{
extern struct hlp help;
extern struct screen_structure scr;
extern struct window_structure w[];

int current_page=0;
int done=FALSE;
int last_load;
int ret_code;

  struct bar_struc browse_menu [5]={
    "Next " ,       "", NULL,1,
    " Previous ", "", NULL,2,
    " Edit " ,      "", NULL,3,
    "Quit ",        "", NULL,4,
    "\0"
  };

if (help.number_pages==0) return(0);

  while(!done){
    alt_screen(ON);
    win_pop_top(help.edit);
    scr.current=win_what_attr(help.edit);
    load_page(current_page);
     status(current_page+1);
     win_pop_top(2);
     alt_screen(OFF);

    ret_code=bar_menu(browse_menu,scr.inverse,scr.normal);

    switch(ret_code){
      case 0: break;
      case 1: current_page++;break;
      case 2: current_page--;break;
      case 3: cls(); win_pop_top(help.edit);
        for(;;){

            /* get edit window attribute */
          scr.current=win_what_attr(help.edit);
            edit(1,1); /* edit window */

            /* pop up the menu and status windows*/
            win_pop_top(help.status);
            win_pop_top(help.menu);
            ret_code=verify_save();
              if (ret_code==0)break;

              if(ret_code==1){
                save_page(current_page);
                break;
              }
```

```
                if(ret_code==2)win_pop_top(help.edit);
                if(ret_code==3) break;
              }/* end for(;;) */
              break;

         case 4: done=TRUE;

      }   /* end switch */

  if (current_page==help.number_pages)
      current_page=help.number_pages-1;
  if (current_page<0)current_page=0;

  } /* end while(!done) */

 win_cls(help.edit);win_redraw_all();
 status(0));  /* update status window */
 return(0);
}


int file(void)       /* get the name of a new help file */
{
extern struct hlp help;
extern struct screen_structure scr;
extern struct window_structure w[];

 char old_name[80];
 strcpy(old_name,help.filename);
 get_name(help.filename);
 if((strcmp(old_name,help.filename))!=0){
   /* delete old edit window, create new one */
   win_delete(help.edit);
   help.edit=win_make(2,3,help.width,help.height,STD_FRAME,
                      "Edit: Then 'Esc' ",scr.normal,scr.normal);
     win_cls(help.status); /* clear status window */
     status(0);            /* create new one */
 }
 return(0);
}


int verify_save(void)   /* verify the user wants to save the page */
{
extern struct hlp help;
extern struct screen_structure scr;
extern struct window_structure w[];

int return_code;
 /* no function pointers, we want return codes only */
   struct bar_struc main_menu [4]={
     "Save",  "", NULL,1,
     "Edit",  "", NULL,2,
     "Quit" , "", NULL,3,
```

```
     "\0"
  };

 return(bar_menu(main_menu,scr.inverse,scr.normal));
}

int add(void)   /* add a new help page */
{
extern struct hlp help;
extern struct screen_structure scr;
extern struct window_structure w[];

int done=FALSE;
char *ptr=NULL;
char *temp;
char far *scrn_ptr;
char ch;
int i,j;
int return_code;

cls();

win_pop_top(help.edit);
scr.current=win_what_attr(help.edit);

/* allocate space, allow for \0 terminator */
ptr=(char *)malloc ((help.width*help.height)*sizeof(char));
status(help.number_pages+1);
win_pop_top(help.edit);
edit(1,1);

while(!done){
   status(help.number_pages+1);
   win_pop_top(help.menu);

   return_code=verify_save();   /* save file?*/

    if ( return_code==1){   /* save help page to file */
      win_pop_top(help.edit);
      /* scan the help window for characters */

      temp=ptr;    /* set temp pointer = pointer */

      for(i=0;i<help.height;i++){  /* get each row */

       scrn_ptr=(char far *)(scr.buffer+(scr.top+i-1)*
               (scr.columns*2)+2*(scr.left-1));

        for(j=0;j<help.width;j++){
         *temp=*scrn_ptr;
         temp++;scrn_ptr+=2;
        }
```

```
          }
           /* save image to file */
           append(help.filename,ptr,(help.width*help.height*
                                        sizeof(char)));
          help.number_pages++;
          ch=' ';

        status(help.number_pages+1);
        win_pop_top(help.menu);

        ceol(1,1);
        print(1,1, "Add another page ");
        scr.bold_caps=TRUE;
        print_here("Y/N? ");
        scr.bold_caps=FALSE;
        while(ch != 'Y' && ch !='N'){
         ch=toupper(getch());
        }

        if(ch=='N') done=TRUE;

        else{                   /* edit a new page */
           cls();
           win_pop_top(help.edit);
           cls();
           edit(1,1);
        }
     } /* end return code==1 */

        if(return_code==2) {
        win_pop_top(help.edit);
        edit(1,1);
        }
        if(return_code==3){
         done=TRUE;

        }

} /* end while !done */

if(ptr!=NULL)free(ptr);
win_cls(help.menu);
win_cls(help.edit);
win_redraw_all(); status(0); return(0);

}

void status(page)             /* display the status line */
{
extern struct hlp help;
extern struct  screen_structure scr;
extern struct window_structure w[];
```

```
char string[20];
win_pop_top(help.status);
ceol(1,1);
scr.current=win_what_attr(help.status);
print(1,1,help.filename);
sprintf(string,"Page %3i of %d",page,help.number_pages);

if(page>help.number_pages)
 strcpy(string,"NEW-PAGE");
print(60,1,string);
win_pop_top(help.menu);
}
```

READHLP.C

```
/*********************  READHLP.C  **************************/

#include "mydef.h"
#include <stdio.h>
#include <io.h>
#include <fcntl.h>

#if defined TURBOC
#include <alloc.h>
#endif

#if defined QUICKC

#include <malloc.h>
#include <sys\types.h>

#endif

void read_help( void)
{
extern struct screen_structure scr;
extern struct window_structure w[];
extern struct help_structure hlp;

static int in_use=FALSE;
int max_pages;
int page;
char ch;
char ext;

/* save text attribute for existing window */
char old_attr=scr.current;
int old_bold_caps=scr.bold_caps; /* save old bold caps setting */

char *buffer;
char far *buffer_ptr;
```

```
char far *scrn_ptr;
int buff_size;
int header_size;
int i,j;

int handle;
long offset;
struct header_struct{
          int width;
          int height;
          }hlp_header;

if(in_use)return;  /* don't invoke help if help already active */
if(hlp.page==0)return; /* return if page =0 (disable help) */

in_use=TRUE;         /* now mark in_use as true */

scr.bold_caps=FALSE; /* we don't want bold caps on */

page=hlp.page-1;

handle= open(hlp.filename,O_RDWR!O_BINARY);

if (handle==(-1)) { /* if file does not exist */
 win_center (40,5,STD_FRAME," Warning: ",hlp.frame_attr,\
          hlp.interior_attr);

  cls();
  print(1,1,"The help file ");print_here(hlp.filename);
  print_here(" is not found");
  print(1,3,"Press any key to continue.");
  get_key(&ch,&ext);
  win_delete_top();

  /* restore the attribute previously in use */
  scr.current=old_attr;
  in_use=FALSE;        /* show that help is no longer active */
  return;
}

/* read the header */
read(handle,(char *)&hlp_header,2*sizeof(int));
offset=lseek(handle,(long)0,SEEK_END); /* how many bytes in file? */
max_pages=(offset-(long)(2*sizeof(int)))/(long)
          (hlp_header.width*hlp_header.height);
if (page>=max_pages) page=max_pages-1;

alt_screen(ON);
win_make (hlp.x,hlp.y,hlp_header.width,hlp_header.height,
          STD_FRAME,hlp.message,hlp.frame_attr,hlp.interior_attr);
alt_screen(OFF);
cursor(NO_CURSOR);
```

```
buff_size=sizeof(char)*(hlp_header.width*hlp_header.height);
header_size=sizeof(int)*2;

buffer=NULL;
/* allocate memory for the help buffer */
buffer=(char*)malloc(buff_size);

/* here we begin the loop to read pages (PgUp,PgDn, or Esc) */
 for(;;){

    /* load help page into buffer */
    lseek(handle,(long)(header_size+ buff_size*page),SEEK_SET);
    read(handle,buffer,buff_size);

    /* copy buffer to active window */

        /* scan the help window for characters */

        buffer_ptr=buffer;        /* set temp pointer = buffer pointer */
        for(i=0;i<hlp_header.height;i++){   /* get each row */

            scrn_ptr=(char far *)(scr.buffer+(scr.top+i-1)*
                    (scr.columns*2)+2*(scr.left-1));

             for(j=0;j<hlp_header.width;j++){

              /* copy char from buffer to screen */
              *scrn_ptr=*buffer_ptr;
               buffer_ptr++;scrn_ptr+=2; /* increment both pointers */
              }
        }

    get_key(&ch,&ext);

    if(ext==PGUP) page--;        /* adjust page according to user input */
    if (ext==PGDN) page++;
    if (ch==ESCAPE) break;
     if(page>max_pages-1)
      page=max_pages-1;
     if(page<0) page=0;
 }

/* finish up before exit */

close(handle);
if(buffer!=NULL) free(buffer);

win_delete_top();

/* restore the attribute previously in use */
scr.current=old_attr;
scr.bold_caps= old_bold_caps;   /* restore bold_caps setting */
in_use=FALSE;                   /* show help no longer in use*/
}
```

```
void get_key(char *ch, char *ext)
{

  for(;;){
   *ch=' ';*ext=' ';

   *ch=getch();        /* get the character */

    if(!*ch){          /* if the character is zero (a special key) */
       *ext=getch(); /* get the extension */
       if (*ext==F1) read_help();
    }

    if (*ext!=F1) break; /* if F1 pressed we must read again */
  }
}
```

Bibliography

COVINGTON, MICHAEL. "The Power of Turbo Pascal." *PC Tech Journal*. Vol. 3, No. 2, February 1985, pp. 112–117. (A discussion of a simple window technique implemented in Turbo Pascal.)

DUNCAN, RAY. *Advanced MS-DOS*. Microsoft Press. 16011 N.E. 36th Way, Box 97017, Redmond, Washington 98073-9717. 1986.

HOFFMANN, THOMAS V. "The IBM Color/Graphics Adapter." *PC Tech Journal*. Vol. 1, No. 1, July/August 1983, pp. 26–166. (Excellent coverage of the CGA adapter)

KERNIGHAN, BRIAN W., AND RITCHIE, DENNIS M. *The C Programming Language*. Prentice Hall, Englewood Cliffs, NJ, 1978.

METCALF, CHRISTOPHER D., AND SUGIYAMA, MARC B. *Beginner's Guide to Machine Language on the IBM PC & PCjr*. Compute! Publications, Inc. P.O. Box 5406, Greensboro, NC 27403. 1985.

NORTON, PETER. *Exploring The IBM PC/Jr. Home Computer*. Microsoft Press. 10700 Northup Way, Bellevue, Washington 98004. 1984.

PINSON, JAMES L. "Pull-down Menus in C." *BYTE*. Vol. 12, No. 5, May 1987, pp. 108–112.

ROCHKIND, MARC J. *Advanced C Programming for Displays*. Prentice Hall, Englewood Cliffs, NJ, 1988.

Appendix A

How to Obtain the Source Code Presented in This Book

By Modem

If you have an account on CompuServe, you may download the code from the Borland Forum 3, library 5. You can get to Borland by typing "GO BPRDGB" at any ! prompt. The source code is compressed in the file "DSIIC.ZIP" (short for *Designing Screen Interfaces in C*).

In order to uncompress the file, you must have a copy of PKUNZIP.EXE, a shareware product created by PKWARE Inc. PKUNZIP.EXE is available on CompuServe.

There is no charge for downloading either of these files. However, the usual connect charges apply.

CompuServe users may send E-mail to me at 73427,2424.

By Mail

If you don't have a CompuServe account, you may obtain the source code diskette from *The C Users Journal* library.

Send $8.00 to:

Attention: KENJI HINO
The C Users Journal
2601 Iowa Street
Lawrence KS 66046

Ask for the source code diskette from *Designing Screen Interfaces in C*.

Index

Cursor:
 and the active window, 25, 31, 42
 attributes, 25–28
 in field editor, 174
 management with multiple windows,
  25, 60–61
 movement via BIOS, 13–14
 position, 25–28, 44
 size, 25, 27, 44
 turning off, 42
 in virtual screens, 56

D

Data input screen editor, 172–84
 data structures for, 176
 data verification using **val__field( )**,
  177–80
 editing commands, 183–84
 features, 173–74
 field editor defined, 173
 getfield( ) function, 175–76, 184
 input( ) function, 176–77, 179, 184
 l__getfield.c module, 175
 l__input, 175
 manipulating text with **chip__**,
  180–82
 purpose, 176
 return codes, 175–77
Desktop metaphor, 17, 24, 29, 42, 43, 47
DESQview, 11, 15, 23, 34, 44, 53, 58–60
 detecting the presence of, 59
 locating the virtual screen, 59
 virtual windows, 58
Dialogue boxes, 117
Direct Memory Access (DMA), 9–10
 and memory models, 9
 using **movedata( )**, 10
 using **movmen( )**, 9
 sample code, 10
 of video buffer, 9–10
Directories:
 accessing from within applications,
  215
 allocating memory for, 218
 as seen in commercial applications,
  215

compiler-specific functions, 218–19
counting entries with **filecount( )**,
 216–17
dir( ) function, 216–17
l__dir.c module, 216
and **list__select( )** function, 220
Disk Transfer Area (DTA), 219–21
 compiler-specific parameter
  sequences, 220
 contents, 221
 defined, 219
 structure, 219
Display adapters:
 Color Graphics Adapter (CGA), 2
 and command line switches, 23
 Enhanced Graphics Adapter (EGA),
  2
 Hercules Graphic Adapter (HGA), 2
 Liquid Crystal Display (LCD), 2
 Monochrome Display Adapter
  (MDA), 2
 setting colors for, 3
 Video Graphics Adapter (VGA), 2
DOS:
 command line interface, 117
 extensions, 11, 219
 mode command, 3, 27–28
 system command, 215
DTA (*see* Disk Transfer Area)

E

Editor, field:
 defined, 173
 getfield( ) function, 175
 insert/overtype mode and the
  cursor, 174
 internal workings, 180
 return codes, 175
 standard features, 173
Enhanced Graphics Adapter (EGA), 2,
  11, 61, 62
Expert mode, 118, 120, 127–29, 151–53
External storage class, 218
External variables, 21–23
 overriding default settings, 23–24
 scr, 21–23, 47–52, 54–63, 130